T0377955

The Brontës and the Fairy Tale

Series in Victorian Studies

Series editors: Joseph McLaughlin and Elizabeth Miller

Katherine D. Harris, *Forget Me Not: The Rise of the British Literary Annual, 1823–1835*

Rebecca Rainof, *The Victorian Novel of Adulthood: Plot and Purgatory in Fictions of Maturity*

Erika Wright, *Reading for Health: Medical Narratives and the Nineteenth-Century Novel*

Daniel Bivona and Marlene Tromp, editors, *Culture and Money in the Nineteenth Century: Abstracting Economics*

Anna Maria Jones and Rebecca N. Mitchell, editors, *Drawing on the Victorians: The Palimpsest of Victorian and Neo-Victorian Graphic Texts*

Mary Elizabeth Leighton and Lisa Surridge, *The Plot Thickens: Illustrated Victorian Serial Fiction from Dickens to Du Maurier*

Dorice Williams Elliott, *Transported to Botany Bay: Class, National Identity, and the Literary Figure of the Australian Convict*

Melisa Klimaszewski, *Collaborative Dickens: Authorship and Victorian Christmas Periodicals*

Sarah Parker and Ana Parejo Vadillo, editors, *Michael Field: Decadent Moderns*

Simon Cooke, *The Moxon Tennyson: A Landmark in Victorian Illustration*

Suchitra Choudhury, *Textile Orientalisms: Cashmere and Paisley Shawls in British Literature and Culture*

Pearl Chaozon Bauer and Erik Gray, editors, *Love among the Poets: The Victorian Poetics of Intimacy*

Jessica Campbell, *The Brontës and the Fairy Tale*

The Brontës & the Fairy Tale

JESSICA CAMPBELL

OHIO UNIVERSITY PRESS
ATHENS

Ohio University Press, Athens, Ohio 45701
ohioswallow.com

Earlier versions of chapters in this book were published in the following articles:

Chapter 4 is reprinted from Campbell, Jessica. "Bluebeard and the Beast: The Mysterious Realism of *Jane Eyre*" in *Marvels & Tales: Journal of Fairy-Tale Studies*, Vol. 30, No. 2. Copyright © 2016 Wayne State University Press, with permission of Wayne State University Press.

Chapter 7 was originally published as "Anne Brontë's Realist 'Bluebeard,'" by Jessica Campbell, *Brontë Studies* 41, no. 4 (2016): 350–360, copyright © The Brontë Society 2016, reprinted by permission of Taylor & Francis Ltd, https://www.tandfonline.com on behalf of The Brontë Society.

Printed in the United States of America
Ohio University Press books are printed on acid-free paper ∞ ™

Library of Congress Cataloging-in-Publication Data
Names: Campbell, Jessica (Jessica A.), 1987– author.
Title: The Brontës and the fairy tale / Jessica Campbell.
Description: Athens : Ohio University Press, 2024. | Series: Series in Victorian studies | Includes bibliographical references and index.
Identifiers: LCCN 2024019022 | ISBN 9780821425640 (hardcover ; acid-free paper) | ISBN 9780821425657 (ebook)
Subjects: LCSH: Brontë, Charlotte, 1816–1855—Criticism and interpretation. | Brontë, Emily, 1818–1848—Criticism and interpretation. | Brontë, Anne, 1820–1849—Criticism and interpretation. | Brontë, Patrick Branwell, 1817–1848—Criticism and interpretation. | Fairy tales in literature. | Folklore in literature. | LCGFT: Literary criticism.
Classification: LCC PR4169 .C36 2024 | DDC 823/.80915—dc23/eng/20240723
LC record available at https://lccn.loc.gov/2024019022

Contents

Acknowledgments

I've struggled to write this acknowledgments section because I have so often been discouraged by those that I have read. Reading the enumeration of fellowships, grants, and armies of research assistants that contributed to a book's completion can be daunting to a scholar who does not have those resources. Most humanities scholars working today do not, and neither did I while writing this book. I got through this process because of many other forms of help and support, which I acknowledge here both to thank the givers and, I hope, to illustrate one path forward for someone living the kind of academic life that so many of us live now.

Thanks to Elizabeth Carolyn Miller, Joseph McLaughlin, Rick Huard, Tyler Balli, Theresa Winchell, the anonymous readers, and all of the other editors and staff members at Ohio University Press. Thanks to fellow scholars in the fields of fairy-tale scholarship and Victorian studies for years of stimulating discussions at conferences on the ideas discussed in this book. Knowing that a community of thinkers was out there for me kept me going when I could only work on this book on Saturdays and summers snatched between weeks and semesters full of teaching and committee work. Thanks also to my colleagues who have listened to me in years' worth of hallway conversations, and to my students, everywhere I have taught, for all the comments and questions in writing and discussion.

Much of the research I did for this book was facilitated by public university libraries: the University of Washington and University of Nevada, Reno. The importance of this resource cannot be overestimated. I thank the friends and other allies who shared online resources from other scholarly libraries—you know who you are. I'm grateful, too, to Debbie Houk, Paula Martin, and Jen Funk, who helped me get the most I could out of the one small scholarly library to which I officially had access for several years.

My doctoral work at UW formed the basis for this project. Professors Charles LaPorte, Marshall Brown, and Jennifer Bean were and have remained the most stimulating and supportive advisers I could have asked for; thanks also, more broadly, to Jesse Oak Taylor, Molly

Clark Hillard, Gillian Harkins, and Raimonda Modiano for additional coursework and other forms of support that contributed to the ideas in this book. The impact, meanwhile, of the academic discussions and moral support provided by my many graduate school friends cannot be underestimated. Despite the brevity of our official relationships, all of these people have undertaken years of uncompensated intellectual and emotional work to provide this support to me.

As an undergraduate, I was fortunate enough to attend a bona fide liberal arts institution, Middlebury College, where I found my first community of thinkers and learned why and how to pursue the history of ideas as a lifelong interest. Brett Millier, Antonia Losano, and Dan Brayton showed me the kind of English professor I wanted to be. Of course, I was able to function at Middlebury in the first place thanks to the dear departed William Brooks, high school English teacher extraordinaire who thought it worthwhile to teach kids at a small school in a small city to write well and read widely.

It takes a great deal of confidence to persist in writing a scholarly monograph despite all the waiting, all the rejection, and all the doubts. My parents, Marianne and Clark Campbell, are responsible for making sure I started off with enough confidence to withstand this process. It was my mom, too, who fostered my love of reading. In more recent years, I'm not sure I could have done any of this without Rachel Shields, who deserves the name of "partner" in every sense of the word. She shared her library when I didn't have one; she read my drafts when I had no colleagues to do so; she followed me to two different states in pursuit of decent jobs; she believed in the book even when I wasn't so sure I did myself; and she made sure there was more to my life than my academic career. This book is dedicated to her.

A final acknowledgment is due to Becky, who didn't live long enough to nibble on the corners of the finished project but was instrumental to the creation of the book and the sanity of its author from start to finish. I think the Brontës would understand.

The Brontës and the Fairy Tale

Introduction

When Charlotte, Branwell, Emily, and Anne Brontë were growing up in the 1820s and 1830s, there was a little room on the second floor of their home that the servants called "the children's study."[1] In this room, the precocious children—whose clergyman father allowed them to read whatever they wished—devoured books, magazines, and newspapers, enjoying a window on the world that belies the lingering popular image of the Brontës as isolated rural geniuses. This world was steeped in fairy tales and folklore, which appeared throughout nineteenth-century England in the form of chapbooks, gift books, paintings, pantomimes, poems, and new fairy-tale retellings. In their reading, the Brontës encountered literary fairy tales from continental Europe, Middle Eastern tales like *The Thousand and One Nights*, and snippets of British folklore in the context of newspaper articles, Romantic poetry, and perhaps folklore books. When the children themselves began to write in the late 1820s, they immediately placed powerful fairies and other supernatural creatures known as genii in control of the imaginary worlds they created together. The Brontës' engagement with fairy tales and folklore did not end with the passing of childhood, however; all four continued to employ these stories in various overt and subtle ways in the poems and novels they went on to publish.

The Brontë sisters captivated critics and casual readers when they burst onto the literary scene in the 1840s, and their popularity has never substantially waned. Their influence on the evolution of literary forms, particularly the novel, was profound—in the Victorian period (1837–1901) and beyond. Scholarship has already begun to demonstrate the role of fairy-tale tropes in making the Brontës such popular writers; for example, some scholars have explored fantastical elements in Charlotte's *Jane Eyre*, and others have noted that fairy tales inspired the siblings' collaborative childhood creation of the imaginary kingdoms of Angria and Gondal. In this book, I argue that the influence of the fairy tale extends further, permeating even the Brontës' soberest adult works.

The Brontës and the Fairy Tale seeks to provide an account of the Brontës' lifelong engagement with fairy tales and other fantastical literature, beginning with childhood reading and ending with the repurposing of these tales in the major works they wrote as adults.

In the following chapters, I contend that fairy tales and folklore, beyond evoking childhood and romance, function across the Brontës' works in a variety of ways—serving, among other things, as plot and character models, subtle commentaries on gender, and modes for the expression of complex (and often negative) internal experiences. I trace not only overt allusions but also unmarked appropriations of various tales' characters, events, and themes—appropriations that would have been more obvious to Victorian readers than to us. I point to the influence of folk and fairy tales on the Brontës' juvenilia, on the extensive writing of Branwell (treated rarely in scholarship), on Emily's and Anne's poetry, and on all the sisters' published novels. Ultimately, that fairy tales matter not only in *Jane Eyre* but also in self-avowedly realist Brontë works, including Branwell's battle narratives and Anne's social-problem novels, attests to the flexibility of fairy tales as models and to their inescapable presence in the Victorian imagination.

Terminology is fraught in studies of fairy tale, folklore, fable, myth, and legend; these stories have a way of leaping over the boundaries with which we attempt to divide them. Although my title refers simply to fairy tales, I write throughout this book of both fairy tales and folklore as those terms are generally understood today. The establishment of and distinction between the two categories has caused much scholarly debate, which has been thoroughly conducted and described in other studies.[2] In essence, "folklore" encompasses all manner of stories, beliefs, and customs transmitted orally within a culture. The Folklore Society defines its purview as "traditional music, song, dance and drama, narrative, arts and crafts, customs and belief . . . popular religion, traditional and regional food, folk medicine, children's folklore, traditional sayings, proverbs, rhymes and jingles."[3] Importantly, folklore incorporates both the mundane and the fantastical. "Fairy tale," meanwhile, is the unfortunate English translation of the French *conte de fées*, or "tale of the fairies" (which could mean "tale about the fairies" or "tale told by the fairies"), even though many stories considered fairy tales in the English-speaking world do not feature fairies. Some scholars have treated "fairy tale" as a subcategory of "folklore": of the many folktales that exist in the world, some treat supernatural subject matter and can thus be considered fairy tales. *Verzeichnis der Märchentypen* (*Tale-Type Index*), the definitive folklore classification first published by Antti Aarne in 1910 and updated over the next century by Stith Thompson and Hans-Jörg Uther, encourages such an approach; of the approximately two thousand folktale types listed, those numbered 300 to 749 are categorized as "Tales of Magic" and include many stories widely considered fairy tales. Vladimir Propp in *Morphology of the Folktale* initially defines fairy tales as "those tales classified by Aarne under numbers 300 to 749," though he later complicates this definition.[4] However, other scholars, such as Elizabeth Wanning Harries, argue that one can trace the history of the fairy tale almost exclusively through print sources as something distinct from (though influenced by) orally transmitted folklore. These scholars emphasize that the majority of the fairy tales we can actually access today are literary—authored by individuals and intended for publication in books—even though some were intended to mimic orally transmitted folklore.

Because of the ephemeral nature of folklore (and, for that matter, of many of the early cheap print editions of fairy tales), the debate over the precise relationship between fairy tale and folktale is impossible to resolve. It seems reasonable, ultimately, to preserve an open mind and to recognize that both oral and written formats have contributed to the development of what we now call fairy tales. Jack Zipes emphasizes the "intricate relationship and evolution of folk and fairy tales," asserting that "together, oral and literary tales form one immense and complex genre because they are inextricably dependent on one another."[5] Tales spread and evolve in both oral and written forms concurrently, overlapping with different versions and with other tales in ways we can never fully describe. While no definition of fairy tales applies universally, Maria Tatar's comes close: she avers that the term "fairy tale" "has been associated with both oral and literary traditions but is above all reserved for narratives set in a fictional world where preternatural events and supernatural intervention are taken wholly for granted."[6]

At some points in the book, I have attempted to maintain a sense of generic flexibility by using the terms "supernatural," "fantastical," and occasionally "magical" to describe nonrealist tales in general terms. "Fantasy" and "fantastical," it should be noted, do not refer in this book to the specific literary genre epitomized by the works of J. R. R. Tolkien, which of course postdated the Brontës significantly; I intend rather the earlier sense of "existing only in imagination; fabulous, imaginary, unreal."[7] The Brontës largely encountered fantastical tales in two forms: literary fairy tales from Europe and the Middle East, and folklore from the British Isles (sometimes in print form, sometimes oral). My discussions of fairy-tale and folklore history in this book focus on the versions of these tales that the Brontës most likely found, even though the tales themselves often have more complex histories. For example, while "Beauty and the Beast" long circulated in oral variants of the animal bridegroom folktale before and after Jeanne-Marie Leprince de Beaumont's influential 1756 literary version, the Brontës are most likely to have read it in literary form, possibly in a collection with other fairy tales from France. I thus treat "Beauty and the Beast" in this book as a literary fairy tale. A tale about a fairy encounter in Devonshire appearing in *Blackwood's Edinburgh Magazine* under the auspices of "popular superstitions" or "popular antiquities," however, I treat as folklore, both because it was relatively local to the Brontës and because "popular antiquities" was precisely the term William Thoms replaced in coining the word "folk-lore" in 1846. The works of Sir Walter Scott and perhaps other print collections also exposed the young Brontës to this type of folklore, as did the oral storytelling of their servant Tabitha Aykroyd.

What matters most for my purposes, though, is that the Brontës, like the Victorians more generally, were surrounded by nonrealist narratives, however they were categorized. The Victorian mania for taxonomy largely postdated the Brontës, and it was not adopted as wholeheartedly by folklorists as it was by scientists.[8] Even during the late-Victorian heyday of folklore study, scholars applied the terms "fairy tale" and "folklore" loosely. As Jennifer Schacker points out,

> Our Victorian scholarly predecessors had remarkably elastic notions of genre and of the narrative forms that fell within the purview of "folklore." The term *fairy tale* is thus used with some frequency throughout the nineteenth century to designate not only the literary tale traditions of French writers like d'Aulnoy, Perrault, Jeanne-Marie Leprince de Beaumont, and others but also the oral traditions introduced in field-based collections.[9]

The liberal application of terminology that Schacker attributes to Victorian folklorists is evident in Victorian writing more broadly. With few exceptions, the Brontës' writing reveals a similarly casual attitude toward the categorization of nonrealist texts and tropes, and they, too, employ the term "fairy tale" in various ways. This is one reason that I have called this book simply *The Brontës and the Fairy Tale* instead of squeezing other types of nonrealist texts into the title. The other reason is that the types of folktales I see most frequently and productively used in the Brontës' writing are those about human beings' encounters with fairies, pixies, brownies, and related supernatural beings; these were sometimes referred to as "fairy lore" or "fairy legends." In the end, the term "fairy tale" most effectively evokes the combination of literary fairy tales and folktales about supernatural creatures that I put in dialogue with the Brontës' works in this book.

The four uses of the term "fairy tale" in Charlotte Brontë's *Jane Eyre* (1847) shed further light on the term's various application in the period. The first time, Jane refers to orally transmitted tales: she reports that a servant told fairy tales in the evenings during her childhood. The next time, later in her childhood, she registers some disappointment with fairy tales because she herself has looked in vain for the elves all over the surrounding countryside; this usage of the term "fairy tale" bears the implications of local origin that we typically associate with folklore as well as a focus on supernatural creatures. Later, Mr. Rochester says to Jane that when he first met her in the wake of a horseback-riding accident, he was put in mind of fairy tales and wondered whether perhaps she had bewitched his horse; events of this kind take place in both literary fairy tales and oral folktales as we define them today. Finally, on the verge of marrying Mr. Rochester, Jane tells him that she can scarcely believe such "complete happiness" could really be achieved; it would be "a fairy tale—a day dream."[10] This fourth use of the term clearly refers to a type of tale that may or may not contain fairies but certainly contains happy endings—a definition that would apply to many (though not all) of the best-known continental literary fairy tales. Thus, across multiple mentions of "fairy tales," Jane refers to supernatural creatures, to malicious magic, and to happiness, and probably to a combination of tales encountered orally and those encountered in literary form.

It is crucial to keep in mind that the Brontës and their contemporaries would not automatically have associated the term "fairy tale" with children and with "happily ever after" as most of us do today; while those associations existed in the nineteenth century as well, they were less preeminent than they are now. In addition to happiness and childhood, fairy tales also signified the magnificent, the beautiful, and the extraordinary. Although many continental literary fairy tales ended happily, others did not, including some tales that were popular in nineteenth-century England, such as Marie-Catherine d'Aulnoy's "The Yellow Dwarf." Moreover, British folktales about fairies and other supernatural creatures often portrayed these beings as capricious, sometimes offering human beings great wealth but other times playing cruel tricks on them or even causing their death. Fairies frequently execute justice in these tales, rewarding the good and punishing the wicked. Nicola Bown notes the "melancholy" nature of many Romantic-era fairies and goes so far as to assert that in the nineteenth century, "fairies were not just for children, nor even mostly for children."[11] Because of the variety of connotations carried by fairies and fairy tales in the nineteenth century, evoking them in fiction and poetry for adults could serve a variety of purposes—many of which I discuss throughout this book.

The Brontës and the Fairy Tale argues for a historically situated understanding of the work fairy tales did for the Brontës. For coming to such an understanding myself, I am indebted to the work of many other scholars on the role of the fairy tale in nineteenth-century Britain. This scholarship has flourished in recent decades, thanks to critics including Jack Zipes, Nina Auerbach, U. C. Knoepflmacher, Jason Marc Harris, Roderick McGillis, Jennifer Schacker, Nicola Bown, Carole G. Silver, Molly Clark Hillard, Caroline Sumpter, Laurence Talairach-Vielmas, and Melissa Dickson. Some of this work has focused on Victorian short stories that heralded themselves as fairy-tale retellings (most of which postdated the Brontës); these scholars have demonstrated that supposedly idle tales of fairies and pixies provided a space for Victorians to work through serious concerns. Other scholars have emphasized the tendency of fairy tales to seep into nineteenth-century texts of other genres, from cartoons to popular science works. This intertextual approach is predicated on one key fact that all this scholarship together has established: the sheer ubiquity of fairies and fairy tales in nineteenth-century Britain. Talairach-Vielmas, having cited Bown and Silver, asserts that "fairies were part and parcel of the Victorian age, and Victorians were experts in fairies and fairy lore far more than their predecessors or followers."[12] Hillard makes a similar claim, emphasizing the effect on literature: "The fairy tale proliferated in every genre of Victorian literature, not whole and unchanged, but retailored to suit every author's particular purpose."[13] My contention in this book that folk and fairy tales permeate the work of the Brontës rests on the findings of previous scholars that such tales were in the air in the first place.

One way my book differs from the scholarship mentioned above is that it focuses substantially, though not exclusively, on the role of fairy tales and folklore in Victorian novels. Jason Marc Harris does consider folklore and the fantastic in Victorian fiction, but he focuses on short stories and novels that are explicitly nonrealist, such as those of George MacDonald and J. M. Barrie. Another exception is Molly Clark Hillard, who explores the role of folklore in several novels, including *Jane Eyre*, as part of a broader study of fairy tales and folklore in Victorian culture; I cite her work throughout this book. My book is modeled on Harry Stone's *Dickens and the Invisible World* (1979), which explores Dickens's evolving but consistent engagement with fairy tales and other fantastical stories throughout his writing career. Considering the popularity of both fairy tales and the novel in the Victorian period, though, less scholarship has examined the two genres together than one might expect. In the next few paragraphs, I will attempt to explain how my book as a whole builds on previous work in the separate fields of fairy-tale scholarship and Victorian studies, as well as why I believe those fields have not yet intersected as much as they have the potential to do. My individual chapters, of course, will take up many works of scholarship in more depth.

Fairy-tale scholarship today bears traces of several distinct phases in its history. It was dominated in the mid-twentieth century by psychological interpretations, then enriched by feminist and historicist perspectives in subsequent decades. Pioneering scholars like Jack Zipes brought a necessary focus to the pernicious ideologies underlying many classic fairy-tale texts, and second-wave feminist scholars uncovered many tales' alignment with patriarchal values. Much recent scholarship unpacks the complexity and updated gender politics of twentieth- and twenty-first-century revisions of fairy tales. More remains to be said, though, about the ways in which readers and writers have always manipulated the fairy tale in unruly ways, even outside the context of explicitly revisionist retellings. Some works of scholarship overstate the conservatism of nineteenth-century tales in the process of applauding later adaptations. I echo Molly Clark Hillard, who has argued persuasively against what she calls the "received idea" that the fairy tale was a "quaint or quiescent form" in the Victorian period; Jennifer Schacker, similarly, disputes "the received narrative about the Victorians' moralizing impulse in fairy tale and children's entertainment."[14] To be sure, the Victorians did sometimes use the fairy tale to moralize: consider Juliana Horatia Ewing's "Amelia and the Dwarfs" (1870), in which an ill-behaved girl undergoes a period of captivity with a group of dwarfs, the sole purpose of which seems to be to teach her to complete her chores and behave selflessly. As Hillard and Schacker have demonstrated, though, this was only one of many ways the fairy tale was deployed in the period. Hillard has shown that in Victorian culture as a whole, the fairy tale was "adaptive, volatile, and eruptive"; Schacker has revealed the same to be true in Victorian theater.[15] Fairy tales, in fact, are promiscuous and adaptable, influencing texts of widely disparate genres in infinitely various ways. A crucial undercurrent of my argument is the contention that the Brontës were not passive recipients of ideologies absorbed from fairy tales; I demonstrate that they were doing important and, in some cases, proto-feminist work with fairy tales even though their plots lack the more obvious rejection of patriarchy that twenty-first-century readers expect of radical texts. My book is indirectly but importantly inspired by the works of fairy-tale scholarship that encourage us to attend to the complexities of pre-twentieth-century tales written by women, especially studies of female writers like Marie-Catherine d'Aulnoy who were Charles Perrault's contemporaries but wrote tales that transcend ideas of the "classic fairy tale" that are based on Perrault and the Brothers Grimm.

Meanwhile, scholars in Victorian studies are well aware that classic fairy tales and other supernatural stories were widespread in the period, and many have commented upon allusions to fairy tales in Victorian novels; some do so in depth and are cited in the following chapters. The associations of fairy tales with childhood and romantic happy endings, however, are the ones that are mentioned most often. Scholars of Charles Dickens's *Great Expectations,* for example, often cite the fairy-tale allusions and motifs in the novel that represent the childish illusions that protagonist Pip must shed; less often do they discuss other uses of fairy tales in the novel that are connected to Pip's adaptation to the reality of adult life.[16] Most of the time, scholarship of Victorian novels containing dry subject matter or unhappy endings does not consider fairy tales as an influence at all, even if those novels have as many fairy-tale allusions as some of their cheerier counterparts. Criticism of the Brontës' work has followed a similar pattern. Scholars know that the Brontës were exposed to fantastical tales as children and readily acknowledge that fairy tales are significant in *Jane Eyre*—a novel with explicit fairy-tale references, a seemingly supernatural event, and a conclusion that showers the heroine with both riches and love. Of all the Brontës' major works, *Jane Eyre* certainly displays its connection to fairy tales and folklore most vividly. Many of their other works, however, simply manifest these tales' influence in different ways, sometimes mimicking the plot of a fairy tale without explicitly alluding to it, other times borrowing motifs from unhappy folktales that have since declined in popularity but would have been familiar to Victorian readers. Folk and fairy tales sometimes subtly advance serious agendas in the Brontës' most realist novels, underscoring social critique ("Bluebeard" in Anne's *The Tenant of Wildfell Hall*) or shedding doubt on a supposedly happy ending (supernatural bride folktales in Charlotte's *Shirley*). Because fewer works of scholarship have explored these uses of folk and fairy tales in the Brontës' writing, my aim is to demonstrate that such tales can and do influence the Brontës' works in more ways than typically supposed. In particular, I endeavor to suggest alternatives to assertions like that of Q. D. Leavis, who does concede the importance of fairy tales and folklore in *Wuthering Heights* but snobbishly opines that "it is a proof of [Emily Brontë's] immaturity at the time of the original conception of *Wuthering Heights* that she should express real psychological insights in such inappropriate forms."[17] Offhand statements such as Sunderland's that "there are . . . clear elements of realism in *Jane Eyre,* even with its romance/fairytale leanings" reflect an assumption that the coexistence of realism and fairy tale in *Jane Eyre* is tenuous or unexpected.[18]

In addition to emphasizing the variety and relevance of fairy tales in the nineteenth century, my insistence upon the harmony between fairy tales and realism is also intended to push on the understanding of realism in Victorian studies. To be sure, realism has never been monolithic, and scholars have never agreed upon any single definition for it; George Levine emphasizes its "variety" and "diversity."[19] But even though scholars of realism often note the presence of allusions to fairy tales in Victorian novels or acknowledge similarities between fairy-tale plots and those of Victorian authors, that is not the same thing as placing references to fairy tales on an equal footing with, say, references to parliamentary procedures when it comes to the construction of a literary real. Most of us would apply the label of realism more readily to Anthony Trollope's *The*

Eustace Diamonds than to *Jane Eyre*. Why? I agree with Audrey Jaffe's suggestion that many literary critics have taken for granted a "consensus not only about realist fiction but about the nature of the real in general within this tradition," an extraliterary real Jaffe argues has been associated at least since Ian Watt's 1957 *The Rise of the Novel* with "the empirical, the material, and the ordinary."[20] To Jaffe's list I would add the category of the visible or external. Other definitions of realism bear out this assertion; Jay Clayton literally calls realism "a form in which the accurate representation of the external scene is paramount," while David Lodge argues that realism represents experience in such a way as to imitate "descriptions of similar experience in nonliterary texts of the same culture."[21] Nonliterary texts nearly always prioritize external over internal information. The writing of the Brontës, in contrast, tends to prioritize internal experience, in all its strangeness, and references to fairy tales often aptly illustrate this experience.

More specifically, I argue that the Brontës often use tools we have been trained to associate with the unreal—references to fairy tales and the supernatural—in order to account for lived experiences that transcend the ability of ordinary realism to articulate. This strategy is especially applicable to the expression of interior experiences. The label of "psychological realism" naturally comes to mind here, but though it does suit the Brontës, it has also been applied to such writers as George Eliot and Anthony Trollope,[22] who brilliantly give voice to characters' rational thought processes but do not stretch the bounds of credibility the way the Brontës sometimes do. What I am observing in the Brontës is a way of reaching into the supposedly unreal in order to convey the feeling of a vitally important real that tends to escape language itself. Explaining how real experience feels can be at odds with conventional forms of literary realism, even psychological realism, because representing reality this way—as filtered through internal experience—sometimes results in descriptions of the external that seem far-fetched. For example, Emily's portrayal of Heathcliff's odd behavior in the latter part of *Wuthering Heights*—which I compare to the behavior of human beings in folklore returned from sojourns with supernatural creatures—seems less odd when one considers that she may have been more interested in capturing the felt experience of grief and obsession than the typical behavior of Yorkshire landowners in the first decade of the nineteenth century. The mystifyingly strange narration of Lucy Snowe in Charlotte's *Villette*, similarly, is riddled with gaps in basic narrative information, but it contains elaborate supernatural and metaphorical passages that provide a startlingly vivid portrayal of the internal experience of loneliness and desire that cannot find expression in ordinary words. In the Brontës' works, passages of conventional literary realism are interspersed with moments like these that strive to express reality from the inside out.

One might object that perhaps some of what the Brontës produced should simply be deemed something other than realism. But the expression of the truth was manifestly their goal. Anne Brontë explicitly stated in her preface to the second edition of *The Tenant of Wildfell Hall* that her "object in writing the following pages, was . . . to tell the truth."[23] Granted, Anne adopted a more conventional form of realism than her sisters did, as we shall see. Yet Charlotte, too, wrote to her publisher in 1848 that "the first duty of an Author is—I conceive—a faithful allegiance to Truth and Nature."[24] These are not the words of a writer who has abandoned realism. Every work of realism offers details selectively; the Brontës sometimes differ from their contemporaries by prioritizing internal over external details at moments in which the most important truth is internal. As part of my argument in this book that we should widen our conception of the affordances of fairy tales in the Brontës' works, I suggest that the Brontës employ particular kinds of realism that are enhanced, not compromised, by fairy-tale models and comparisons.

Part and Chapter Summary

My chapters show that fantastical references are far more frequent in the Brontës' works than readers usually appreciate, even though some works engage them more deeply than others do. Moreover, because folk and fairy tales are less monolithic than modern readers sometimes expect, they can contribute to a wide variety of poetic and novelistic purposes, serving as keys to interpretation, cautionary tales, behavior models, indicators of gender relations, expressions of unspoken desires, and counterexamples. I take my cues from the Brontë texts themselves: in some, references to fairies and related supernatural creatures take precedence, while in others literary fairy tales provide clear structural models even though they do not appear in direct allusions. In many cases, I show that fairy tales play into issues long identified as central to the works at hand, offering a fresh approach.

Part 1, "Once Upon a Time," begins with an analysis of the Brontës' earliest collaborative writings, in which they created several fantastical kingdoms. I then consider the siblings' subsequent forays into individual writing, all of which involve experimentation with fantastical intertexts. Chapter 1 first explores the ways in which the Brontë children read and heard fairy tales, folklore, and supernatural literature more generally, then discusses the fictional worlds the Brontë children created together beginning in the late 1820s. Both of their primary fictional worlds are overseen and controlled by supernatural forces, essentially fairies in one and genii in the other; I will demonstrate the centrality of supernatural creatures to these early texts and their clear derivation from tales the Brontës read. Finally, I argue for the wide-ranging importance of folk- and fairy-tale models in Charlotte's individual juvenilia, discussing both early stories that rework British folktales and late-1830s novellas that are primarily realist but nonetheless feature many figurative references to fairies and fairy tales. In chapter 2, I consider the voluminous extant writings of Branwell Brontë, which feature a fascinating combination of explicit disdain for the supernatural (which he came to see as overly feminine and exotic) and deployment of supernatural references. Long after Branwell abandoned the all-powerful "Chief Genii" who originally controlled the Brontës' fantastical kingdoms, he continued to include supernatural references in his writing in order to provide a counterpoint to the real, to illustrate an experience of extraordinary power or intensity, and to describe women. Chapter 3 assesses the role of the supernatural in the poetry of Emily and Anne Brontë, arguing that both used references to supernatural forces and creatures in an attempt to explain crucial aspects of life in the world that frustrate explanations in ordinary language. For Anne, the religious supernatural took precedence: many of her poems refer to the powers of God. Magic arises sometimes as an inferior counterpoint to this divine puissance and other times as one of several ways of articulating it. For Emily, the supernatural provided a way to convey the human individual's experience of nature. Nature sometimes appears in her poems in the form of supernatural creatures or spells that intensify the human speaker's feelings of fear or longing. Both Emily and Anne used these strategies throughout their writing careers; there is no noticeable decrease in supernatural references as they grew older.

Part 2, "Happily Ever After," focuses on *Jane Eyre*. In chapter 4, after weighing previous scholarly explorations of the role of fairy tales and folklore in *Jane Eyre* (1847), I argue that we can further understand the novel by reading it as a contest between the narrative models of "Bluebeard" and "Beauty and the Beast," two French fairy tales widely reproduced and adapted in nineteenth-century England. These tales occupy two sides of the same coin—both featuring a heroine's entrapment with a suspicious male figure—but require vastly different responses from the young women at their centers. Charlotte Brontë's use of elements from these tales anchors her brand of realism; oriented around the truth of the individual's experience, this realism is thus often but not always faithful to the laws of the everyday external world. That part 2 contains only one chapter is intended to reinforce the argument that happy endings are only one of many tropes that can be taken from fairy-tale models.

The title of part 3, "Farewell to the Fairies," reflects the shift from *Jane Eyre*'s happy ending to two other Brontë novels in which references to folklore advance plots that are ambiguous or simply unhappy. The two chapters in part 3 interrogate the role of folklore in Charlotte's *Shirley* (1849) and Emily's *Wuthering Heights* (1847). I first show in chapter 5 that the realist novel *Shirley*, despite heralding itself on the first page as "unromantic as Monday morning," repeatedly invokes folktales about creatures like fairies and mermaids, particularly as emblematic of a desirable but lost past. In this novel, supernatural creatures are clearly aligned with the feminine against the masculine and with nature against industrial development. The novel's evocations of the supernatural or animal bride tale—in which marriage resembles captivity and ends in separation—cast a pall over the novel's supposedly happy double-wedding resolution. In chapter 6, I demonstrate that the continental fairy tale is evoked primarily as a stark counterpoint to the disastrous central events of Emily Brontë's *Wuthering Heights;* British folklore, however, aptly underscores the unpredictable behavior and tragic ends of many of the characters. Most prominently, characters in *Wuthering Heights* constantly compare Heathcliff to negatively connoted supernatural creatures from folklore, even as the author more subtly associates his endless mourning for Catherine with the struggle of human beings in folktales who are lured away—literally or figuratively—by creatures like fairies, pixies, and will-o'-the-wisps. Taken together, these two facets of the supernatural in the novel suggest opposite conclusions about Heathcliff, underscoring the complexity of this character who has drawn so much critical debate.

Finally, part 4, "What Is Real?," argues that Anne and Charlotte Brontë incorporate fairy tales into novels that seem on the surface to be at odds with such tales. I argue in chapter 7 that Anne's fiercely realist novels, *Agnes Grey* (1847) and *The Tenant of Wildfell Hall* (1848), are deeply indebted to traditional continental fairy tales. *Agnes Grey*, for all its somber didacticism, is in many ways a textbook Victorian Cinderella retelling: Anne uses the plot of "Cinderella" to provide a recognizable framework for a narrative whose primary purpose is to provide instruction and encourage moral behavior in her readers. I then read *The Tenant of Wildfell Hall* as a retelling of "Bluebeard" animated by contemporary concerns. This novel contains key thematic elements of "Bluebeard"—chiefly, a naive heroine's relationship with a dangerous husband—as well as specific details that suggest a deliberate allusion to the tale. Critics have treated Anne's work as the opposite of all things fairy tale; however, the murderous husband at the center of "Bluebeard" makes this tale a perfect underlying structure for a realist novel advocating for temperance and the right of women to divorce. Finally, chapter 8 considers Charlotte's final novel, *Villette* (1853), and argues that first-person narrator Lucy Snowe's notoriously obfuscated account of her experience is an instrument of enchantment. Lucy, I argue, offers what is to a significant extent a conventionally realist narrative of the struggles of a young single woman without resources in the nineteenth century, but intersperses it with metaphors and detours that leave us with an "enchanted" picture of her life: one that masks and replaces certain details but leaves others intact. Allusions to fairy tales and supernatural creatures abound in this novel, putting to rest any doubt that Charlotte would deploy fantastical references lavishly throughout her writing career.

Although I have organized the book by a combination of chronology and theme, it is also worth briefly considering each Brontë in terms of which aspects of fairy tale and folklore she or he embraced or repudiated. Anne, for example, made most productive use of classic continental literary fairy tales, including their moral lessons, their mostly happy endings, and the seriousness of their villains. She did very little with folklore. Emily, conversely, seems to have used the continental fairy tale only in the happy but pale "Beauty and the Beast"–like story of young Cathy and Hareton in *Wuthering Heights*, otherwise preferring to incorporate the nature spirits, ghosts, and other supernatural creatures of folklore. Branwell, too, drew on English folklore, particularly its dark supernatural creatures and grim heroic figures. He had no use for any of the aspects of continental tales that appealed to Anne. Thus, though Branwell and Anne are united in that they use fantastical tales less than their sisters and avow a commitment to the real, they make exceptions for opposite kinds of nonrealist tales in ways that reflect divergent priorities (his for legendary masculine heroism and hers for instruction in the modern world). Charlotte, meanwhile, seems to have loved it all. Although in her last works she casts eloquent doubt on the classic romantic happy ending, there seems to have been no aspect of folklore or fairy tale that she did not find a way to use in one story or another. The lessons and rewards of continental tales, the terrifying and magnificent supernatural creatures, exotic tales and local legends—all appear in Charlotte's work. The freedom to stretch the bounds of plausibility was a crucial affordance of fantastical tales for both Charlotte and Emily; the compatibility of continental tales' morals with realist goals was equally crucial for both Charlotte and Anne.

Common to all three Brontë sisters, and to Branwell to a lesser extent, was the use of fantastical tales and creatures to convey the vividness of internal experiences. Charles Dickens called fairy tales a "precious old escape" from a difficult world, but they could just as well be described as the key to understanding the world in deeper ways. Importantly, "the world" as the Brontës saw it was not only the observable world: it was also the world of the mind and emotions. The Brontës have long been considered virtuosos in telling compelling stories that capture internal and external realities in a way that no one else ever has. *The Brontës and the Fairy Tale* argues that fairy tales and folklore constituted a crucial element of the Brontëan literary real.

PART I

Once Upon a Time

1 From Haworth to Glass Town

Reading and Writing in "the Children's Study"

Awful Brannii gloomy giant
Shaking oer earth his blazing air
Brooding on blood with drear and vengeful soul
He sits enthroned in clouds to hear his thunders roll
Dread Tallii next like a dire Eagle flies
And on our mortal miseries feasts her bloody eyes
Emii and Annii last with boding cry
Famine fortell and mortal misery.

—Branwell Brontë, "Ode on the Celebration of the Great African Games" (1831–32)

When the Brontë children began to write, they immediately wrote themselves into their stories in the form of powerful supernatural creatures. In the fictional worlds they invented together, human characters might be helped or hurt at any moment by four imposing figures with names very similar to "Branwell," "Charlotte," "Emily," and "Anne." Depending on the story, these figures were sometimes fairies, sometimes genii (mighty spirits from *The Thousand and One Nights* and other Middle Eastern stories, enduring in the West today in the "genie in a bottle" trope). Although we tend to think of supernatural creatures today as exclusively good or evil, and of fairy tales as invariably ending happily, these certainties did not prevail in the stories the Brontës would have read and heard; for them, drawing on fairy tales and on the folklore of supernatural creatures could take infinite forms. While these forms include the serious poetry and realist novels the Brontës wrote as adults, the use of the supernatural in their juvenilia is much more prominent than it would be in later texts; even in the earliest stories the Brontës wrote as children, however, their deployments of fantastical literature were already multifaceted.

One of the most distinctive episodes in the Brontë family biography is the literary play that Charlotte, Branwell, Emily, and Anne undertook together as children. Their clergyman father, Patrick Brontë, prioritized the education of all four children and allowed them to read whatever they wished—a remarkable decision, especially for a father of girls, in the early nineteenth century. Although the popular imagination, fueled by Elizabeth Gaskell's foundational biography *The Life of Charlotte Brontë* (1857), situates the Brontës in a rustic cottage on an isolated, wind-swept moor, they were very much part of the world. Haworth Parsonage, where they lived from 1820 on, was essentially "the last house in the village," overlooking the moor but near the church and plenty of other buildings.[1] Haworth was a small town but stood within just a few miles of three larger ones. The Brontës read multiple newspapers every week even in childhood and had ample access to books of all kinds; they were well aware of current events and of contemporary discourses within numerous fields. Meanwhile, Patrick also gave his children free rein to compose stories and poems in the room in the parsonage dubbed "the children's study" by the servants.[2] The result was the massive body of writing now known as the Brontë juvenilia. Although the children initially invented stories together, most of the surviving texts were physically written by Charlotte or Branwell; particularly with the earliest texts, it is impossible to say for sure whether each story's author invented it or merely recorded a collective narrative. We do know that, in general, the children began by concocting stories as a group of four but gradually broke off into pairs: Charlotte and Branwell continued the stories of Glass Town and Angria that had originated as the whole family's Young Men's Play, while Emily and Anne established their own imaginary world of Gondal. Another difficulty in approaching the Brontë juvenilia is the magnitude: these texts span hundreds of pages, amounting in modern editions to three volumes of Branwell's writing, three volumes and a projected fourth of Charlotte's, and scantier surviving outputs from Emily and Anne.[3] Yet, as voluminous as this body of writing is, many texts the Brontës wrote as children have been lost or destroyed, most notably the entirety of the prose chronicles of Gondal. Consequently, the Brontë juvenilia can feel at once overwhelming and disconnected. Nevertheless, these tales and poems offer unparalleled insight into the development of the Brontës as writers. For my purposes, they also reveal a case study in the reception of fairy tales, folklore, and other supernatural texts by one nineteenth-century English family—albeit an extraordinary one.

In this chapter, I first provide an overview of the sources in which the Brontë children encountered or might have encountered fairy tales, folklore, and the literature of the supernatural more generally. In some cases, we know for sure that the Brontës read a given text. In many others, we do not. For example, no surviving evidence in the Brontës' home library or personal writing indicates precisely where they encountered Charles Perrault's "Bluebeard"; we know they encountered it, however, because Charlotte names the tale explicitly in all her major novels. Similarly, we cannot be sure of the exact oral or print sources for the Brontës' ideas about fairies, but the mentions of fairies in their own writing demonstrate that they were familiar with contemporary discussions of fairies in literature and folklore. In part, the scarcity of concrete evidence speaks to the ephemeral nature of the texts in which fairy tales and folklore were disseminated in the eighteenth and nineteenth centuries: they often appeared in periodicals and very cheap books that were not preserved. It also speaks to the pervasiveness of folk and fairy tales in any culture: one often knows the basic outline of a famous tale but cannot say precisely where one read or heard it. In the following pages, I discuss how folk and fairy tales were available to nineteenth-century English children in general, as well as sources that are particularly likely to have reached the Brontës. I then discuss the Brontës' storytelling collaborations of the late 1820s, which they called the Islanders Play and the Young Men's Play. Both fictional worlds are overseen and controlled by supernatural creatures: fairies in one and genii in the other. I will demonstrate the centrality of the supernatural in these early texts and its clear derivation from tales the Brontës read. Finally, I gesture toward the ubiquity of folk- and fairy-tale references in Charlotte's individual juvenilia, demonstrating how her use of these models evolved over the course of the 1830s from full-fledged retellings of folktales about fairies to more subtle metaphorical allusions within longer realist narratives.

The Brontës' Sources for Folk and Fairy Tales

Fairy tales were virtually unavoidable even for less avid readers of the Brontës' generation, because of the sheer number and variety of print and oral forms they took in the late eighteenth and early nineteenth centuries. The voracious reading of the Brontë children provided ample opportunity to encounter fairy tales from all over the world. Although it is impossible—and undesirable—to distinguish completely between folklore and fairy tale, I proceed in the following paragraphs by discussing the ways the Brontë children could have encountered literary fairy tales (in books), followed by the ways in which they could have encountered folklore (orally and in periodicals, as well as in books; see the introduction for a fuller discussion of the fraught question of fairy-tale taxonomy). My goal is not to argue for specific versions of tales as the most likely sources for the Brontës; rather, I hope to provide a sense of the tapestry of folk- and fairy-tale models available in the popular culture from which the Brontës drew.

The major sources of the literary fairy tale in nineteenth-century England were *The Thousand and One Nights* (to which I will generally refer in this book as the *Arabian Nights' Entertainments* because of the prevalence of the eighteenth-century English translation with that title) and tales from continental Europe. *The Thousand and One Nights* gained popularity in Europe when Antoine Galland began translating the stories into French, in multiple volumes, between 1704 and 1717. Galland's translation both capitalized on and fueled the vogue for literary fairy tales in France, begun in the late seventeenth century partly by Charles Perrault's *Histoires ou contes du temps passé* (1697) but also by a myriad of tales authored by female aristocrats. The leader of these so-called *conteuses* was Marie-Catherine Le Jumel de Barneville, Baroness d'Aulnoy, who launched the literary fairy tale in France by embedding a tale called "L'île de la félicité" ("The Island of Happiness") in her 1690 novel *Histoire d'Hypolite, comte de Douglas* and went on to produce an astonishing number of stand-alone fairy tales. Other women, including Charlotte-Rose de Caumont de la Force; Marie-Jeanne Lhéritier; Catherine Bernard; Henriette-Julie de Murat; Louise de Bossigny, comtesse d'Auneuil; and Jeanne-Marie Leprince de Beaumont, followed suit. English translations of Galland appeared by 1706; throughout the eighteenth century, translations of d'Aulnoy, Perrault, and their compatriots became available to Britons as well.[4] It is possible that the Brontës could even have read French fairy tales in the original language—French was a regular subject at Roe Head School, attended by all three Brontë sisters in the 1830s, and considering that Charlotte translated the entire first volume of Voltaire's *La Henriade* at age fourteen, reading these tales would have been well within her reach.[5] Literary fairy tales also seized public interest in other European countries, notably Germany, where a number of leading Romantic writers produced fairy tales based on traditional stories. The famous *Kinder- und Hausmärchen* of Jacob Grimm and Wilhelm Grimm were first published in 1812 and 1819 (and reissued repeatedly in the following decades). They were soon translated into English by Edgar Taylor, who published *German Popular Stories* in two volumes (released in 1823 and 1826).

These translations were extremely popular in England, where publishers could easily combine them with homegrown tales like "Jack the Giant-Killer." Historians of children's literature—including F. J. Harvey Darton, Mary V. Jackson, and M. O. Grenby—provide substantially similar accounts of the rise of children's literature as a publication category in the eighteenth century and the subsequent surge in fanciful literature for children. Although many children's books were didactic, imaginative works became increasingly popular; in the latter half of the eighteenth century, according to Jackson, "more and more, fairies, magic, and fantasy found their way into the trade wares stocked in the juvenile libraries."[6] Fairy tales were published in a number of formats, including collections of tales by the same author and collections containing the works of various authors. Publisher John Harris released numerous collections of fairy tales in the early nineteenth century—editions of d'Aulnoy and Perrault's tales in 1802–3, for example, and a collection containing tales by multiple authors called *The Court of Oberon; or, Temple of the Fairies* in 1823, the same year that Edgar Taylor's translations of the tales of the Grimms began to appear. Many other "respectable booksellers," too, published "fairy tales . . . English folklore, and ballads" in the first decade of the nineteenth century, notably Benjamin Tabart.[7]

Historians also agree that a great deal of children's literature in the eighteenth and early nineteenth centuries appeared in the form of chapbooks. These flimsy editions of fairy tales and other popular literature were designed for children and minimally educated adults; they often came without covers and would not have been seen as worthy of preservation, which of course poses problems for scholarship. We know, however, that chapbooks were ubiquitous and that they frequently featured fairy tales. According to Mary V. Jackson, "It would be impossible to even list a tenth of the chapbook publications in this area [fairy tales, folktales, and romances] in England, Ireland, and Scotland. A complete list would require many sizable volumes. . . . Chapbooks regularly offered adventures, fairy tales, romances, and Eastern tales and continued to do so after respectable publishers had joined in completely."[8] F. J. Harvey Darton agrees that "single tales, *Cinderella* especially, came out in chapbook form quite early"; he also mentions "Jack the Giant-Killer," "Tom Thumb," and individual editions of the various fairy tales of Charles Perrault as favorite chapbook subjects.[9] Historians also have assembled evidence that children from nearly all strata of society actually read fairy tales in chapbook and other forms. Such evidence is "abundant," according to Grenby, who provides examples such as Thomas Carter's *Memoirs of a Working Man*, in which Carter specifically mentions having read chapbook versions of "Tom Thumb," "Jack the Giant-Killer," and "Little Red Riding Hood" during his childhood.[10] Although the Brontës were of a higher and more educated class than the average nineteenth-century chapbook reader, they still might well have encountered fairy tales this way or interacted with other children who did.

Ultimately, Jackson deems the 1820s—the decade in which Charlotte, Branwell, Emily, and Anne, born in that order between 1816 and 1820, began to read and write in earnest—a "watershed" in children's books; at this point, moralistic and religious opposition to the publication and reading of fairy tales and other imaginative stories largely faded away, and fairy tales had become widely available in low- and high-quality forms.[11] Although we cannot conclusively prove that the Brontës owned or read any particular editions, we know that they encountered them somewhere, considering that their writings would explicitly mention tales including "Cinderella," "Bluebeard," and various tales from the *Arabian Nights' Entertainments*, while also strongly evoking "Beauty and the Beast," "Little Red Riding Hood," and others. It would have been impossible for the Brontës to have avoided encountering fairy tales in some form or other—and since they demonstrably encountered some, it is reasonable to conjecture that they were also familiar with related tales that they do not mention by name.

The Brontë children's exposure to specific books of any genre is a matter of debate for their biographers because the books extant in the library at Haworth Parsonage (now the Brontë Parsonage Museum) represent only a small fraction of the material with which the Brontës demonstrated familiarity even at an early age. Elizabeth Gaskell wrote in *The Life of Charlotte Brontë* that the children would walk to the larger nearby town of Keighley to obtain library books, but she does not specify which library.[12] Clifford Whone suggests the library of the Keighley Mechanics' Institute as a source of reading material.[13] Some scholars, including Rebecca Fraser and Bob Duckett, have suggested that the children used the extensive library at Ponden Hall, three miles from the parsonage.[14] Juliet Barker argues that the regular circulating libraries in Keighley are the most likely repository of books for the Brontë children.[15] In any case, we cannot know for sure where the Brontës borrowed books or what they might have obtained there. Lists of library holdings from the period are tantalizing (Duckett offers the Ponden Hall library catalog from 1899, and Whone the Keighley Mechanics' Institute library catalog from 1841); they include books of science, history, biography, and ancient and modern literature. But the dates of the existing catalogs are too late to provide definitive evidence of the Brontës' access, and no records remain to indicate what they actually borrowed from any library.[16] It seems to me that we have insufficient evidence to completely rule out any of the possible sources for Brontë book borrowing. Obviously, they read far more than was available to them in their home; they borrowed liberally from one or more libraries and perhaps from acquaintances. Our best clue to the Brontës' reading remains their own writing.

Despite the difficulty of documenting the Brontës' exposure to literary fairy tales, we can more easily trace their access to folklore. The Brontë children almost certainly heard folktales about fairies from their longtime servant Tabitha Aykroyd. Affectionately known as "Tabby," she joined the Brontës in 1824 and remained until she died shortly before Charlotte in 1854. According to Elizabeth Gaskell, Tabby

> had known the "bottom," or the valley, in those primitive days when the fairies frequented the margin of the "beck" on moonlight nights, and had known folk who had seen them. But that was when there were no mills in the valleys; and when all the wool-spinning was done by hand in the farmhouses round. "It wur the factories as had driven 'em away," she said. No doubt she had many a tale to tell of by-gone days of the country-side.[17]

Some of Gaskell's statements have been debunked, but usually her misrepresentations were intended to smooth over unseemly details such as Charlotte's unrequited love for her married employer Constantin Héger; there is no reason not to believe her account of Tabby.[18] Moreover, Charlotte's novels offer what seem to be reflections of Tabby's storytelling: Jane Eyre notes that servant Bessie used to tell stories on "winter evenings . . . passages of love and adventure taken from old fairy tales and older ballads,"[19] and an old housekeeper at the end of *Shirley* muses about the sightings of fairy tales she once experienced. Shirley herself remarks, "When I was a very little girl . . . my nurse used to tell me of fairies being seen in that Hollow . . . before my father built the mill."[20] This image of the female domestic worker recounting fairy stories to the children in her care became something of a cliché, but it seems to have been authentic in the case of the Brontës. Unfortunately, we do not know any specific tales that Tabby shared; the notions of fairies loving the moonlight and eventually departing from the countryside in the face of industrialization, however, were widespread cultural tropes that also appeared in the Brontës' writing.[21]

Folklore had also found its way into numerous published collections by the time the Brontë children had learned to read. Jennifer Schacker has demonstrated that "from the 1820s onward, dozens of folklore books were issued by London publishers."[22] Richard Dorson's *The British Folklorists* names several collections of stories based on folklore that were available during the Brontës' youth, including Thomas Keightley's *The Fairy Mythology* (1828) and Allan Cunningham's *Traditional Tales of the English and Scottish Peasantry* (1822).[23] Another influential folklore book from the period, Thomas Crofton Croker's *Fairy Legends and Traditions of the South of Ireland* (1825), is of particular interest because of the Brontës' Irish heritage; their grandfather Hugh Brontë was, according to Patrick in a letter to Elizabeth Gaskell, "a native of the South of Ireland."[24] If Hugh was a storyteller, as some scholars have suggested, he might have known the same stories included in Croker's collection.[25] Regardless, Croker's book was quite popular, issued in a second edition in 1826; reviews appeared in the *Quarterly Review* and in *Blackwood's Edinburgh Magazine*, which the Brontë children read religiously. During this period, book reviews tended to include much longer excerpts than they do today. The excerpt in the *Blackwood's* review of Croker's book included two stories in their entirety: "The Legend of Knocksheogowna," in which a fairy plays a prank, and "Master and Man," in which a fairy grants a wish, then enforces servitude on the recipient, but ultimately is outwitted. Overall, *Fairy Legends and Traditions of the South of Ireland* offers lively tales of fairy capriciousness and fairy justice, of changelings, of banshees, and of merrows (creatures similar to mermaids or seal maidens). These are all representative of the ways in which fairies tended to be portrayed in traditional tales of the British Isles.

The writing of Sir Walter Scott—identified by Emma Butcher as crucial context for the Brontës' conceptions of war[26]—was also an indispensable resource for folklore in the early nineteenth century. The Brontës owned copies of Scott's long poems *The Lay of the Last Minstrel* (1806), *The Vision of Don Roderick* (1811), and *Rokeby* (1813), as well as his children's history of Scotland, *Tales of a Grandfather* (1827), and George Allan's *Life of Sir Walter Scott* (1834). The Brontës' published and unpublished writings are full of admiring references to Scott, including many other works besides those we know they owned; in 1827, Emily chose Scott as her "chief man" in the Islanders Play discussed later in this chapter.[27] In long poems of Scott's that we know the Brontës read, they would have found all manner of supernatural creatures and magic. For example, *The Lay of the Last Minstrel* features a malicious creature usually referred to as a goblin but also called an "elf," an "imp," and a "vile malignant sprite" (Canto Fourth, stanza 15, ln. 270 and 277). As he often does, Scott includes a substantial footnote explaining the Scottish superstitions that underlie the various actions of this character. Other long poems of Scott's feature a wide array of supernatural creatures; for example, fairies, giants, enchanters, and dwarfs appear in *The Lady of the Lake* (1810).

Scott's nonfiction writings on "popular antiquities," which included supernatural beliefs, were crucial to the study of the subject in their day and would have been appealing to the young Brontës. For example, the extensive introduction to *Minstrelsy of the Scottish Border* (1802–3) contains a section about the superstitious beliefs of the border region. Creatures including fairies, brownies, bogles, and kelpies are described in fairly typical ways: fairies are the "chief" creatures, brownies are "meagre, shaggy, and wild," bogles prefer "rather to perplex and frighten mankind, than either to serve, or seriously to hurt, them," and kelpies live in the water (lxxxi–lxxxvi). The text also includes a lengthy story about a brownie with all the traditional elements: he attaches himself to a family, helps them, demands compensation (a green coat), and finally disappears forever (lxxxiii). In a detailed discussion of fairies, Scott traces the English fairies' origin to the Peris of the Middle East (fairy-like creatures from Persian mythology, associated with beauty in Western appropriations), noting that they are similarly angelic in appearance and rather less than angelic in behavior. The stories of the fairy Melusina and the Erl-King are told. Fairies play pranks and steal babies. All in all, *Minstrelsy of the Scottish Border* contains a wealth of popular superstitions of its day and of days past.

Supernatural happenings and creatures from English folklore appeared in all kinds of sources, including highly literary texts. The works of William Shakespeare, such as *A Midsummer Night's Dream* and *Macbeth,* feature fairies, witches, and numerous folk beliefs. Shakespearean allusions in the Brontës' writings of 1829 and 1830 indicate that they were already familiar with his plays at a young age. *A Midsummer Night's Dream* features prominent fairy characters and encapsulates traditional English fairy belief in the figure of Puck. Also named Robin Goodfellow, Puck can shape-shift, work magic, or turn into a will-o'-the-wisp; he addresses himself as "Goblin" (III.1.103–6, III.2.399). He wreaks domestic mischief and, famously, deems mortals "fools" (III.2.115). Throughout, *A Midsummer Night's Dream* demonstrates the power of fairy actions and fairy magic to influence human beings. This interference temporarily ruins Hermia's happiness, then ultimately secures the happiness of everyone. Oberon, king of the fairies, declares at the end of the play that he will bless the three mortal couples so that their children "ever shall be fortunate" (V.1.398). A reader of the play comes away with a keen impression of the ease and carelessness with which fairies can make or break human lives.[28]

In addition to books, the Brontës read newspapers and magazines voraciously as children; twelve-year-old Charlotte noted in one of her earliest extant texts that "we take 2 and see three newspapers a week," as well as *Blackwood's Edinburgh Magazine,* which she confidently deems "the most able periodical there is."[29] The family had regular access to current and past issues of *Blackwood's* through December 1831, when the neighbor from whom they borrowed the magazine died. They continued to see *Blackwood's* after that at least some of the time, as evidenced by various sources.[30] *Blackwood's* was an eclectic monthly publication, offering articles on current affairs, political commentary, travel accounts, letters to the editor, reviews of works of literature, and original poems and stories. Mentions of fairy tales and supernatural creatures appeared frequently in the magazine in poems, stories, and reviews. Fairies, in particular, permeated the pages of *Blackwood's* just as they permeated the rest of nineteenth-century English culture, often in the form of fairy poems contributed by unnamed or little-known authors (see, for example, "The Fairy Well" in April 1833 and "The Faëry Bank" in April 1835). The attributes of the fairies in these poems are thoroughly traditional and would be reflected in the Brontës' own writing; for example, fairies often wear green and revel in the moonlight, and they are both attractive and threatening to human beings. A lengthy poem published in 1831, "Unimore, a Dream of the Highlands," refers to other supernatural beings that appear in later Brontë works, including naiads, mermaids, and nereids. The May 1832 issue contained an article on Tennyson that disparaged his two poems "The Mermaid" and "The Merman" but nevertheless quoted them both nearly in full. The June 1837 issue included a fascinating article called "Source of Medieval Legends and Superstitions." Here, the Brontës would have found mentions of Dick Whittington and his cat, Jack the Giant-Killer, Prince Ahmed of the *Arabian Nights' Entertainments*, Melusina, and Thor; even werewolves make an appearance. *Fraser's Magazine for Town and Country*, a comparable monthly to which the Brontës subscribed as of May 1832, contained similar mentions of fairies and other supernatural creatures, including fairy poems and reviews of longer works that dealt with folklore. Both magazines, too, frequently contained offhand allusions to fairy tales from continental Europe in articles of all kinds; "Bluebeard" was a particular favorite.

During the 1820s and 1830s, many of the most memorable fairy stories and poems in *Blackwood's* and *Fraser's* were contributed by James Hogg, a Scottish poet and novelist who often published under the name "The Ettrick Shepherd." Hogg, who had in fact been a shepherd, called himself "king o' the mountain and fairy school."[31] Young Charlotte refers to him by name in "The History of the Year" (1829), declaring him "a man of most extraordinary genius."[32] Hogg's series for *Blackwood's* called "The Shepherd's Calendar" often involved tales of encounters with supernatural creatures, including the comparatively well-known tale "Mary Burnet" (1828), which I will discuss in chapter 5. Hogg's writing in *Blackwood's* disseminated traditional beliefs about supernatural creatures including fairies, witches, and brownies.[33]

Clearly, fairy tales and folklore pervaded the early nineteenth-century print culture in which the Brontës were immersed. Even though accounts of the Brontës' reading specific folk and fairy tales are few, it is likely that they encountered them often. Reading, however, did not satisfy the Brontës: while still quite young, they began to write, imitating the styles of texts they read and fashioning their own versions of stories and genres encountered in print. The influence of some of the sources I have mentioned, especially the continental literary fairy tales, will not be apparent until later chapters; we will see now, however, that the earliest texts the Brontës wrote were inspired by the *Arabian Nights' Entertainments* and by the portrayals of fairies and other supernatural creatures they found in books and periodicals.

Once Upon a Time

The Brontës organized the multiple fictional worlds they created together under the name of "plays"; the most lasting were the Islanders Play and the Young Men's Play, the latter of which would develop into the extensive writing of Charlotte and Branwell on Glass Town and Angria. Each "play" refers to a fictional world that encompasses various characters and multiple stories of varying genres; these plays began in the late 1820s with the four children inventing stories aloud together, sometimes acting them out with toys, and later writing some of the stories down. The term "play" refers to the act of playing in general (tangibly and intellectually), not only to the specific genre associated with drama; the meaning of the name "the Islanders Play" is more equivalent to "the Star Wars universe" than to "the Scottish play," in that it refers to an entire fictional world within which numerous stories of varying types and genres could be told. It is apparent that the children were impressed by the portrayals of supernatural creatures in the folk- and fairy-tale texts they had encountered at this point: in their own stories, fairies control the world of the Islanders Play while genii control that of the Young Men's Play. These supernatural forces are integral to the Brontës' earliest writing.

The Islanders Play began in December 1827, at which point Charlotte was eleven years old, Branwell ten, Emily nine, and Anne nearly eight. Much of what we know about the play comes from two surviving texts written later by Charlotte: the section entitled "The origin of the Islanders" in "The History of the Year," an 1829 account of the origins of the

Brontë siblings' fictional worlds, and *Tales of the Islanders,* a collection of stories from the Islanders Play written in four short "volumes" between June 30, 1829, and July 30, 1830. Charlotte's account of the Islanders Play begins with a frame providing the occasion for storytelling (in the fashion of Giovanni Boccaccio or Giovanni Francesco Straparola, though it is unlikely that the children had encountered those tales): "One night, about the time when the cold sleet and dreary fogs of November are succeeded by the snow storms and high, piercing, night winds of confirmed winter, we were all sitting round the warm, blazing kitchen fire" when Branwell declared that he was bored.[34] To relieve the boredom, each Brontë child chose an island off England for his or her own, then imaginatively populated it with important men (in Charlotte's case, the same Duke of Wellington who would star in the Young Men's Play). But by chapter 2 of the first volume, they had moved on together to a "fictitious island" which "appeared [more] like the region of enchantment or a beautiful fiction than sober reality" (6). This island is obviously—and explicitly—"fairy land" (23). Charlotte details its natural beauty and introduces the "Little King and Queens" (8): the Brontë children themselves in supernatural form, sometimes referred to in the text as "fairies." Like the genii of the Young Men's Play discussed below, the Little King and Queens can participate in and influence events on the island; they sometimes appear as human beings and other times adopt a more imposing fairy form.

It is crucial to appreciate that fairies in traditional folklore are rarely exclusively "good" or "evil"; rather, when human beings encounter fairies, they are as likely to lose their lives as to gain fabulous rewards. Thomas Crofton Croker's "The Legend of Knockgrafton," included in *Fairy Legends and Traditions of the South of Ireland,* swiftly illustrates both possibilities. A man with a hump on his back, hearing a group of fairies singing, waits for a pause and builds harmoniously on their tune; the delighted fairies invite him to be one of their own because they respect his musical skill, and they remove his hump. Then, another man with a hump, having heard of the other's good fortune, attempts to replicate it, but when he sings along with the fairies, he ignores their tune. Now furious, the fairies punish him by adding another hump to the one he already has; this excess weight leads "soon" to the man's death.[35] From the human beings' perspective, the fairies dispense relief one moment and death the next; from the fairies' perspective, however, this is not capriciousness but justice. Fairies clearly see themselves as superior to mortals: they take human beings as slaves, for example, in many traditional tales (including Croker's "Master and Man," which was printed in *Blackwood's* in July 1825, and Allan Cunningham's "Elphin Irving, The Fairies' Cupbearer"). Fairies are neither particularly malicious nor particularly benevolent toward human beings: they simply act without reference to human desires.

Tales of the Islanders blends this indifference to human beings with the "fairies' farewell" of traditional English folklore. As discussed above, the Brontës' own storytelling servant Tabby Aykroyd referred to a centuries-old belief that the fairies who once dwelt in England are departing or have departed in the face of modern developments (such as Christianity or industrialization) that make the land uninhabitable for them.[36] Charlotte refers to this belief in both *Jane Eyre* and *Shirley; Tales of the Islanders* arrives at the same result from a different direction. In the second volume, not long after a rebellion at the school on the island, the Little King and Queens grow "tired" of the school and send the children home; thenceforth, "only fairies dwell in the Island of a Dream."[37] The third and fourth volumes then take place not on the fairy island but in England, though fairies and other supernatural creatures still appear frequently. In other words, in *Tales of the Islanders,* the fairies dismiss human beings from their land rather than being driven away by human inventions. It is thus the human beings' farewell to fairyland that effects the separation of mortal and immortal that heralds modernity.

This inversion of the fairy lore tradition—evocative of the expulsion of human beings from the Garden of Eden—showcases the power the Brontës bestow upon their supernatural alter egos. The same Little King and Queens who swiftly apply "fairy remedies" to rescue the Duke of Wellington's son from the brink of the grave decide in the very same chapter to dismiss mortals from their land.[38] In this case, the banished mortals are not being punished for any particular breach of conduct as in tales like "The Legend of Knockgrafton"; the fairies simply "tire" of them. Moreover, this power over human beings operates in tandem with the narrative power Charlotte confers on the Little King and Queens by writing the text of *Tales of the Islanders* from a first-person perspective: "we" are always in charge, of the action and the point of view. The perspective of the mere mortals in the story does not concern the storyteller and, implicitly, ought not concern the reader. Charlotte ends *Tales of the Islanders* with a final reminder of ownership:

That is Emily's, Branwell's, Anne's and my land
And now I bid a kind and glad goodbye
To those who o'er my book cast an indulgent eye

(81, italics in original)

Notably, the land is "ours," but the book is "mine."

While the Brontës participated in and ultimately controlled their human characters' lives in the Islanders Play in the form of fairies, they did the same in the Young Men's Play in the form of genii. The Young Men's Play began in June 1826, when Branwell received a set of twelve toy soldiers. He shared the soldiers with his sisters, and each of the four children claimed one and named it after a prominent man: Charlotte's was the Duke of Wellington, Branwell's was Napoleon Buonaparte, Emily's was at first dubbed "Gravey" but later evolved into explorer William Edward Parry, and Anne's was at first "Waiting Boy," later explorer John Ross.[39] Then they began to imagine what these men might do—and thus was born the play that would continue in various forms for the next two decades. In the earliest extant text describing the Young Men's adventures, a ship sets out from England in 1793 bearing twelve men. They arrive in Africa, defeat the Ashanti inhabitants in battle, and make a peace treaty with the Ashanti king. The British adventurers then build a city that they will call "Glass Town" or "Verdopolis"; this becomes the setting for dozens of stories the young Brontës (especially Charlotte and Branwell) would go on to write.

Branwell soon instituted a magazine for the citizens of the new land, called *Branwell's Blackwood's Magazine*. Like the real *Blackwood's*, the new monthly magazine—edited by Branwell but with many contributions from Charlotte—contains articles on art, current events, literature, and politics, as well as advertisements and letters to the editor.[40] The magazine's tiny physical form (about two inches by one inch) suited the toy soldiers, and the articles were pitched to the Young Men of Glass Town. The early issues of 1829 do not survive, but the June issue contains Branwell's poem "Dirge of the Genii," Charlotte's tale "The Enfant" (in which a menacing fairy foretells the story's events), a letter to the editor passionately defending the authenticity of Ossian,[41] a brief drama called "Nights" modeled on the *Noctes Ambrosianae* feature in *Blackwood's*, and several fictional advertisements. As this list demonstrates, the magazine mingles fantasy and verisimilitude. By August, Charlotte had taken over as editor under the name "The Genius CB" and renamed the publication *Blackwood's Young Men's Magazine;* she would continue as editor until the magazine was apparently abandoned in 1831.

The "Genius CB" was, of course, the Genius Charlotte Brontë. Although "genius" in this period could indicate exceptional intelligence, the kind of genius referred to here (sometimes rendered "genie") was a formidable supernatural creature, often associated with a particular space—one might be a genius of the lamp, as in certain famous Middle Eastern stories, while another might be a genius of a portion of land. The Brontë children named themselves the four Chief Genii of their fictional kingdom, writing themselves into the stories as Tallii, Brannii, Emmii, and Annii (the spelling sometimes varied). According to Branwell's map, the land surrounding Glass Town was divided into regions named after the Brontës' Chief Men: "Sneaky's Land" (Sneaky or Sneachi was another name for Branwell's hero), "Parry's Land," "Ross's Land," and "Wellington's Land."[42] Each Chief Genius ruled in the land named for his or her "chief man"; the four Genii also work in tandem to protect the Twelve Adventurers. They have magnificent powers to influence events and subdue mere mortals; as we will see in the next chapter, Branwell grew to think that the Genii's sway verged on tyranny.

Yet tyranny was endemic to the invented city of Glass Town because it was located in the decidedly real land of the Ashanti tribe in Africa, for which land the British were actually fighting in the 1820s. As Firdous Azim has stated with reference to Charlotte in particular, "Far from being the escapist 'dream world' which Fannie Ratchford once claimed them to be, Brontë's early stories are thus fully implicated . . . in the colonial enterprise with which they are coeval."[43] Indeed, the Brontë children learned about the British Empire from their avid reading of periodicals, including *Blackwood's Edinburgh Magazine;* in fact, the June 1826 issue of *Blackwood's* contained a map of northern and central Africa that Branwell adapted to serve as the map of the Glass Town Federation and the kingdom of Angria. Gayatri Chakravorty Spivak identifies in *Jane Eyre* "the unquestioned idiom of imperialist presuppositions."[44] While I find this assertion somewhat reductive in the case of *Jane Eyre,* it is unfortunately fair enough if applied to the Brontë juvenilia. The Brontë children's minds clearly functioned like sponges, soaking in the ideas, plots, and rhetorical strategies they encountered in their reading. What strikes me most in reading the juvenilia alongside contemporary discussions of Africa and Africans in the periodical press is how little the Brontë children deviated from those models. Take, for example, the article "The British Settlements in Western Africa," which appeared in the September 1829 issue of *Blackwood's*. This article's discussion of the Ashantis devotes much space to their prowess in battle, then goes on to explain how they are ultimately defeated militarily and how little "gratitude" and "fidelity" the ones who subsequently work for the English demonstrate.[45] Ashantis are also described as lazy and superstitious. It is quite likely that the Brontës read this particular article, but if not, a steady stream of similar articles appeared in other issues of their favorite periodicals; as Azim has noted, "Nearly every issue of the 'real' *Blackwood's Edinburgh Magazine* during the late 1820s and early 1830s contained articles dealing with the colonial question: debates regarding the efficacy of British territorial expansion, trade, slavery, on the phenomenon of displaced and mixed races and peoples and explorations in natural history and geography."[46] Ashantis are singled out in more than one English text from the period as the most formidable rebels against English rule in West Africa. It is for this reason, presumably, that the Brontë children chose them as the adversaries most fit to showcase their heroes' strength. Throughout the juvenilia, Ashanti characters—whether individualized or discussed as a group—predominantly reflect contemporary stereotypes of military skill, superstition, laziness, licentiousness, and ingratitude. The character who most often figures in the stories as an individual, Quashia Quamina, is, like the Duke of Wellington and several other characters in the juvenilia, named and modeled after a real historical figure. Nevertheless, the Brontë children do not seem particularly interested in real African people; it is almost as though, for them, Africans exist only as fictional characters. Relative to the vast overall number of characters in the juvenilia, only a few Black characters are individualized enough to be named; their stories are told only insofar as they interact with White characters, and none of them feel like real people.[47]

One character of color is sometimes associated with creatures from folklore: Finic, the hated son of Charlotte's White principal character, Arthur Wellesley, and an Ashanti woman he loved in his youth named Sofala. Finic is described in *A Leaf from an Unopened Volume* as having "more the appearance of some hideous and unpropitious sprite than of a human being. It was not more than three feet high, broad set, and having a head which in itself, disproportionately large, derived a frightful increase of size from the matted coal-black elf-locks with which it was profusely covered."[48] He is also mute until his final moments. Apparently Finic's dwarfism and otherwise unusual appearance are not congenital: rather, Sofala on her deathbed prayed that the child would shame his father; accordingly, he then transformed (376). This transformation is not dramatized or commented on by the narrator, merely recounted by Finic's uncle years later in a pair of sentences in *A Leaf from an Unopened Volume;* should we assume that an Ashanti or Christian deity is responsible, or perhaps the Chief Genii? Judith Pike has discussed the mutual amplification of race and disability in the character of Finic, comparing him to *Jane Eyre*'s Bertha as a racialized character whose disabilities chiefly seem monstrous, in contrast to the more noble disabling of Rochester.[49] His father does indeed call him a "hideous monster," and his dwarfism may evoke in readers' minds images of supernatural creatures.[50] Still, there is no implication in *A Leaf from an Unopened Volume* or in *The Foundling,* in which he also briefly appears, that Finic is literally inhuman. Instead, like a less fully drawn version of Heathcliff, as we will see in chapter 6, he is portrayed as a human being whose fellow characters often discuss him using the language of supernatural creatures in order to convey the strength of their feelings about him.

Susan Meyer considers at some length the question of why Charlotte, in particular, would have turned so early to imperial writing. Meyer finds an implicit answer in Charlotte's very first surviving manuscript:

> There was once a little girl and her name was Anne. She was born at a little village named Thornton and by and by she grew a good girl. Her father and mother was very rich. Mr and Mrs Wood were their names and she was their only child, but she was not too much indulged.
>
> Once little Anne and her mother went to see a fine castle near London, about ten miles from it. Anne was very much pleased with it.
>
> Once Anne and her papa and her Mama went to sea in a ship and they had very fine weather all the way, but Anne's Mama was very sick and Anne attended her with so much care. She gave her her medicine.[51]

As Meyer observes, this initial literary attempt begins at home, featuring as protagonist a girl much like Charlotte and her sisters, only wealthier.

Yet Charlotte "comes repeatedly, at the end of each paragraph, to the same literary dead end" and must send her heroine to a new space in order to create further incident.[52] The British colonies, in contrast to the English domestic space, "provided a region primarily defined by strife and conflict" (36). This seems to me a plausible assessment of Charlotte's thought process, and it is consistent with fundamental insights like Edward Said's that the "Orient," broadly defined to include Africa, the Middle East, and Asia, appealed to European writers and artists by virtue of seeming to be a categorically "distinct" and more eventful space than their own countries.[53] This conceptualized Orient, of course, often bore little resemblance to the peoples and nations it purported to depict; instead, it simultaneously underscored European superiority and allowed the portrayal of more exotic, decadent, and dramatic events than generally deemed acceptable in a European context. The Brontës had numerous models for such orientalism in the works of the Romantic poets they admired and, of course, the *Arabian Nights Entertainments,* which I discuss in greater detail at various points throughout this book.

But, to follow Meyer's supposition further, it turned out that for the Brontës, setting stories in a foreign land was not enough; it needed to be a version of that foreign land that permitted alternative histories and fantastical happenings. Except for the occasional presence of the Chief Genii, especially in the earliest tales, most of the stories that deal directly with military and political conflict with the Ashantis are remarkably unimaginative, considering the creativity on display in so many of the other stories and poems. As Said has observed, orientalism, in its essential belief in complete difference between East and West, "imposed limits upon thought about the Orient," even in the case of "the most imaginative writers of an age."[54] Indeed, racial difference seems to have presented something of an imaginative stumbling block for the young Brontës: the creative plotting and astute psychological insights sometimes applied to White characters even in the earliest writings simply do not extend to Ashanti characters. Instead, while the Brontës' treatments of Black human characters mostly mimicked what they read in the periodical press, they had no difficulty exploring the creative potential of the supernatural creatures in whose hands they placed their kingdom's fate.

Like many of their contemporaries, the Brontë children adored the *Arabian Nights' Entertainments* and drew on it eagerly in their own writing, clearly untroubled by any ideas of cultural appropriation as a negative or disrespectful act. Among other things, the *Arabian Nights' Entertainments* taught them a great deal about genii; as Tanya Llewellyn has argued, these genii functioned as "enticing symbols of power that the Brontës could imaginatively appropriate."[55] The activities and moral status of the genii in the *Arabian Nights' Entertainments* vary widely across tales. In "The Story of Noureddin Ali, and Bedreddin Hassan" (which Anne and Charlotte each would later reference in *Agnes Grey* and *Villette*), a genie joins forces with a fairy to thwart an evil sultan and contrive a marriage between handsome Bedreddin and a beautiful young girl (for whom he turns out to have been destined all along); the scheme sometimes involves magically lifting a sleeping Bedreddin and transporting him to other locations. The human protagonist of "The Merchant and the Genie" must beg for his life after he accidentally kills a genie's son. In another story, a fisherman liberates a genie from a bottle only to find that the genie plans to kill the one who frees him; the fisherman manages to trick the genie back into the bottle and tells a series of tales that persuade him to repay the fisherman with an enchanted lake full of fish rather than death. Prince Zeyn Alasnam undergoes what turns out to be an elaborate test set by the king of the genii in order to prove his worthiness to assume his father's throne. All in all, the genii of the *Arabian Nights' Entertainments* exert extraordinary control over human life, and they often vacillate or seem to vacillate between offering assistance and threatening harm within the same story. However, they can also be subdued by human machinations—a weakness with which the Brontës did not saddle their own genius alter egos.

As formative as the *Arabian Nights' Entertainments* was for the Brontës, Jane W. Stedman (1965) has argued that the Brontë children's genii more closely resemble those found in *Tales of the Genii* by James Ridley, writing under the name Sir Charles Morrell (1764). Beloved by Charles Dickens, this orientalist story collection gave the eighteenth- and nineteenth-century English more of the "exotic" fiction for which they had developed a taste after the early translations of *The Thousand and One Nights*. Although no evidence conclusively proves that the Brontës read it, *Tales of the Genii* was widely accessible and monumentally popular, and Stedman makes a compelling case for its influence on the Brontës' genii. In particular, Stedman observes that Ridley's genii, more than those of the *Arabian Nights' Entertainments*, function as guardians of particular people or places; in the frame story of *Tales of the Genii,* a genius takes charge of a group of siblings and proceeds to tell them stories with both moral import and fantastical entertainment value. The Chief Genii of the Brontës' juvenilia, too, each claim one of the Twelve Adventurers early on as his or her special responsibility; their interactions with human beings often originate in an effort to assist their wards. The Brontës may also have been inspired by Sir Walter Scott, whose poem *The Vision of Don Roderick* (1811) refers twice to the idea of a Genius presiding over a certain geographical spot (1811, 27.7 and 44.6), while *Marmion* (1808) imagines a metaphorical "Genius of Chivalry" which has been sleeping due to "talisman and spell" and must be woken by, presumably, the poet (introduction to Canto First, ln. 289). The Brontës' Chief Genii often function in the plot as *dei ex machina* and appear with the intimidating splendor of biblical angels. Here, too, Stedman advocates for the influence of Ridley, whose narrative is stuffed with "awe-inspiring details," offering particularly elaborate depictions of the genii's palaces.[56] Ultimately, the Brontës' conception of genii—as of much else in the juvenilia—grew from various sources within their wide childhood reading.

The splendor of genii is on display in "A True Story by CB" (that is, by Charlotte Brontë), which appeared in two parts in the August and September 1829 issues of the *Young Men's Magazine.* Protagonists Arthur and Charles Wellesley (young sons of the Duke of Wellington) are visited by a pair of goblins who offer to take them to see the Feast of the Genii—a phenomenon no mortal has ever witnessed. They eagerly accept, despite the goblins' warning that "if you are discovered, you will pay for it."[57] When the feast begins, "a strange bloody light spread itself over all the cave, glittering pillars rose to the roof which sparkled exceedingly, four diamond thrones appeared, sounds of music were heard at a distance, troops of genii and fairies began slowly to glide into the cave till it was full and then a very bright light shone on all, which announced the approach of the Chief Genii" (63). This description foregrounds the strange and threatening aspects of the genii as well as their magnificence. The Chief Genii initially look like "pyramids of fire" and then "chang[e] into red lurid flames" as "black clouds and terrible peals of thunder" surround them (64). The feast ends with this ominous alteration, yet Arthur and Charles are safely transported home with the help of their goblin guides. "How magnificent and yet how awful, and without hurt we have seen what no mortal has ever before seen," reflects young Arthur

(64). Indeed, despite the goblins' warning, the boys do not "pay" for their glimpse of the genii's glory. If Charlotte did have Ridley's *Tales of the Genii* in mind while composing this story, then she borrowed Ridley's emphasis on splendor but not his interest in imparting moral lessons.

Emily Brontë, in poetry written later in her life, drew on the concept of genii as guardians of particular spaces in the natural world, as we will see in chapter 3. Although Emily and Anne were originally involved in imagining the Glass Town stories, no Glass Town manuscripts of their authorship survive. Their influence lingers, though, in that their Chief Genius alter egos exist as characters in certain narratives penned by Charlotte and Branwell. A representative portrayal of Charlotte's attitude toward her sisters' writing can be found in "A Day at Parry's Palace," included in the *Young Men's Magazine* for October 1830. Chronicler Charles Wellesley[58] reports exasperation at the dullness of life in the palace of Parry's Land, in which Sir Edward Parry and "Lady Emily" preside over a series of silent meals. The palace boasts a significant number of animals, which may be a reference to Emily's fierce love for her pets. Although the visit bores Charles, Charlotte allows the fictional Emily to preside: Captain John Ross, Anne's "chief man," appears at one of these meals and makes himself ill from overeating, prompting a visit from "the Genius Emily . . . at a most opportune period; and when the disorder had reached its crisis, she cured with an incantation and vanished."[59] Charles barely remarks upon this supernatural visitation, closing the story with a perfunctory paragraph about his return to Glass Town. But Charlotte, despite her mockery, seems to take it for granted that the Genius Emily should play the climactic role in the story of Emily's realm.

The surviving accounts of the Brontë children's early collaborative plays of the Young Men and the Islanders raise as many questions as they answer—Which Brontë really came up with each story? Did the children dispute plot developments? Why did they pursue the Young Men's Play for more than a decade but abandon the Islanders after three years?[60] We may never know. But two things, at least, are clear. First, that the Brontës' earliest stories depended on fantastical creatures, both in terms of the prominence of fairies and genii in the narratives and in terms of the control these creatures exerted over events within the fictional worlds. Second, that the children's conception of supernatural beings and their power clearly derived from the tales they were reading, including the *Arabian Nights' Entertainments*, Ridley's *Tales of the Genii*, and the fairy lore encountered in the works of various Romantic writers, *Blackwood's Edinburgh Magazine*, and perhaps other folklore sources. To launch their literary careers, the Brontës seized the license these texts gave them to imagine other worlds.

Fairy Lands and Fairy Allusions in Charlotte Brontë's Juvenilia

In the top margin of the manuscript for "The History of the Year" (1829), one of the earliest surviving Brontë texts, Charlotte has written, "Once upon a time there was a king whose name was Ethelbert Eleance who Governed all Caledonia" (Bonnell Collection, B80[11]). From the beginning, Charlotte Brontë used the fairy tale as a model for her own writing, using the "once upon a time" opening popularized by French fairy-tale writers like Marie-Catherine d'Aulnoy and Charles Perrault as *il était une fois*. Charlotte apparently invented this King Ethelbert of Caledonia; it is King Aethelbert of Kent who is known to history. But Caledonia—the old, romantic name for Scotland—frequently provided the setting for Sir Walter Scott's legends of encounters with elfin peoples. The full story of Charlotte's King Ethelbert is lost, if it was ever completed. Yet with "once upon a time" and "Caledonia," its one surviving sentence encapsulates Charlotte's liberal deployment of both literary European fairy tales and the folklore of the British Isles in the creation of her own imaginative narratives.

Throughout the 1830s, Emily and Anne broke away to begin their own saga of Gondal (discussed in chapter 3). Meanwhile, Charlotte and Branwell wrote hundreds of pages of stories, many of which were interlocking (and sometimes warring) accounts of events in Glass Town and, later, Angria, as the kingdom of the settlers expands and Arthur Wellesley ultimately names himself Emperor of Angria and environs. The stories that Charlotte appears to have written alone (Angrian or otherwise) are bursting with allusions to the supernatural of all kinds. Evocations of and explicit references to continental literary fairy tales appear repeatedly, as do fairies, genii, and magical objects, which often play significant roles in the tales of the early 1830s. This is less true of Charlotte's longer narratives of the mid to late 1830s, but in these narratives, she continues to draw on folk and fairy tales for figurative language. The sheer volume of both offhand references to and sustained engagements with folk and fairy tales in Charlotte's juvenilia is impressive; this clear evidence that she was familiar with such tales underlies my arguments later in this book about the ways she would use them in the novels she wrote as an adult.

Charlotte Brontë's juvenilia received comparatively little attention in scholarship before the publication of detailed editions of them (edited by Christine Alexander) in the 1980s and 1990s. Alexander's groundbreaking editions and scholarly works on the juvenilia have, as Judith Pike puts it, provided other scholars with an "atlas" with which to approach this formidably large and heterogeneous body of early writing.[61] Sometimes, scholars have overstated the juvenilia's difference from Charlotte's "mature" writing; for example, even Alexander states that Charlotte's "first novel *The Professor* represents a distinct break with her juvenilia."[62] While *The Professor* does indeed bear very little resemblance to the juvenilia, their influence is much easier to detect in every other novel Charlotte would go on to write in adulthood, particularly in the form of references to folklore and fairy tales; any break was only temporary. Fortunately, recent works of scholarship have complicated the idea of such a split. For example, Tanya Llewellyn has shown that "although the significance of the *Arabian Nights* to Charlotte Brontë's work has generally been relegated to the sphere of childhood fantasy, in fact references to the *Nights* are interwoven through her adult fiction with a complexity that surpasses simple nostalgia for childhood."[63] Several other scholarly works since Charlotte's bicentennial in 2016 have addressed her engagement with race (as discussed above), stressed the variety and sophistication of her early writings, and compared those writings to the novels for which she later became famous. I am indebted in a fundamental way to these scholars' insights. For example, Diane Long Hoeveler's argument that several of Charlotte's early texts reflect the influence of "down-market" Gothic novels is a model for my argument later in this section that several of Charlotte's other early texts reflect the influence of journey-to-fairyland folktales.[64] Zak Sitter and Tamara Silvia Wagner, meanwhile, though they too are interested in different aspects and texts within the juvenilia than I am, precede me in insisting that the once-prevailing notion of a strict demarcation between Charlotte's juvenilia and her "mature" novels is tenuous at best. Sitter argues that Charlotte's juvenilia "demonstrate something more complicated than mere inadequacy to the demands of realism."[65] Wagner contends that in scholarship, Charlotte's juvenilia

> have generally been considered apprentice pieces that envisioned a wildly imaginative realm. This fantasy world of epic drama had to be left behind before Charlotte Brontë could embark on narratives rooted in the everyday realities of Victorian Britain. Careful reassessments of the juvenilia, however, have revealed that such a dichotomous view of her works is not merely simplistic, but deeply flawed. . . . In all its fantastic elements, Angria [the Brontës' chief fictional kingdom] is thus already rooted in the contemporary and the everyday.[66]

Indeed, Charlotte's frequent focus on perfectly realistic social and political relations among the Angrians, as well as the references to real topical issues, historical figures, and the prominent men of nineteenth-century England, render much of the juvenilia rather more mundane than was once acknowledged.

These commentators' discussions of the realism of much of the juvenilia are valid and exciting, and they also entice new readers who might have dismissed juvenilia they believed to be purely fantastical. Moreover, as I will demonstrate later in this book in keeping with scholars like Llewellyn, the "mature" writings of the Brontës are also not so strictly bound to the real as the formerly prevailing dichotomous view of the oeuvre suggests. Nevertheless, it is still true that fairy tales and folklore are ubiquitous in Charlotte's juvenilia, including in some ways that scholars have not yet discussed. In this section, I show the range of Charlotte's use of folk and fairy tales in her juvenilia by using two examples: first, her retellings of folktales about mortals' journeys to fairyland; and second, the late-1830s novellas that, despite their focus on the decidedly unfantastical exploits of the Angrian leisure class, include numerous offhand comparisons to fairies and fairy tales.

Charlotte's stories of sojourns with the fairies clearly show the influence of similar tales in contemporary folklore. For example, in "Llewellyn's Dance," from Thomas Crofton Croker's *Fairy Legends and Traditions of the South of Ireland,* a man named Rhys is distracted by fairy music while walking home one evening; he runs after this music and lives with the fairies for one year. When his friends find him and bring him back to the human world, he is "sad, sullen, and silent," and he soon dies.[67] James Hogg's poem "Kilmeny" (1813) and tale "Mary Burnet" (1828) both tell of young girls spirited away by fairies. Both girls dwell with the fairies for seven years, then return home to assure their families of their safety. Soon, however, realizing they no longer belong in the human world, they choose to return to the fairies. In Allan Cunningham's "Elphin Irving, The Fairies' Cupbearer," a young man aptly named Elphin is abducted by fairies and made the queen's slave; his twin sister, Phemie, attempts to save him by seizing him as he passes by with the fairies at night. But the fairies transform him into an angry bull, then a river, and finally a burst of fire, which Phemie cannot hold onto. Phemie vows to try again on All Hallows' Eve; all we know of this attempt is that the townspeople find her dead the following morning, with no sign of Elphin. The Scottish tale of Tam Lin or Tamlane, included in Sir Walter Scott's *Minstrelsy of the Scottish Border,* offers a similar attempt to rescue a fairy captive that ends successfully. Despite exceptions like this one, however, endings like those of the other tales I have just mentioned are more common in traditional folklore. Taken together, these tales imply that mortals cannot survive fairy sojourns unchanged—and that they may not survive at all.

The complex and capricious nature of fairies and other similar creatures as they were understood in the early nineteenth century suited them well to Charlotte's fondness for surprising and ethically ambiguous situations. The strict moral boundary we envision today between good, beautiful creatures like fairies and evil, ugly creatures like goblins barely existed in the early nineteenth century; it was the mid- to late Victorians, with their passion for taxonomies of all kinds, who solidified these distinctions.[68] According to the tales Charlotte would have read, the spectrum of possibility was extremely wide: a fairy encountered on a walk in the woods might do or say nearly anything. In the folklore of the British Isles, encounters with fairies and similar creatures are frequent and varied, sometimes leading to the captivity or brief disorientation of human beings. Some creatures, particularly pixies and will-o'-the-wisps, are famous for leading human travelers off the path but do not tend to hold them captive for extended periods of time; their effects on human beings are similar to those of a moonless night or a dense fog. The tales that young Charlotte Brontë reworked, however, are those that tell of mortals who dwell with fairy folk for years, beginning sometimes with outright abduction and other times with a human being's imprudent eagerness to witness fairy revels. These mortals sometimes cannot be recovered from fairyland; even if they do return, they often struggle to readjust to human society, expressing symptoms consistent with insanity, intoxication, or excessive melancholy. Carole Silver has argued that fairies traditionally caused anxiety precisely because of the resulting in-between status of human beings believed to have returned from fairy sojourns: "With actual death, at least, came certainty; with abduction and apparent death came the possibility of a flawed resurrection and a resultant uncertainty about status."[69] Death would be preferable, Silver points out, because it can be reconciled with religious faith and is more definitive, whereas "the dead person's reappearance in material form suggested a transgression of the boundaries—a sort of cosmic disorder" (172). A bind results: mortals who have dwelt with supernatural creatures often wish to return home because they do not belong in fairyland, but having lived with supernatural folk also renders them unfit to rejoin human society.

Charlotte's tales of journeys to and from fairyland closely resemble traditional models, with one crucial difference: not a single one of her protagonists is damaged by the experience. In "Leisure Hours" (1830), the most traditional of these tales, Charlotte's narrator begins, "I once knew a man who said he had been caught by fairies one night as he was travelling on a lonely moor, and that he had lived 5 years among them. He used often to relate his adventures to me."[70] Discussion of the scene of storytelling itself was common in folklore narratives like those of Thomas Crofton Croker, James Hogg, and Allan Cunningham. The manner of the protagonist's capture, too, taking place on a lonely moor at night, is taken straight from contemporary tales of pixy-led wanderers and those abducted more permanently by fairies. "Leisure Hours" is quite short, stylistically similar to contemporary folktales. The fairies initially strike fear into the man's heart as they eat a feast of lambs, dance and yell strangely, and shape-shift into crows—not to mention that they promptly assign him as a slave to one of their number. From the perspective of their human witness, these are creatures of power and otherness. The rest of the story, however, showcases more benevolent fairy behavior. The man and his new fairy master see a human girl in the forest saving a nest of baby birds from a boy on the verge of killing them; she then offers food to the fairy and the man. At this point the fairy rewards her with a large bag of gold, saying, "Charity and mercy shall have their reward" (179). Charlotte stops short of having the fairy quote any specific Bible verse, but his words do echo the spirit and much of the language of Matthew 6:1–18, from the Sermon on the Mount, in which Jesus promises that good deeds done in secret will be rewarded by God. This fairy—despite participating in the killing and enslavement of innocents—also hastens the recompense for good deeds promised by Christianity.

"Leisure Hours" ends here; we do not learn how the protagonist returned to human society or what happened in the intervening five years. On the whole, though, Charlotte offers a relatively optimistic outlook on a stint in fairy captivity. The man apparently undergoes no abuse other than bondage itself, and the narrator leaves us with the fairy master's act of justice and generosity. The human sojourner appears to return from fairy control changed only in that he now possesses a fount of stories with which to cheer his associates. In this most traditional of Charlotte's fairy narratives, she still breaks with traditional models in refusing to attribute any lasting consequences to the period spent with supernatural masters. She retains the suspense afforded by the demonstration of fairies' potential to do harm but resolves events in the human character's favor.

While the protagonist of "Leisure Hours" was "caught" by the fairies against his will, another of Charlotte's fairy stories from 1830 hedges on the question of the protagonist's consent to the journey to fairyland. The titular hero of "The Adventures of Ernest Alembert" immediately reveals an awareness of the kinds of tales Charlotte is reworking, including their typically unhappy endings. When a man "clothed in a dark mantle" appears at Ernest's door, identifies himself as Rufus Warner, and requests shelter, Ernest welcomes him, but "dim, dream-like reminiscences passed slowly across his mind concerning tales of spirits who, in various shapes, had appeared to men shortly before their deaths."[71] Among other "spirits," he may be thinking of banshees or black dogs, whose primary traditional function is to herald death; his initial suspicion is thus actually worse than the truth, which is that Warner is a fairy. When Warner announces that he comes from a land where "the trees bear without ceasing . . . the sun shines for ever, and the moon and stars are not quenched even at noonday," Ernest becomes more worried than ever (156). But "a secret charm seemed to have been cast upon him which prevented him from being overcome by terror," and he asks "under the influence of a secret fascination" to visit this land (156). In a way, Ernest is kidnapped. But it becomes evident that Warner has no evil intentions; the story implies that he wishes to reward Ernest for his hospitality by taking him to a beautiful land in which he suffers no harm. As in "Leisure Hours," Charlotte creates suspense by alerting the reader early on to the danger of interacting with fairies, but her human protagonist is ultimately safe.

Ernest dwells in "the land of fairies" for some time (160), providing Charlotte ample opportunity to describe fairyland at length—at much greater length, in fact, than contemporary British folktales of fairy encounters tended to do. In addition to the *Arabian Nights' Entertainments* and *Tales of the Genii*, the literary fairy tales of Marie-Catherine d'Aulnoy may have provided a model for Charlotte's elaborate descriptions. As noted previously, d'Aulnoy was one of the French fairy-tale writers most widely translated and anthologized in the English fairy-tale publications of the eighteenth and nineteenth centuries. Looking at the fairy king's palace, which is made of "liquid diamond," Ernest "beheld only a star of light, for the palace was formed of certain materials too brilliant for any but fairies to behold distinctly" (164, 163). Similarly, when the human queen in d'Aulnoy's 1698 "The Hind in the Wood" (also translated as "The White Doe") approaches a fairy palace, her "eyes were struck by the incomparable brilliance of a palace made entirely of diamonds" ("ses yeux furent frappés par l'éclat sans pareil d'un palais tout de diamant" [trans. mine]);[72] the human prince of d'Aulnoy's widely anthologized "The White Cat," too, "could hardly see anything beyond the rays cast by the gate's carbuncles" when he approaches the enchanted cat's magnificent palace.[73] In general, d'Aulnoy's tales provide extensive descriptions of magnificent settings more than most other supernatural tales the Brontës would likely have encountered; many of d'Aulnoy's tales could have inspired Charlotte's liberal depictions of supernatural splendor.

While deviating from traditional folktale models in enumerating the sights, sounds, and scents that would greet a visitor to fairyland, Charlotte hews more closely to these models in portraying impressive fairy behavior. Repeatedly, Ernest Alembert witnesses

> their midnight revels in many a wild glen and wood, when they feasted beneath the solemn moon. . . . He often watched their sports on the 'beached margin of the sea' and saw the rolling billows fall calm under the magic influence of their muttered incantations. He heard and felt the sweet witchery of their songs chanted at unearthly banquets, and when the sound swelled to a starlit, lofty sky, all the revolving worlds arrested their mighty course and stood still in the charmed heavens to listen.[74]

Even in this mostly positive portrayal, the fairies are alien to Ernest, considering the "witchery" in their music and the "unearthly" quality of their feasts. For all its beauty, fairyland can be too much for mortal beings. The fairies are dangerous; although Ernest's fairy hosts never harm him, he witnesses "the spells by which they drew the lonely traveller into their enchanted circlet" (164). Chiefly, though, Ernest eventually "longed once more to dwell among human beings" and to walk beneath "earthly trees" simply because he does not belong in fairyland (165). This basic incompatibility between the mortal and the immortal drives innumerable folk and fairy tales that Charlotte could have read or heard, notably the tales of supernatural brides that I identify in chapter 5 as important models for *Shirley*. Tales of mortal men who fall in love with creatures like mermaids, seal maidens, or swan maidens almost invariably contain an interlude in which the mismatched pair dwell together in either the human or the supernatural world; in the end, however, the longing for one's own kind usually prevails, severing the couple. As folklorist Katharine Briggs observes of supernatural bride tales, "There is no lasting union between fairies and mortals."[75] Charlotte's early fairy stories do not feature romance, but the principle is the same. In "The Adventures of Ernest Alembert," the fairies make no attempt to detain Ernest: they sanction his longing for humankind and send him away from fairyland by means of a magical draught.

Ernest does not, however, go all the way home. Instead, the draught takes him to a valley where he meets an elderly man who reveals that he once encountered supernatural beings "of a less gentle nature" than Ernest's fairies.[76] The story ends with the information that the two men dwell happily together in this valley for many years; we learn of no full return to human society for either of them. Their reintegration into the mortal world is thus only partial; they apparently have no supernatural company in this valley, but they also have no mortal company apart from each other. Charlotte gives them a happy ending, but she does not imagine either of them completely at home again in the human realm. Considering that Ernest is deemed most suited to live neither with fairies nor with ordinary humans but rather with another mortal man who has also dealt with supernatural creatures, this story reinforces the implication of many traditional tales that everyone should keep to their own kind.

Clearly, folktales of encounters with fairies held sufficient interest for Charlotte to write her own versions of such tales—happier versions that allowed her to revel in elaborate descriptions of the fantastic without having to dramatize the usual consequences for such encounters. Over the course of the 1830s, Charlotte's tales of excursions into fairyland give way to longer, more realist narratives usually connected to the larger saga of Glass Town and Angria. These narratives chronicle political conflicts, courtship, adultery, and the more mundane features of high-society life in a British colony that may be fictional but is nonetheless designed to resemble those the Brontës read about in the periodical press. As stated earlier, I entirely agree with critics who have insisted on the realism in much of Charlotte's juvenilia. But this realism—like that of her published novels—has plenty of room for the fantastical: even as actual fairies gradually recede from Charlotte's plots, she continues to make frequent figurative references to fairies, the *Arabian Nights' Entertainments*, and continental literary fairy tales. Charlotte wrote hundreds of pages in the 1830s; she had ample opportunity both to play with fairy tales and folklore in numerous ways, and to make sophisticated experiments with realist narrative.

Take, for example, *Caroline Vernon* (1839), which centers on fifteen-year-old Caroline's experience of falling in love with the Duke of Zamorna and eventually becoming his mistress despite the efforts of her father—Alexander Percy, who is Branwell's chief hero and Zamorna's enemy—to prevent it. Late in the text, the narrator describes the eponymous heroine as "moping by the hearth like Cinderella."[77] This explicit reference to "Cinderella" is comparatively unusual for Charlotte—which is surprising, considering the cachet of "Cinderella" in nineteenth-century England. Moreover, this text's narrator, the ironic Charles Townshend (a later evolution of Charles Wellesley), adopts a detached and less-than-sympathetic attitude toward Caroline throughout the narrative; this, along with the word "moping," suggests that the Cinderella reference could be intended comically. Caroline is, after all, hardly as downtrodden as Cinderella: she mopes in this scene only because of what she believes to be unrequited passion for the Duke of Zamorna. Soon, though, Zamorna reveals that he does desire a sexual relationship with her, and he addresses her as "my fairy" while describing the woodland cabin in which he plans to keep her as his mistress (307). Characterizing women as fairies was one of the most common metaphorical uses of fairies in the nineteenth century—one that Charlotte would problematize in later works.

Caroline is herself clearly aware of magic and fairy tales. Specifically, she twice expresses a desire for the kind of magical power often described in such tales. Early in the story, she muses, "I wish a fairy would bring me a ring or a magician would appear & give me a talisman like Aladdin's lamp that I could get everything I want" (256). Magical fairy rings have largely not survived the vicissitudes that have fashioned our contemporary understanding of fairy tales, but they appeared in many old stories, including some of Marie-Catherine d'Aulnoy's tales and both Villeneuve's and Beaumont's eighteenth-century versions of "Beauty and the Beast." In addition to magic that offers wish fulfillment, Caroline also considers magic that confers knowledge: "If there was such a thing as magic & if His Grace could tell just how much I care for him & could know how I am lying awake just now & wishing to see him, I wonder what he would think?" (291). Clearly, Charlotte imagined the *Arabian Nights' Entertainments* and European fairy tales to have been part of Caroline's reading.

As would be the case in all of Charlotte Brontë's published novels, fairy tales and the supernatural appear in the narrative of *Caroline Vernon* even when nothing fantastical is literally taking place. After all, this 1839 text also resembles Charlotte's published novels of the next decade and a half in another way: it is primarily not fantastical. As Heather Glen has insisted, it is above all a "tale of fashionable life," a variation on the "silver fork" novel that was so popular in the 1820s and 1830s.[78] Although *Caroline Vernon* contains several allusions to fairies and fairy tales, it contains far fewer than *Jane Eyre*, *Shirley*, or *Villette*, even accounting for the differences in length between the novella and the published novels.[79] Around the same time as *Caroline Vernon*, Charlotte wrote a text generally known as "Farewell to Angria," a two-paragraph fragment in which she vows to stop writing melodramatic stories about the balmy fictional kingdom of her juvenilia: "The mind would cease from excitement & turn now to a cooler region, where the dawn breaks grey and sober."[80] This, clearly, was the same frame of mind in which she wrote her first novel, *The Professor*, several years later. Based on her experiences living in Brussels in the early 1840s, this manuscript was rejected for publication and ultimately published only after her death. A dry realist novel, *The Professor* contrasts sharply with the fairy stories and tales of Byronic heroes that Charlotte wrote in her youth. In a preface to *The Professor*, she asserts that by the time she wrote the novel, she had given up "ornamented" writing and had "come to prefer what was plain and homely" in literature.[81] But she also claims in the same sentence that her juvenile writings were "destroyed almost as soon as composed."[82] The latter, obviously, is untrue, considering the hundreds of pages of juvenilia that survive; we should be careful, therefore, about taking any of these statements literally, including the supposed partiality to plainness. Certainly, many factors render *The Professor* less compelling to readers than *Jane Eyre*, *Villette*, and even *Shirley*. But readers commonly complain that *The Professor* is simply dull compared to Charlotte Brontë's later works. One aspect contributing to the impression of dullness is the minimal quantity of references to fairy tales and supernatural creatures. No tales are explicitly mentioned, and few creature comparisons appear. Clearly, after the failure of *The Professor* to secure publication, she decided that the supernatural world had an important role to play in her writing. *Caroline Vernon*, the other late-1830s novellas, and *The Professor* do not constitute a step on a direct path from childhood fantasy to mature realism; rather, they represent the nadir of her use of fairy- and folktale models. Fairy tales and the supernatural were integral to every other novel Charlotte Brontë would go on to write.

2 Branwell Brontë, the Fantastical, and the Real

Branwell Brontë (1817–48) has always been something of an outlier. In the popular imagination, the Brontës are usually "the Brontë sisters," occasionally accompanied by a vague sense that there was a brother with a disreputable or tragic story. A brief overview of his life will partly bear out this impression. Branwell, one year younger than Charlotte, was specially taught ancient Greek and Latin but otherwise mostly educated alongside his sisters. As the only boy in the family, he was treated with more indulgence and higher expectations—a combination that ultimately probably harmed more than it helped him. Although he considered careers in painting and music as well, he desperately wanted to be a man of letters, sending poems to prominent Romantic writers, including William Wordsworth, Thomas De Quincey, and Hartley Coleridge (Samuel Taylor Coleridge's son, and the only one of the three who responded). When James Hogg died in 1835, Branwell—then eighteen years old—wrote to *Blackwood's Edinburgh Magazine* offering himself as a replacement. In almost all these cases, the pompous tone of his letters clashed with the amateur quality of the accompanying poetry. Like his sisters, Branwell had to earn his own living. Yet he was dismissed from multiple positions throughout the 1840s—as a tutor, as a train station clerk—for various bad behaviors. At the same time, he worked hard enough on his writing during his year as a station clerk to produce the first of eighteen poems that would be published in local Yorkshire newspapers during his lifetime, most under the synonym "Northangerland," the name of his chief character in the Glass Town and Angria stories. His family evidently did not know of these publications; however, they were unfortunately well aware of the scandal that arose out of his final position as a tutor to the Robinson family at Thorp Green, in which he apparently had an affair with Mrs. Lydia Robinson. Anne worked as a governess in the same household. Lydia Robinson chose not to marry Branwell even after her husband died a year after Branwell's dismissal; ultimately, Branwell could not recover from this disappointment, falling into the alcoholism and drug addiction that led to his death in 1848. He was apparently never told about his sisters' first successful efforts at publishing poems in 1846 and all their first novels in 1847; the brother and sisters' mutual ignorance of their success in writing is particularly sad in view of the close literary collaboration with which all these remarkable writing careers began.

Thus far, as Bob Duckett's 2017 annotated bibliography attests, scholarly work on Branwell Brontë has focused predominantly on his personal life (particularly his adulterous relationship with Lydia Robinson) and on his relationship to *Wuthering Heights* (as a model for Heathcliff or as a potential author—the latter of which is a tantalizing but ultimately unconvincing suggestion). For much of the twentieth century it was very difficult for scholars to access the majority of Branwell's writing; as a result, the amount of scholarship on Branwell is minimal in comparison to what has been written about his sisters. Fortunately, as is the case with Charlotte's juvenilia, we can now read hundreds of the pages Branwell wrote over the course of his lifetime; I consider this body of writing as a whole in this chapter. Branwell's oeuvre is various, including multiple revisions of the poems he ultimately published, as well as lengthy prose texts about Glass Town from his youth that seem never to have been revised at all, apparently composed in a rush to write as quickly as he could think.[1] Like Charlotte, Branwell wrote voluminously from a young age and delighted in mimicking the rhetorical styles found in *Blackwood's Edinburgh Magazine* and other contemporary texts. He differed substantially from Charlotte, however, in his preferred subjects and his stated attitude toward writing: while Charlotte tended in her juvenilia and published writing to deal with the supernatural, with personal relationships, and with the politics of society, Branwell often focused on the military aspect of political struggles (though he too explored personal relationships) and explicitly scorned fantastical subjects.[2]

This chapter, therefore, will focus on an aspect of Branwell's writing that Branwell himself might have denied was there: his use of fantasy.[3] Charlotte, as we have already seen in chapter 1, began early to integrate European literary fairy tales into her writing; Branwell virtually ignored these tales. But he engaged in various ways with other stories that fall within the broader categories of the supernatural or fantastical. He was, with Charlotte, one of the leaders of the four Brontë children's early fictional collaborations, which involved creation of powerful "genii" (the plural of "genius" or "genie"), supernatural creatures from the *Arabian Nights' Entertainments* and its imitators. Even after he stopped writing about actual supernatural creatures, he continued to allude casually to stories or characters from the *Arabian Nights' Entertainments* throughout his writing career, often to describe something of extraordinary power or intensity. Fairies and other supernatural creatures from English folklore, too, would persist in offhand references. In fact, on two occasions, Branwell criticizes those who write about fairies or genii and then almost immediately proceeds to allude to supernatural creatures or tales himself, apparently unaware of the inconsistency. This type of allusion precisely *does not* indicate any deliberate interest in fairy tales on the part of the writer; rather, it indicates that the fairy tale was so prevalent in nineteenth-century Britain that some writers drew on fairy tales hardly knowing they were doing so.

The references Branwell makes to fantasy and supernatural creatures that seem more deliberate are consummately Victorian: he uses the supernatural to describe women and to provide a counterpoint to the real. He compares beautiful women to fairies throughout his writing career in a way that anticipates the emerging understanding of fairies as merely dainty, as opposed to being simultaneously beautiful and threatening. Meanwhile, he explicitly associates magic and fantasy with both dreams and the past, in contrast to the waking world of the present; although the contrast between fantasy and reality is obviously not a new one, Branwell articulates a sense of incompatibility between the two that lines up well with an incipient Victorian idea of realism as constructed by naturalistic portrayals of external and observable social realities. Charlotte seems to have held a similar view briefly during the late 1830s and early 1840s. Ultimately, though, while she and Emily (and even Anne, to a lesser extent) arrived at a kind of realism that incorporated fairy tales and folklore in a vivid presentation of internal experience, Branwell's idea of realism remained more literal and conventional. This also means that most of Branwell's extant works do not engage with anything supernatural at all. Because of both the comparative paucity of supernatural references and the kinds of references he does include, Branwell represents a more conventional strain of Victorian writing that throws the experiments of his sisters, especially Charlotte, into relief.

In this chapter, I begin by unpacking Branwell's role in the creation and portrayal of genii in the Brontë children's early fictional collaborations; I then consider Branwell's early fascination with *The Poems of Ossian*, a work of Scottish pseudo-folklore which the Brontës owned and annotated. The second section of the chapter provides an analysis of Branwell's use of supernatural references throughout his writing career to describe women and to underscore the distinction between fantasy and reality. In the final section, I point to Branwell's many casual allusions to various supernatural creatures and tales from the folk and fairy lore tradition, including those that immediately follow an overt criticism of the use of fantasy in writing.

Genii and Warriors

All the Brontës read widely as children and were deeply influenced by much of what they read when they themselves began to write. In the late 1820s, all four siblings, particularly Branwell and Charlotte, enthusiastically invented the city of Glass Town, an imaginary British colony in Africa. This fictional world was heavily reliant on the supernatural, controlled as it was by the four powerful Chief Genii (Tallii, Brannii, Emii, and Annii), alter egos of the Brontë children themselves. The Brontës had learned about genii from various texts they had read, including the *Arabian Nights' Entertainments*, various Romantic poems, and James Ridley's *Tales of the Genii*. In chapter 1, I discussed the extensive power the Brontë children granted the Chief Genii to control events in Glass Town; human characters—both native inhabitants and British settlers—were entirely at their mercy. Even in his earliest texts, Branwell displays more uneasiness about the Chief Genii's supernatural powers than is evident in Charlotte's writing. More often than not, his references to the Genii emphasize the dark side of such power or criticize it outright. Two poems he wrote in 1829 illustrate the aggression of the Genii: "Adress to the Genius" is full of lines like "Onward thou rushest in glory and might / Onward thou rushest all men to affright," while a Genius in "Song 1" soars menacingly in the sky, sounding "the dreadful note of war."[4] Branwell's basic descriptions of the Genii do not vary substantially from Charlotte's; what distinguishes him is his immediate sense that the level of power with which the siblings endowed their creations was fundamentally oppressive.[5] Branwell's early play *Nights* prominently features the human characters' desire to escape the rule of the Genii.[6] Similarly, the July 1829 issue of *Branwell's Blackwood's Magazine* includes a letter to the editor lamenting the Chief Genii's declaration that unless the Young Men (the Brontës' name for the early English inhabitants of Glass Town) carry out several arduous tasks, the Genii will incinerate the earth (32).[7] All four Genii soar threateningly over the scene of Branwell's 1832 "Ode on the Celebration of the Great African Games." All these texts reflect on the tyrannous potential of the Genii's might.

Branwell's 1830–31 text "The History of the Young Men," which offers his version of the same Glass Town origin story that Charlotte recorded in 1829 as "A Romantic Tale," encapsulates the tension in his conception of the Genii—for clearly he was fascinated by the Genii's power even as he emphasized its danger for human beings. The narrator praises the Twelve Adventurers for "resisting the cruel and Infamous oppressions of the Genii" and describes Chief Genius Brannii in particular as a "dreadful monster."[8] Yet one of the leaders of the Twelve Adventurers, Crashey, successfully seeks help from the Genii three times as he and his companions attempt to establish a settlement. Chief Genius Brannii participates in this assistance, and it is all the Genii together who are described, from the beginning of the Twelves' arrival, as both causing terror and vowing to protect their charges (150, 153). Charlotte often vividly illustrated the might of supernatural creatures such as genii and fairies, only to pull back from the implications of that power. For Branwell, too, the splendid powers of supernatural creatures were an attraction, but his stories illustrated the destructive exercise of those powers much more often than Charlotte's did. Even though both of them were drawn to potentially dangerous creatures (and, later, dangerous Byronic heroes), Branwell's outlook was fundamentally more negative than Charlotte's from the beginning of their writing careers.

In Branwell's writing as in Charlotte's, the Chief Genii decline in prominence over time. Eventually, the Genii remain merely in the characters' language, functioning in Branwell's later juvenilia as gods do in a minimally devout society: "By the Genii" is uttered often as a mild oath in the place of "By God," but no one appears to believe that the Genii have any meaningful existence or influence on human affairs. The ultimate heir to Branwell's Genii is a human being: his chief character Alexander Percy (also known as Rogue, Lord Ellrington, and the Earl or Duke of Northangerland). A former pirate and the primary adversary to Charlotte's dubious hero, the Duke of Zamorna, Percy attains and habitually abuses political and sexual power. Like Zamorna, Percy seduces and abandons numerous women; he also frequently leads insurrections both before and after ascending to legitimate political positions under Zamorna. Branwell clearly sees Percy's power, like that of the Chief Genii, as both fascinating and dangerous.

Branwell's shift in focus from observing tyranny in the Chief Genii to observing it in Percy reflects his general preference for human rather than supernatural subjects. It is unsurprising, then, that the folkloric text that seems to have influenced Branwell most was *The Poems of Ossian*. James Macpherson originally published this work in 1760, presenting it as a translation of the authentic writing of the ancient Gaelic poet Ossian. Controversy arose immediately, with prominent figures like Samuel Johnson expressing doubt about the poems' supposedly ancient provenance. Although we now know that much of the book was Macpherson's invention, the controversy remained unresolved in the early decades of the nineteenth century; it was mentioned several times in *Blackwood's Edinburgh Magazine* during the years the Brontës read it. The September 1826 issue, for instance, contains an extensive article by editor Christopher North, a section of which begins by asking, "Was there ever such a man as Ossian? We devoutly hope there was" (North 1826, 410). North proceeds to extol the charms of the poems, without precisely entering the debate over their authenticity. By 1829, the Brontës have joined the debate themselves: Branwell writes in an issue of *Branwell's Blackwood's Magazine* that "Chief Genius Taly" (namely Charlotte) had given him a copy of the poems of Ossian. He expresses enthusiasm about the poems and asserts that they were surely written by "OSSIAN who lived 1000 years ago."[9] Clearly, Branwell knew about the authorship controversy, and he preferred the story of a Celtic warrior-poet to that of a modern-day literary charlatan.

The poems of "Ossian" themselves are generally classified as folklore, but they bear more resemblance to epic poetry like the *Iliad* than to folklore collections like Thomas Crofton Croker's *Fairy Legends and Traditions of the South of Ireland*. Macpherson was interested not in the remarkable experiences of ordinary folk but rather in the exploits of bygone war heroes; his poems primarily consist of one legendary battle account after another. The Brontës owned a copy of the 1819 edition of *The Poems of Ossian*, annotated and available to researchers at the Brontë Parsonage Museum. We cannot definitively state which member of the Brontë family is responsible for any given annotation in the volume; the name "Charlotte" is written on one page of the prefatory "Critical Dissertation on the Poems of Ossian, the son of Fingal, by Hugh Blair, DD, One of the Minsters of the High Church, and Professor of Rhetoric and Belles-Lettres, Edinburgh,"[10] but most of the annotations consist of stars and underlinings rather than words. Typically, the sentences or paragraphs marked are the more poetic moments in the text, often featuring extensive similes; for example, "Then dismal, roaring, fierce, and deep the gloom of battle poured along, as mist that is rolled on a valley when storms invade the silent sunshine of heaven" is noted, as is "We shall pass away like a dream. No sound will remain in our fields of war" (286, 333). A long passage in Book 1 of *Fingal* is marked:

> Like autumn's dark storms pouring from two echoing hills, towards each other approached the heroes. Like two deep streams from high rocks meeting, mixing, roaring on the plain; loud, rough, and dark in battle meet Lochlin and Inisfail. Chief mixes his strokes with chief, and man with man; steel, clanging, sounds on steel. Helmets are cleft on high. Blood bursts and smokes around. Strings murmur on the polished yews. Darts rush along the sky. Spears fall like the circles of light which gild the face of night. As the noise of the troubled ocean, when roll the waves on high. As the last peal of thunder in heaven, such is the din of war! Though Cormac's hundred bards were there to give the fight to song; feeble was the voice of a hundred bards to send the deaths to future times! For many were the deaths of heroes; wide poured the blood of the brave! (276)

Charlotte, Branwell, or Emily could be responsible for any of these annotations, interested as they all were in such vivid Romantic descriptions. But I attribute the notes on the descriptions of battles to Branwell; as far as we know, none of his sisters wrote extensive descriptions of military conflicts. Of all the Brontës, it is Branwell who seems to have been inspired by such stirring presentations of warlike events to write his own.

The influence of Ossian on Branwell's writing is clear in his many battle narratives. Branwell's account of a war between the Glass Town settlers and the Ashantis in *Angria and the Angrians* I(d), for instance, reflects Ossian's close attention to the physical details of battle as well as his penchant for simile:

> I saw a whole <park> of flying artillery galloped by trains of Horses rapidly down the street under the window. The terrific rattle of their metal carriages made the house shake as if it was about to grind them to dust. This was no time for staying to see the sight so I hurried on my cloth[e]s and took my arms to go down as I was about to leave the room (the cannon had some minutes ago passed by) up again rose such a Thunder and beating of Drums without that there was not a pane in the windows which did not shake and quiver to its centre. Oh how they rolled and rattled and rose in such a storm of sound as I had never heard equaled before directly the shrill exhilarating thrilling of fifes joined in on this Terrific reveillé.[11]

This passage is typical of Branwell's writing—the first-person perspective, the focus on violence and destruction, the poetic touches (here, analogy and alliteration), and the evidence of hasty and exuberant composition. Like Macpherson as Ossian, Branwell constructs an extensive and vivid description of the sights and sounds of battle. In addition to the poems of Ossian, Branwell seems to have been familiar with Arthurian legends, given that the eponymous hero of his verse drama *Caractacus* (1830) was connected to the Arthurian tradition. Caractacus, also known by the name Caradoc or Cradoc, was a Welsh king immortalized in various folktales and ballads, by some accounts also serving as a knight of the Round Table. However, Branwell's drama focuses narrowly on the aftermath of Caractacus's defeat by the Romans; Branwell does not make any particular use of the Arthurian tradition more generally, and there is no mention of any of that tradition's supernatural elements.

It seems clear that Branwell enjoyed these heroic legends in spite of their fantastical components, responding instead to a manliness and seriousness he found in their focus on war and political conflict. Even the exclusively human portions of the traditions of Arthur and Ossian, however—like the stories of the Chief Genii—are by no means drily realist. They are, instead, dramatic portrayals of powerful men in extraordinary circumstances. Branwell would go on to write poems and fictionalized prose texts about military heroes including Napoleon and Admiral Nelson (victor of the battle of Trafalgar); Napoleon even became a character in his Glass Town stories. These texts of Branwell's lie outside the scope of this chapter, but one could argue that they are the ultimate manifestations of what Branwell learned from folkloric texts he read in childhood, even though they usually contain no supernatural references. Branwell would never again write about supernatural creatures like the Genii; however, he would continue to use supernatural references as metaphors for very real concerns.

Fairy Women and Distant Fantasies

Branwell's decreasing interest in genii and increasing interest in human affairs was not accompanied by a total dismissal of mentions of the supernatural. His writing about relationships between men and women, for example, reveals that he, like Charlotte, absorbed the popular nineteenth-century strategy of using fairies in figurative descriptions of women's physical appearance. In a fairly early text, *The Politics of Verdopolis* (1833), Branwell notes Mary Henrietta Percy's "fairy hands and feet" among her many attractions.[12] Branwell's last prose text, "And the Weary Are at Rest" (1845), features a comparison of a beautiful woman to a sylph.[13] Throughout his writing, minor female characters sometimes have "fairy hands," in one case accompanied by "beautiful little feet."[14] In all of these instances, the word "fairy" essentially functions as a synonym for "dainty"; for Branwell, to compare a woman's appearance to that of a fairy or sylph is simply to state that she is beautiful. Similar phrases occur in Charlotte's juvenilia; Charlotte, however, also wrote numerous tales in her youth that portrayed fairies more negatively, demonstrating their power over human beings and indifference to human notions of morality. Even though fairies do not usually cause lasting harm to human beings in her stories, she sometimes created suspense by exploiting the traditional understanding of fairies as formidable; the fairy in her tale "The Enfant," for example, speaks "in a loud and terrible voice," and, "spreading her large, white wings, she rose majestically above the city."[15] Charlotte would later make far more sophisticated and complex analogies between women and supernatural creatures in all her published novels, evoking the beauty and the danger of these creatures simultaneously. The potential Branwell saw in fairies to express something about women, by contrast, seems to have had only one dimension.

Charlotte embraced the traditional understanding of fairies and other supernatural creatures as dramatically unpredictable; in traditional folklore, a fairy encountered on an evening walk might offer a human being anything from riches to death, depending on the fairy's assessment of the human being's merit. Branwell, meanwhile, seems early on to have sensed an impending shift in attitudes toward supernatural creatures: as the nineteenth century progressed, a clearer divide gradually emerged between supernatural creatures understood as inherently good (such as fairies, elves, and sprites) and those understood as inherently evil (such as goblins, ogres, ghouls, hags, and vampires). Fairies in later Victorian writing continued to symbolize the seeming capriciousness of women toward men, but they often lacked the true menace of figures like the dissembling fairy bride of Keats's "La Belle Dame Sans Merci" (1819), who leaves her mortal beloved to waste away and die. Tennyson's "Lilian," from *Poems, Chiefly Lyrical* (1830), encapsulates the emerging Victorian attitude toward fairies (and engendered the term "airy-fairy," meaning insubstantial or idealistic, which Branwell used in a context I will discuss later). In the first stanza, the speaker warbles,

> Airy, Fairy Lilian,
> Flitting, fairy Lilian,
> When I ask her if she love me,
> Claps her tiny hands above me,
> Laughing all she can;
> She'll not tell me if she love me,
> Cruel little Lilian

This woman resembles a fairy in that she is small (both "tiny" and "little"), light ("airy"), agile ("flitting"), merry ("laughing"), and noncommittal ("she'll not tell me if she love me"). Her "cruelty" consists merely of a refusal to confess love to the presumably male speaker. She poses no serious threat—as is shockingly indicated in the final stanza, in which the speaker asserts that if Lilian will not heed his supplication, "Like a rose-leaf I will crush thee, / Fairy Lilian" (stanza 4). Crucially, this fairy-woman is "cruel" but also "little": she can affect the male admirer's emotions but not his safety. The kind of connection Tennyson makes between fairies and women is the one that would rise in currency over the course of the Victorian period; Branwell's comprehensive association of fairies with the beautiful and diminutive qualities of women—as opposed to Charlotte's use of fairies as both feminine and formidable—is somewhat ahead of his time.

Branwell often deployed the supernatural in emphasizing the distinction between fantasy and reality—specifically, between fantasy as associated with dreams, the past, and all that is pleasant, and reality as associated with the harsh waking world of today. From writing of his qualms about the Chief Genii's possession of magnificent powers within the context of a fictional world, Branwell progressed to registering skepticism that there was anything to be gained by dwelling on illusory impressions—a different kind of distrust of the power of fantasy. One text that associates magic with dreams is the multivolume collection *Angria and the Angrians*, which contains a poem that begins,

> Morn comes and with it all the stir of morn
> New life new light upon its sunbeams born
> The Magic dreams of Midnight fade away
> And Iron labour rouses with the day.[16]

Magic is here associated with night and dreaming, and placed in opposition to action, light, and physical work. Branwell may even have had in mind the old wisdom that iron was a threat to fairies and other supernatural beings.[17] The 1837 poem "An Hours Musings on the Atlantic," too, forces the speaker to move from dream to waking reality:

> Life alone on its midnight sea
> The Terrible Reality!
> Sleeper awake! Thy dream is flown
> And thou-rt on Ocean all alone![18]

Dreams are like magic to Branwell in that they can be perceived but are ultimately illusory—and, arguably, having had the beautiful dream makes the harsh reality all the more difficult to bear.

Other texts associate magic with the past; it is from dwelling on memories that these characters and speakers must awake. The line "Ah World!—why wilt thou break Enchantment's chain!" laments a man returning to his childhood home and finding it less than he remembered; this line persists across various revisions of the poem, ultimately titled "Sir Henry Tunstall."[19] Interestingly, Branwell chose to figure enchantment here as a chain—usually a negative image. This choice may reflect the fact that Branwell usually *does* see enchantment as negative, but in this case the shattering of the enchantment of memory is a painful experience. The speaker of another poem, "Calm and clear the day, declining," hears a funeral bell and is transported back to the memory of her deceased sister.

> This scene seems like the magic glass
> Which bore upon its clouded face
> Strange shadows that deceived the eye
> With forms defined uncertainly;
> That Bell is old Agrippa's wand,
> Which parts the clouds on either hand
> And shows the pictured forms of doom
> Momently brightening through the gloom:
> Yes—shows a scene of bygone years.[20]

In this poem, to remember is to be deceived by dramatic but ultimately false images that distract from the painful reality of death. As with "enchantment's chain" in the previous poem, the images here are complex. The memories themselves seem initially to be the "shadows" that render the face of the magic glass "clouded," but later the clouds are the barriers that must be removed in order to reveal the "bright" images of memory. At the same time, these bright images are described ominously as "the pictured forms of doom," even though the memory she goes on to describe is a pleasant one. In any event, Agrippa's wand and the magic glass are the sources of the vivid memories that ultimately cede their place in the end of the poem to the speaker's sad awareness of her sister's death. Both of these poems reveal adult Branwell's conflicting attraction to memory and certainty that the real world of the present must always prevail.

In Branwell's late work "And the Weary Are at Rest" (1845), memory and fantasy are aligned several times, always negatively. Maria Thurston seems quite sinister to Alexander Percy when he notices that her eyes hold no light "save the ignus fatuus of decay which lights up the charnel remnants of time past."[21] Branwell is referring to the *ignis fatuus,* or will-o'-the-wisp, the "false light" of folklore that leads travelers astray; in his allusion, that which illuminates the past is inherently a false magic trick. The ignis fatuus should always be avoided, and it is clear in this case that any rekindling of the bygone romance of Percy and Maria would be ill-advised, considering the use of the word "charnel" to describe the past and the fact that Maria is currently married to someone else. The narrator of "And the Weary Are at Rest" also refers to fairy tales in order to register Maria's disappointment with her marriage: "The remembrance of her bridal days caused the astonishment which one feels when thinking that one's childhood took for truth the gibberish of a nursery tale" (460). Nineteenth-century writers alluded to fairy tales in part because they could assume near-universal familiarity with them; Branwell assumes that a concept of the falseness of such tales is universal as well. He also explicitly associates fairy tales with children here in a way that would become more common later in the Victorian period.

Thus, in both his association of women with fairies and his association of fantasy with memory and the past, Branwell registers an impression of the supernatural as both alluring and other. In the works of Charlotte and Emily Brontë, the supernatural is consistently endemic to the real world. For Branwell it is often in mind but always apart—in the mystifying and ultimately incomprehensible opposite sex, in the past, in the world of the imagination. On the whole, more Victorian writers held Branwell's view than those of Charlotte and Emily; obviously there were exceptions, but Branwell's ideas were the ones on the rise throughout the Victorian period. Considering Branwell's view thus provides a glimpse of the broader Victorian attitude, even as it also puts the innovations of his sisters into perspective.

The Persistent Fairy-Tale Allusion

Despite all the suspicion of fairy tales and fantasy registered in the previous section, Branwell made numerous offhand references to supernatural tales and creatures throughout his writing. In general, these allusions do not seem to be deeply considered and do not add significantly to the import of the texts in which they appear. Rather, they speak to the immediate availability of fantastical subjects as metaphors in nineteenth-century England. One key source for such metaphors is the *Arabian Nights' Entertainments*, to which Branwell continues to refer even after the Chief Genii cease to play an active role in the Glass Town stories.

Like Charlotte, Branwell often makes these allusions in order to convey the magnificence of a scene. For example, in the first volume of *Angria and the Angrians* (1834), Branwell twice likens the Houses of Parliament of Verdopolis (another name for Glass Town) to structures from the *Arabian Nights' Entertainments*. First, the narrator compares them to "the famed pavilion of Prince Ahmed" for their splendor and then later to the magnetic "Loadstone mountain [in] the Arabian Tale" for their ability to "attract toward them every heart and foot in the city of Verdopolis."[22] In these offhand uses of "exotic" tales to epitomize unearthly splendor, Branwell participates in a common trend in nineteenth-century English writing and art; the *Arabian Nights' Entertainments* and other tales of the broadly defined East seemed to many English authors simply available for comparisons their readers would quickly understand.

In addition to allusions to Middle Eastern tales, unremarked-upon references to other forms of supernatural and fairy lore also permeate Branwell's poetry and prose texts. The first volume of *Angria and the Angrians* contains yellow balls shining like jack-o'-lanterns, children with elfish faces, and civil servants with the tenacity of harpies, the last of those perhaps paving the way for the "Harpies of Democratic Tyranny" in a later volume.[23] In one of Branwell's last works more than a decade later, the poem "Juan Fernandez," he describes the sunshine as gilding "fairy-like" the rills that flowed into the ocean.[24] In between, Zamorna smiles a "witching smile," a funeral bell is described as "the Enchanter's stern command," a character tells her sister stories of fairies and "Benshees" (banshees), a lady is oppressed by a "goblin dream," and a feeling like an "incubus" prevents Percy from pursuing an object of desire.[25] At least eleven times, Branwell uses the word "majic" or "magic" to describe an awe-inspiring sight[26]—a technique Charlotte uses throughout her juvenilia, novels, and personal writing. This selection of Branwell's offhand references to magic and supernatural creatures demonstrates that Branwell maintained throughout his writing career the casual habit of such allusion that pervades nineteenth-century writing.

So instinctive are supernatural references for Branwell that more than once in his writing of the 1830s, he criticizes the practice of writing about fantastical subjects but then immediately refers to supernatural tales or creatures himself, apparently unaware that this might strike a reader as contradictory. First, in "The Life of Field Marshal the Right Honourable Alexander Percy" (1834), Branwell's narrator scorns those who believe that in poetry, "every thing real in this world's ongoings must give place to some pretty tale of true or false love or the Orisons of some simple maiden or the gambols of fairies in a flowery vale."[27] Thus far, the message is clear enough: Branwell wants to write about the real world, while his sisters want to write about love, silly girls, nature, and innocuous fairies. But he concludes the diatribe this way: "I for one will always fly from the sickly tales of mental concoctions or monstrositys sentimental decoctions or airy fairyism and shadowy fancies of what has never been a Barmecideal feast which can never satisfy my hunger" (149). The rest of the narrative offers an account of Alexander Percy's life, implicitly contrasted with the "airy fairyism" the other Brontës are writing. The "Barmecideal feast" appears in a popular story from the *Arabian Nights' Entertainments* about an imaginary feast served to a beggar by a man from the wealthy Barmecide family.[28] To be fair, the story turns out to have been a portrayal of trickery rather than magic. Nevertheless, Branwell seems, unironically, to be explaining what he finds dissatisfying about fantastical tales by alluding to a story from the book that epitomized supernatural storytelling in the era.

The second, and starker, instance of inadvertent hypocrisy occurs in the fourth volume of *Angria and the Angrians* (1837). He begins by criticizing Charlotte: "I would doubt the genius of that writer who loved more to dwell upon Indian Palm Groves or Genii palaces than on the wooded manors and cloudy skies of England."[29] In other words, Branwell positions foreign and fantastical settings as a less worthy subject for great writing than the natural, unglamorous, local reality. But on the very next page, Branwell describes a spot in the Outer Hebrides of Scotland by observing that the tallest of the "gloomy firs" tower over the buildings "like the Genii of that desolate scene" (187). Once again, figurative uses of the supernatural are so instinctive for Branwell that he refers to genii almost immediately after asserting the inadequacy of foreign and fantastical subjects, including genii in particular.

One might object that in both cases I have identified, Branwell implies a distinction between writing about actual supernatural happenings and using them in a merely figurative sense. However, only a few lines after the comparison of trees to genii in *Angria and the Angrians,* he goes into great detail about the legend of the "Darkwall Gytrash," which is treated as a plausible story within the world about which he is writing. Readers of *Jane Eyre* will recall the moment when Jane first sees Rochester's dog, Pilot, on a nighttime walk and initially believes him to be the shapeshifting "North-of-England spirit, called a 'Gytrash.'"[30] Branwell, however, spends far more time discussing the Gytrash than Charlotte would go on to do:

> A Gytrash is a Spectre neither at all similar to the Ghosts of those who once were alive nor to fairys and silvan Creatures nor to Demons and the powers of the air it does not confine its forms to the Human and indeed most seldom appears in such a form a Black Dog dragging a chain a dusky calf nay even a rolling stone or self impelled cart wheel are more commonly the mortal coil of the Sullen Spectre But the Darkwall Gytrash was known by the form of an Old Dwarfish and hideous Man as often seen without a head as with one and moving at dark along the naked fields which spread round the Aged House its visits were connected in all mens minds with the fortunes of the family he hovered round and evil omens were always drawn on such occasions and if tradition spoke true fulfilled upon them.[31]

Soon after criticizing Charlotte's focus on the supernatural, then, Branwell devotes more than 150 words to a description of a specter. So detailed is Branwell's description that this very text is the primary source cited in the entry for "guytrash, gytrash" in *A Dictionary of English Folklore*.[32] Branwell begins by anxiously distancing the Gytrash from ghosts, fairies, woodland creatures, demons, and aerial spirits. Rather, he emphasizes the belief that this spirit shifts between forms that are ordinary in and of themselves—a dog, a calf, a stone, a wheel, or a man, albeit one without a head.

The question, then, is what Branwell believed to be the fundamental difference between the Darkwall Gytrash and the "Indian Palm Groves or Genii palaces." One obvious distinction is geographical and cultural: the Gytrash was an English legend, and a North-of-England one at that. Brontë biographer Winifred Gérin notes that Branwell's description of the Gytrash corresponds to local folklore about a spirit associated with Ponden House, the manor house near Haworth that served as a model for Thrushcross Grange in *Wuthering Heights*. This spirit was believed to appear in various forms, including that of a dog, a horse, a cow, or even a "flaming barrel bowling across the fields"; apparently, members of the family that owned Ponden House would see the spirit whenever disaster was approaching.[33] The intensely local nature of this tradition is crucial: when Branwell contrasts "Indian Palm Groves or Genii palaces" with "the wooded manors and cloudy skies of England," the distinction between the foreign and the local seems to be more prominent than that between fantasy and reality. In Branwell's mind, the English story of the Gytrash apparently could belong to the here and now in a way that genii could not.

However, as we saw in previous chapters, there were many English folktales of fairies as well; why was the Gytrash acceptable to Branwell while fairies were not? His term "airy fairyism" provides the answer. In contrast to the complex way Charlotte conceived of fairies, Branwell seems to have seen them as irredeemably "airy"—that is, as inherently feminine and forever floating above the earth. The vast majority of Branwell's references to fairies have to do with women. Recall that his criticism in "The Life of Field Marshal the Right Honourable Alexander Percy" takes aim in one breath at "love or the Orisons of some simple maiden or the gambols of fairies in a flowery vale";[34] he sees fairies as inextricably bound up with love, prayers, girls, and flowers—all clearly objects of his scorn. He presents the Gytrash, by contrast, as a very earthly and masculine spirit, physically and spiritually dark. These distinctions correspond to Branwell's treatment of fantasy as fundamentally a falsehood, liable to dissipate and leave the dreamer with a harsh dose of reality. As we have already seen, that which was bleak always seemed more real to Branwell than that which was pleasant or attractive. Branwell clearly concluded that an ominous supernatural creature of the here and now could be worthy of discussion in literature, while cheery, foreign, or feminine creatures could not.

Working out which types of these references seemed sufficiently "real" to Branwell is useful for my broader interrogation of how the literary real was constructed in this period and what that meant for folk and fairy tales. Branwell's ringing defense of the authenticity of Ossian in *Branwell's Blackwood's Magazine* suggests that he saw that material as real, or at least as possessing literary or cultural validity. We can identify several commonalities between the poems of Ossian and the story of the Darkwall Gytrash, the other folkloric subject on which Branwell is happy to dwell: they are masculine; they are native to the British Isles; and their subject matter is inherently negative, involving war, death, and dark omens. These are the qualities a folkloric subject must have in order to be admitted into Branwell Brontë's literary real—which was dominated, of course, by content that had nothing to do with folklore at all, let alone fairy tales. As a result, Branwell's view had much in common with the emerging concept of the Victorian literary real more generally. The idea held by some that fairy tale and realism are in conflict is bound up with assumptions that the darker perspective is always the more realist one; it is also bound up with fairy tales' association with women and, later in the Victorian period, children. I will demonstrate in future chapters that Charlotte Brontë in particular found fairy tales especially useful for constructing an authentic illustration of internal experience. Our understanding of realism, however, tends to prioritize its more observable, external aspects—aspects that were, on the whole, more available to Victorian men than to Victorian women. Perhaps it should not surprise us, then, that the one Brontë son had a conception of the literary real that was in keeping with his time; Anne Brontë, too, wrote novels that are generally considered unimpeachably realist, but she did so by building plots modeled on European literary fairy tales. I would not assert a one-to-one correspondence between Victorian realism and the masculine; I am instead building a more complex argument that will emerge over the course of this book. For now, the important point is that Branwell embraced a conventional concept of realism that explicitly excluded the fairy tale and that would not be shared by any of his sisters.

I have attempted to demonstrate throughout this chapter, however, that Branwell Brontë's stated dismissal of the fantastical is not entirely borne out by his own writing. In addition to participating in the Brontë children's collaborative creation of Glass Town and its Chief Genii, Branwell uses supernatural references several times in order to describe women and to underscore the contrast between fantasy and reality. He also makes numerous casual references to enchantment, supernatural creatures, and stories from the *Arabian Nights' Entertainments*. Unlike all of his sisters, however, Branwell never seems to have used folk or fairy tales as models for his own plots. This difference is important: I identify deliberate and strategic engagements with folk and fairy tales in the novels of Charlotte, Emily, and Anne (albeit very different ones), while much of what I observe in Branwell's work is an uncritical and possibly nearly unconscious use of folk- and fairy-tale allusions. That these allusions were sometimes unconscious is emphasized by their appearance immediately after an explicit criticism of writing about fairies and their ilk. He usually seems not to have intended these allusions to reinforce the content of the texts in any substantial way; rather, the fact that he used them at all speaks to the ubiquity of folk and fairy tales in the oral and print culture within which Branwell lived.

Branwell, unlike Charlotte, continued to write stories and poems based on the characters or setting of Angria well into adulthood, "never fully quitting this dream-like realm," as Conover puts it.[35] There was a brand of overt fantasy that he found deeply distasteful, but he never let go of the imaginary world of his childhood. Perhaps even more than his sisters', Branwell's life story is indisputably a sad one; he might have blamed himself for holding onto a happier world of the imagination, but surely no one else would think the same.

3 Natural, Supernatural, and Divine in the Poetry of Anne and Emily Brontë

In 1831, Emily and Anne Brontë, then twelve and eleven years old, abandoned the Glass Town world they had invented with Charlotte and Branwell in order to create their own fictional kingdom. Its primary setting was Gondal, an imaginary island in the North Pacific whose environment was modeled on that of Scotland and Yorkshire. Like Glass Town, Gondal was populated with various larger-than-life characters, some of whom actually participated in both sagas. Also like Glass Town, Gondal was home to adventurers: the Gondals discover and explore an island in the South Pacific called Gaaldine. Unfortunately, most of Emily's and Anne's writing about Gondal has been lost. We know from a few surviving "diary papers" written by Emily and Anne that extensive prose chronicles once existed, but they exist no longer.[1] Most of the surviving poems are lyrics, consisting of emotional outpourings from a Gondal character; modern scholars thus often see the reaction to an event without having the chronicle of the event itself.

Fannie E. Ratchford, in *Gondal's Queen: A Novel in Verse* (1955), valiantly attempted a reconstruction of the Gondal narrative based on the surviving documents. But Ratchford's reconstruction is ultimately hypothetical: we actually cannot say for sure which of Emily's and Anne's poems originally belonged to the Gondal story, much less where they fit in it. In 1844, Emily copied numerous poems she had written into two notebooks: one labeled "Gondal Poems" and one containing poems without references to Gondal, now known as the Honresfeld manuscript.[2]

Some scholars use this separation to distinguish entirely between Gondal and non-Gondal poetry, often going on to criticize the Gondal poems as melodramatic and immature.[3] But no evidence suggests that Emily divided her poems so starkly before 1844, and since most of her poems are lyrics, any given poem could just as easily express the feelings of a Gondal character as those of Emily herself or any other imagined poetic persona. When she prepared poems from both notebooks for publication in 1846, she simply deleted a few names of Gondal characters and references to Gondal events, which emphasizes the tenuousness of the 1844 division.[4] Moreover, Emily and Anne themselves often do not distinguish between Gondal and Haworth at times we expect them to; as their joint diary paper of November 24, 1834, reports, "The Gondals are discovering the interior of Gaaldine Sally Mosley is washing in the back kitchin."[5] Not even a punctuation mark separates the exploration in Gaaldine from the domestic labor in Haworth. This is one reason that some scholars, including me, ultimately choose not to impose a strict partition between "Gondal" and "non-Gondal" poems. Any attempt to divide the poems of Emily in particular into juvenilia and "mature" writing also fails, considering that she wrote poems about Gondal throughout her life.

I also choose not to treat Gondal poems separately because there is no evidence that Gondal was home to many supernatural creatures like the genii and fairies of Glass Town and Angria. Certainly, Gondal was not a particularly realist world; Emily's and Anne's writing about Gondal owes much to the work of Sir Walter Scott, Lord Byron, and the Gothic mode in general, as the surviving poems indicate (characters are forever languishing in dungeons and nursing desperate passions, for example). But, at least in the texts that survive, figurative and literal references to supernatural forces or creatures from folklore are not noticeably more prominent in Gondal poems than in verses clearly written outside that fictional context. The poems in which Emily and Anne most productively employ the supernatural span many years of their lives and exist both within and without the Gondal story. Emily, in particular, wrote several poems featuring supernatural creatures and magic spells, only some of which explicitly take place in Gondal.

In this chapter, therefore, I discuss the role of the supernatural in the poetry of Emily and Anne Brontë as a whole. For Anne, the religious supernatural took precedence: many of her poems refer to the powers of God. She most often refers to the nonreligious supernatural figuratively, the better to illustrate the experience of love and faith. Divine puissance, however, virtually always emerges as stronger than any other kind of enchantment. For Emily, the supernatural was intertwined with the natural. Several of her surviving poems—ranging from 1837 to 1844—feature spells or supernatural spirits of some sort, many of whom are closely associated with nature. Like the protagonists of Charlotte's early fairy stories, Emily's speakers in these poems are typically human beings surprised by the supernatural encounter. These poems use the supernatural to explore the question of human beings' alienation from nature (and, sometimes, from God)—usually arriving at only ambiguous answers to that question.

Both Emily and Anne thus utilize supernatural references in order to interrogate what they evidently believed to be the most important issues in human life. These are also the issues that are most difficult to corral into language. Something feels "like magic" when we cannot understand how it works; God and nature are crucial examples of forces that often defy human explanation in this way. Scholars do not tend to use the term "realism" in reference to poetry, but I am identifying essentially the same technique in Emily's and Anne's poetry as in the adult novels of all the Brontë sisters: they use tools we have been trained to associate with the unreal in order to address real experiences in the world that transcend the power of ordinary realism to articulate. This technique is especially applicable to the expression of interior experiences, as conventional realism tends to focus on the external and observable. Although psychological realism deals with interior experience, it is most successful in giving voice to rational thought processes that can be articulated in ordinary language. What I am observing, by contrast, is a way of reaching into the supposedly unreal in order to convey the feeling of a vitally important real that tends to escape language itself.

"Make My Trancéd Spirit Blest": Anne Brontë

Anne Brontë was no aficionado of fairy tales and fantasy. Consider the conclusion of the diary paper written on July 30, 1841, in which 21-year-old Anne imagines the future: "For some time I have looked upon 25 as a sort of era in my existence it may prove a true presentiment or it may be only a superstitious fancy the latter seems most likely but time will show."[6] Superstitious fancies may be experienced, this statement suggests, but no credence should be given to them; like Branwell, Anne explicitly advocated writing about the real world. Although her novels draw on fairy-tale themes and narrative structures, this is less true of her poetry, which tends instead to deal with religion, memory, and internal experiences of sadness and reflection. For Anne, the power of God was the most important reality; it is also, though, a reality that can be difficult to reduce to ordinary language. Therefore, Anne sometimes uses language of magic and enchantment as one of many metaphorical devices for describing the experience of the divine.[7] Although the concepts of both the magical and the divine provide ways to articulate experiences of extraordinary power, Anne characterizes magic as ultimately an illusion, whereas the true origin of that experience almost always turns out to be the divine.

Considering Anne's religious beliefs and priorities, it is actually noteworthy that she never explicitly criticizes the practice of writing or reading about the nonreligious supernatural. Many other commentators did in the late eighteenth and early nineteenth centuries. The way in which Anne does use folkloric supernatural language is instructive: she primarily uses it to better explain how an experience feels (be it memory, human love, or the exhilaration of faith itself). Anne was religious but not rigid: she rejected Calvinism in favor of a doctrine of universal salvation. The confidence and openness implied in this belief seems to me in keeping with Anne's willingness to draw on the nonreligious supernatural in her writing: for someone who truly believes that everyone will be saved and that God's power is the strongest force in the universe, what is the harm in comparing a spiritual experience to magic or enchantment?

Using language about charms and magic enables Anne to describe real spiritual experiences that are extremely difficult to articulate. For example, in the undated "Farewell to thee! But not farewell," published in 1848, the speaker describes the lingering effect of the departed beloved by using both religious language and several terms connected to magic. We learn early in the poem that this beloved exceeded even the rosy hopes of the speaker's youthful imagination:

> If thou hadst never met mine eye,
> I had not dreamed a living face
> Could fancied charms so far outvie
>
> (ln. 6–8)[8]

Although at this point in the poem one might expect that enchantment is fully quelled by the superiority of reality to the "fancied charms," the speaker goes on to describe the beloved's actual effects by using similar language:

> That voice, the magic of whose tone
> Could wake an echo in my breast
> Creating feelings that, alone,
> Can make my trancéd spirit blest
>
> (ln. 13–16)

The effect of the voice is described in the present tense: while the voice "could" wake an echo in the past, the resulting feelings still "can" benefit the spirit precisely because it is still "trancéd," an unusual synonym for "enchanted." Taken together, these lines indicate that the speaker once merely fancied the "charms" a lover might have, but the beloved transcended that fancy to the point where the speaker remains "trancéd" and "blest" even now that the beloved has gone. The final stanza expresses the hope that "Heaven / . . . May answer all my thousand prayers" and reunite the speaker with the beloved in the future (ln. 25–26). Unlike Jane Eyre in love with Rochester, the speaker of this poem apparently does not worry that she has made of the beloved an idol; rather, her spirit can be at once "trancéd" and "blest," as is reinforced in the form of the poem by the fact that the word "spirit" is literally surrounded by those two words. This poem thus does not present magic and spirituality in conflict, even as it focuses on the seemingly magical effects human beings may have on each other more than on the power of God.

In one of Anne's best-known religious poems, the religious and non-religious supernatural operate in complete harmony: she uses the word "magic" to express the force of religious faith. In "The Three Guides," dated 1847 and published in *Fraser's Magazine* the next year, the speaker considers the Spirit of Earth, the Spirit of Pride, and finally the Spirit of Faith, deeming the first two specious and only the last worthy. Some critics, including Muriel Spark and Edward Chitham, have associated the Spirit of Pride with Emily, considering the Spirit's fiery strength.[9] To the Spirit of Faith, the speaker says,

> And still to all that seek thy way
> This magic power is given,—

E'en while their footsteps press the clay,
Their souls ascend to Heaven

(ln. 165–68)[10]

Faith is not magic, of course, and that difference was especially significant in light of the popular British Protestant association between magic and Catholicism—which Charlotte Brontë develops extensively in *Villette.* Yet Anne nevertheless finds magic the best illustration of the remarkable real experience religious faith can bring about: that of feeling spiritually liberated even while physically limited in a human body. Making a positive reference to magic seems to be acceptable to Anne because the message of the poem is obviously the supremacy of faith.

In another poem, Anne again presents magic and God as working in tandem but explicitly deems God superior. Called "Memory" and dated May 29, 1844, the poem reverently recalls childhood in a way that, as many critics have noted, clearly evokes William Wordsworth.[11] After recalling her childhood adoration of the beauties of nature for several stanzas, the speaker directly addresses Memory, using the language of magic as she enjoins it to remain: "Forever hang thy dreamy spell, / Round golden star and heatherbell" (ln. 31–32).[12] Memory here functions as a spell—a word she applies to it again in line 46—that lends additional beauty to various ordinary objects in nature. The speaker goes on to consider the possibility that childhood was not inherently the most joyful time of life, but that the spell cast by memory itself makes it seem so. In the final stanza, however, she subordinates the magic power of memory to the power of God with the line "Nor is the glory all thine own" and the new description of the spell's effect as a "holy light" (ln. 43, 45). Ultimately, she seems to suggest that remembering can feel like falling under a spell, but that in fact only the divine is responsible for the feeling. As with the reference to magic power in "The Three Guides," it is interesting that she uses the word "spell" twice in a poem that works so hard to attribute its observations to the influence of God. Again, Anne sees experiencing the power of God as supremely real but difficult to explain; the imaginary sensation of falling under a spell comes closer to describing that experience than a comparison taken from the everyday world would have.

Ultimately, what is true of Branwell is also true of Anne: both resort to the descriptive language of enchantment and fantasy despite deeming it inferior to something else (in his case, historical and military exploits;

in hers, Christian faith). Branwell, as discussed in the previous chapter, often seems to use this language without realizing it, especially considering that he sometimes rails against supernatural subject matter just before using it himself in passing. Anne does not explicitly criticize those who write about the nonreligious supernatural and seems unconcerned about occasionally doing so herself, confident that only divine power possesses any real force. Religious experience is real but difficult to explain; she is clearly happy to take advantage of any method of explanation. Emily, too, strives to articulate the human being's relationship with the divine, but Emily's divine is more diffuse, incorporating nature and the cosmos in addition to a Christian God. Elizabeth Hollis Berry has distinguished Emily's and Anne's conceptions of nature by suggesting that "whereas for Emily the wild, natural world is a pantheistic embodiment of a great spirit, for Anne the realms of heaven and earth are imagined as separate spaces, with various linking bridges, portals and paths offered to the earthbound traveller who has faith and hope."[13] Nature and spirituality blend for Emily in a way that they do not for Anne. In some poems, Emily also seems to see the nonreligious supernatural as endemic to the natural world in a way that her sister does not. Like Anne, however, Emily often takes up a subject that defies conventional explanation—in her case, the place of the human individual in a natural world that is both divine and material—and uses the language of the supernatural in order to do so.

Spirit, Nature, and the Individual: Emily Brontë

Emily Brontë's poetry poses a particular challenge to scholars because of its often-fragmentary nature, our uncertainty as to the role of Gondal in any given poem, and the near-total lack of personal writings from which to draw illuminating commentary from Emily herself. As with *Wuthering Heights,* readers have made widely varying interpretations of Emily's poems; early commentators' confident literal readings of her references to God, for example, are matched in certainty by the contrasting view of later critics like Margaret Homans that Emily could not possibly have believed her own statements of religious faith. Scholars of Emily's poetry have not tended to comment on the role of the supernatural, with the exception of some discussion of her treatment of ghosts.[14] Her engagement with nature in her poetry, though, has generated wide-ranging debate, which I will only touch on here. Robin Grove observes that "while [Emily Brontë's] reputation as a 'nature poet' has stood high, a firm basis for it is hard to discover," considering what he terms her "surprisingly few poems of landscape."[15] But ultimately he acknowledges that landscape does function in Emily's poetry by vividly "mapping out inner shifts, in energy and time" (47). For Barbara Hardy, similarly, nature "suggest[s] what is unnatural" and also allows Emily to "imagine spirit through nature."[16] Like William Wordsworth, whose poetry all the Brontës admired, Emily Brontë is popularly considered a nature poet but rarely wrote poems simply about nature for its own sake; rather, she, like him, typically interrogated nature's relationship to the human being or used nature as a site for poetic reflection on other concerns.

Of course, articulating nature's relationship to the human being is a far more difficult proposition than simply describing the natural world would be. In real lived experience, nature can feel by turns safe and threatening, kin and alien to a human individual. It often seems to house some sort of unseen but essential spirit. Such impressions defy illustration in straightforward language; Emily Brontë, therefore, uses supernatural comparisons and figures in her poetry to capture something of the experience. Like many Romantic writers such as Samuel Taylor Coleridge, she was something of a pantheist, and the supernatural tends to overlap with both the natural and the divine in her writing. Sometimes, like Anne, she uses the language of enchantment to describe the power of God, though more often such language explores the relationship between human beings and nature. Unlike Anne, she peoples some of her poems with supernatural spirits, who tend to be figures capable of bridging the gap between nature and the human speaker—a rapprochement that may or may not be desired by either party, depending on the poem.

Spells and enchantment are often associated with nature in Emily Brontë's poetry, but whether natural forces themselves cast the spells is not always clear, as in the poem beginning

> The night is darkening round me
> The wild winds coldly blow
> But a tyrant spell has bound me
> And I cannot cannot go
>
> (ln. 1–3)[17]

Although Emily provides no title for this poem, dated November 1837, many editions have given it the title "Spellbound." The speaker goes on to give no detail about this "tyrant spell," but it is clearly potent, as the speaker does indeed remain in the stormy wilderness. The word "tyrant" suggests that the spell is unwelcome, but, as Gezari points out, "there is no evidence in the poem that the lyric speaker feels threatened" by the growing storm.[18] Moreover, by the end of the poem, the speaker seems to exert agency even as she also is constrained: "I will not cannot go" (ln. 12).[19] The spell has no distinct point of origin; the poem's final line raises the possibility that the speaker has effectively cast a spell on herself. It is unclear whether the force that cast the spell actually has any relationship to nature. All we know is the spell's outcome: to detain the speaker outside on a stormy winter night, and to do it so thoroughly that the speaker can finally no longer distinguish its will from her own. In other words, we do not know what precisely has occurred in the story implied by the poem, but Emily's reference to a spell permits her to evoke a real feeling of entrapment, particularly any entrapment whose potency has outlasted the memory of its cause. One could also easily imagine this poem being uttered by Heathcliff in the second part of *Wuthering Heights*—as I will discuss in chapter 6, his behavior, though always possible according to the rules of the real world, often resembles that of human beings who have been bound by some sort of supernatural influence.

The speaker of "Loud without the wind was roaring," dated November 11, 1838, is glad to be enthralled by nature. Included in the non-Gondal Honresfeld manuscript, this poem refers twice to a spell of somewhat uncertain provenance. Early in the poem, the speaker is suffering through a stormy November night when an "ancient song" comes and "awaken[s] a spell" that transports the speaker to a memory of spring on the faraway moors of her home (ln. 9, 12).[20] The origin of this ancient song is unclear, and the speaker provides only two of its lines; later in the poem, however, she kneels on a foreign heath and hears the heath speaking. Although what it whispers to her is that it is dying, she asserts nonetheless that there is no "spell more adored and heart-breaking / Than in its half-blighted bells lay—" (ln. 61–62). Whether the spell of the ancient song and the spell of the heath are identical is not clear. However, the result is increased optimism in the speaker: having begun the poem on a "dreary eve" feeling "repining grief," the speaker reflects in the final stanza,

> Well, well the sad minutes are moving
> Though loaded with trouble and pain—
> And sometime the loved and the loving
> Shall meet on the mountains again—
>
> (ln. 67–70)

The speaker remains homesick at the end of the poem, but the spell or spells revive a sufficiently detailed memory of her moors to lead to confidence of a future return. Though treated as literal rather than figurative, the spell functions in the poem as a metaphor for powerful impressions created by the perception of nature—in this case a positive impression in which one landscape evokes another so vividly as to seem the result of magic.

In contrast to the abstractions of the foregoing poems, some other poems feature personified nature spirits. Traditional supernatural creatures have often been associated with aspects of nature: mermaids represent all the dangers of a voyage at sea, fairies often wear green and are associated with the forest or other specific places in nature, and some genii claim guardianship of particular landscapes. The many folktales about human beings' interactions with such creatures (as well as folktales about animal brides and animal grooms) speak to human interactions with nature more broadly, often at once demonstrating nature's appeal and danger for human beings. Charlotte Brontë would deploy these tales in *Shirley* to comment on the destruction of nature, of supernatural belief, and of the feminine at the hands of industrial and masculine forces. Emily Brontë's creatures, though, are even more closely connected to nature than Charlotte's, seeming to embody and give voice to it (the latter of which is, of course, a key function in lyric poetry). Nymphs fulfill essentially this role in Greek mythology, personifying mountains, trees, and various bodies of water. A more local traditional example of this kind of spirit is the Spirit of the Storm in the Ninth Bard's Song of *The Queen's Wake* (1813) by James Hogg, discussed in earlier chapters as a favorite writer of the young Brontës. In this narrative poem, a human seer who has previously ventured into the wilderness to see fairies and other spirits without harm witnesses the Spirit of the Storm atop a mountain. This spirit has red eyes and a ghostly face, as well as a cap of "the mooncloud's silver gray" and a staff made out of a constellation.[21] Furious at the intrusion, the Spirit of the Storm berates the seer and condemns him to "ride the blast" with him forever (100); a terrible storm ensues immediately, and the seer's body is discovered the next day.[22] This spirit does not merely dwell in nature; he embodies an aspect of nature, and he wields the same power over a human being as that aspect of nature could in reality (that is, he poses precisely the danger of a winter storm). In Emily Brontë's poetry, we find somewhat more benevolent versions of this kind of spirit. Emily's poems of human encounters with magical nature spirits vividly illustrate the various ways being in nature can feel, as though nature itself were bidding the human individual either to come closer or to stay away.

To run afoul of a winter storm is a real experience so overpowering that Emily Brontë, like James Hogg, stages it as a meeting between a human being and a supernatural spirit who may choose to ruin or to release him. There are seasons and places in the natural world in which human beings seem not to belong, and "The night was dark yet winter breathed," dated January 12, 1839, describes one of them. The second line explicitly sets the poem in Gondal, though Ratchford was not able to work it into her organization of all Emily's poems into stages in the Gondal narrative.[23] In addition to possibly responding to Hogg's Spirit of the Storm and similar tales, the poem evokes traditional folktales about solitary travelers who encounter supernatural creatures after losing their way, which I also discuss in the context of Charlotte Brontë's juvenilia in chapter 1 and of *Wuthering Heights* in chapter 6. In Charlotte's early tales, the human beings tend to return unharmed. *Wuthering Heights* instead portrays adult Heathcliff behaving like someone who has returned from a supernatural encounter with his life but not his stability intact. "The night was dark yet winter breathed" lies somewhere in between, as the following large excerpt shows:

> How deep into the wilderness
> My horse had strayed, I cannot say
> But neither morsel nor caress
> Would urge him further on the way
>
> So loosening from his neck the rein,
> I set my worn companion free
> . . . .
> I paused, confounded and distressed
> Down in the heath my limbs I threw

. . . .

It was about the middle night
And under such a starless dome
When gliding from the mountain's height
I saw a shadowy spirit come.

Her wavy hair on her shoulders bare,
It shone like soft clouds round the moon;
Her noiseless feet like melting sleet
Gleamed white a moment then were gone.

'What seek you now on this bleak moor's brow
Where wanders that form from heaven descending?'
It was thus I said as her graceful head
The spirit above my couch was bending

'This is my home where whirlwinds blow
Where snowdrifts round my path are swelling
'Tis many a year 'tis long ago
Since I beheld another dwelling

'When thick and fast the smothering blast
O'erwhelmed the hunter on the plain
If my cheek grew pale in its loudest gale
May I never tread the hills again

'The shepherd had died on the mountain side
But my ready aid was near him then
I led him back o'er the hidden track
And gave him to his native glen

'When tempests roar on the lonely shore
I light my beacon with sea-weeds dry
And it flings its fire through the darkness dire
And gladdens the sailor's hopeless eye

'And the scattered sheep I love to keep
Their timid forms to guard from harm
I have a spell and they know it well
And I save them with a powerful charm

'Thy own good steed on his friendless bed
A few hours since you left to die
But I knelt by his side and the saddle untied
And life returned to his glazing eye

'And deem thou not that quite forgot
My mercy will forsake me now
I bring thee care and not Despair
Abasement but not overthrow

'To a silent home thy foot may come
And years may follow of toilsome pain
But yet I swear by that Burning Tear
The loved shall meet on its hearth again.'

(E. Brontë, *Poems*, 92–94)

The nature of this "shadowy spirit" is vaguely defined but falls somewhere between that of a nymph and of Hogg's Spirit of the Storm (though she stops short of exacting the punishment of death that Hogg's spirit demands of the human being who intrudes in his territory). Emily's speaker compares the spirit's hair to clouds and feet to melting sleet, underscoring her physical kinship with nature. The spirit's powers are various: she does not seem to control the elements as Hogg's spirit does, but she knows how to work with them, especially in that she mediates between them and the human beings and animals at their mercy. The sheep are clearly the favored beneficiaries of her ministrations: the spirit uses the word "love" in speaking of them, apparently finding them more deserving because they are "timid." Moreover, the sheep "know" the "spell" or "charm" she uses to protect them, which clearly differentiates them from the clueless human speaker. The spirit also has some sovereignty over life and death, knowing "hidden" pathways by which to guide a dead shepherd back to the living world and bringing the speaker's horse back to life merely by sitting near him and removing his saddle. So closely are the spirit's person and powers tied to the natural world that she functions as an aspect of that world—not the storm itself, as in Hogg's poem, but the branch of nature that seems to decide who lives and who dies.

The human speaker, meanwhile, begins much like pixy-led travelers of traditional folktales, becoming "confounded and distressed" in the stormy night. Pixies, though, tend to lead travelers astray deliberately for a lark, letting them find their paths again after a short while. In this poem, the human being wanders unbidden into a realm where he does not belong and meets resistance from the supernatural creature who dwells there;[24] this scenario is more common in folktales of fairies who become angry at the interruption of their revels or of formidable spirits like those in tales such as Hogg's Ninth Bard's Song. Emily's spirit implicitly punishes the speaker for his intrusion, even though his ostensible crime is the abandonment of his horse. The spirit emphasizes that the punishment could have been worse: she will inflict not "despair" but "care," not "overthrow" but "abasement." In her decree, the spirit emphasizes the human being's own "home" and "hearth": as he has invaded her domain, her influence will reach his. As in many traditional folktales, however, the punishment seems disproportionately severe. The speaker does not appear to have harmed the spirit by entering her realm, and there is no indication that he intended to abandon the horse permanently; the speaker simply dismounts and proceeds alone because the horse will go no farther. Nevertheless, like his predecessors in traditional folklore and like many a winter traveler in the real world, the speaker of this poem will pay a heavy—though not fatal—price for attempting to engage with nature in an inappropriate way.

The poem's formal characteristics reinforce the spirit's accord with her environment and the speaker's status as an intruder: the poem coheres more tightly when the spirit is being described by the speaker or is speaking herself. The internal rhymes, in particular, are stronger in the first and third lines of these stanzas; contrast, for example, the speaker's early "How deep into the wilderness" and "But neither morsel nor caress," containing no internal rhymes, with the spirit's "The shepherd had *died* on the mountain *side*" and "I led him *back* o'er the hidden *track*" (emphasis mine). The transition takes place when the speaker begins to describe the spirit: the first and third lines of this stanza read "Her wavy hair, on her shoulders bare" and "Her noiseless feet, like melting sleet." In part, the increase in rhyme underscores the spirit's harmony with her environment; everything fits together, naturally and poetically. I would also attribute the spirit's association with rhyme to the traditional tendency of supernatural creatures to speak in verse[25]—Christina Rossetti's "Goblin Market" is another classic nineteenth-century poem that reflects this pattern. It is true that not all of the spirit's stanzas contain perfect internal rhymes; "Thy own good steed on his friendless bed" is one example, as is the final stanza, offering "home/come" and "swear/tear," which only appear orthographically to rhyme. But in both these stanzas, the spirit is speaking of the human intruder, and in the first, internal rhyme returns in the third line with the spirit's intervention in the abandonment of the horse: "But I knelt by his side and the saddle untied." The speaker's physical intrusion is echoed in his disruption of the spirit's poetic patterns. Poetic form, nature, and the spirit are thus connected throughout the poem—and the human being cannot join them. This poem thus illustrates the human being's unmistakable (and, to him, mystifying) alienation from the natural world and any other transcendent forces the spirit might represent.

But nature does not always demand the same behavior of the human being: in some of Emily Brontë's other poems, representatives of nature wish for humans to be closer to, not farther from, their domain. This is the case in the poem beginning "Shall Earth no more inspire thee," dated May 16, 1841, and included in the Honresfeld manuscript. Charlotte wrote of this poem when she published it after Emily's death that "in it the Genius of a solitary region seems to address his wandering and wayward votary, and to recall within his influence the proud mind which rebelled at times against what it most loved."[26] Subsequent commentators have suggested that the speaker of the poem may be Pan or the wind, but Earth itself, Gezari's suggestion, is the most obvious interpretation.[27] Nevertheless, Charlotte's identification of the speaker as a genius has the merit of emphasizing that the speaker of the poem reads as a creature with feelings and desires, rather than as an abstract entity. The poem begins,

> Shall Earth no more inspire thee,
> Thou lonely dreamer now?
> Since passion may not fire thee
> Shall Nature cease to bow?
>
> (ln. 1–4)[28]

Chiding the addressee for "roving" and "moving" elsewhere, the speaker calls him or her home. This genius uses the language of the supernatural to insist on its influence over the human being:

> I know my mountain breezes
> Enchant and soothe thee still. . . .

I know my magic power
To drive thy griefs away

(ln. 9–10, 19–20)

This poem portrays a different version of the problem at the heart of "The night was dark yet winter breathed": humankind's alienation from nature. If the speaker of the earlier poem were not so alienated, he would not be an intruder in the spirit's realm. In "Shall Earth no more inspire thee," the genius of the natural region seems to be attempting to prevent such an estrangement. Like a lover, the genius avers that it continues to have power over the addressee—specifically, to mitigate emotional distress. The explicitly supernatural language is accompanied by the language of consolation: "enchant" is paired with "soothe," "magic" with "drive thy griefs away." Whereas the shadowy spirit essentially warns that she will use (super)natural power in order to punish, the genius rather pleads to be allowed to continue to use that power in order to comfort. One could also locate the difference in the human beings rather than in the representatives of nature. In this view, the human speaker of "The night was dark yet winter breathed" has so separated himself from nature that a return to it carries for him the same shock that one might feel in encountering a supernatural creature, whereas the human addressee of "Shall Earth no more inspire thee" is (if we take the speaker's word for it) someone who has been so close to nature as to gain solace from it that possesses the strength of magic, or someone whose effect on nature has been so noticeable that nature seems to cry out for her when she is gone. Supernatural language enables Emily to convey the intensity of these situations in a way that ordinary language cannot.

The final poem I will consider uses the supernatural both to interrogate the cycles of nature and to express the final undecidability of questions of religious faith and doubt. "A Day Dream," dated March 5, 1844, and included in the non-Gondal Honresfeld manuscript, features supernatural spirits that may have been generated in nature, in heaven, or in the speaker's own mind. The speaker reposes on a hillside on a beautiful spring day but feels dejected nonetheless, specifically upon reflecting that everything alive in the present, such as the birds and plants around her, must one day perish. Interestingly, she does not explicitly name herself among those doomed to mortality; she seems rather to ask whether a human individual can respond to nature in general with happiness despite the knowledge that its denizens cannot endure. As if in response, the atmosphere seems to light up with sparks and music. Thousands of "little glittering spirits" appear and sing to her that sadness is inappropriate, for

> could we lift the veil, and give
> One brief glimpse to thine eye
> Thou wouldst rejoice for those that live,
> *Because* they live to die
>
> (ln. 51, 65–68)[29]

The speaker of the poem concludes with some doubt as to the verity of the vision:

> The music ceased; the noonday dream
> Like dream of night, withdrew;
> But Fancy, still, will sometimes deem
> Her fond creation true
>
> (ln. 69–72)

Whether or not the speaker actually heard these spirits speaking in the fictional world of the poem, she is sufficiently impressed by her perception of their optimistic words that she does not revisit the dejection with which she began.

The origin of the speaker's perceptions is a tantalizing question in the poem: are they a natural phenomenon, a divine vision, or merely "Fancy"? Simon Marsden has described the passage as a moment of "apocalyptic unveiling."[30] Homans observes that the little glittering spirits offer a transcendent message that may be "couched in pagan or fanciful terms, but [is] as orthodox in spirit" as Emily's more overtly religious writings.[31] Homans, though, is ultimately unconvinced by this poem, precisely because it reminds her of a fairy tale: "Are we really to put our faith in 'little glittering spirits,' and to believe that Brontë does too? The most persuasive lines in the poem, the ones that seem to describe heartfelt experience rather than the outlines of a fable, are not in the vision itself" (146). Like many readers (and Branwell Brontë), Homans is skeptical that authenticity can coexist with fairy tale and the supernatural, a view with which I obviously do not agree; moreover, claims about which poetic lines are more heartfelt than others seem to my mind tenuous. Ultimately, however, the question of the poem exceeds the little glittering spirits, and the answer must leave room for doubt: in the final stanza, the speaker explicitly suggests that she was merely dreaming but leaves the reader with the word "true" and the statement that sometimes—if only sometimes—she has faith.

It is worth pausing, however, on the question of the spirits' source. Nature is a strong possibility; the speaker is surrounded by and closely observing nature when they appear, and she has already believed nature to be speaking to her: "The very grey rocks, looking on, / Asked, 'What do you do here?'" (ln. 15–16).[32] Moreover, earth and air are pervaded by the spirits:

> Methought, the very breath I breathed
> Was full of sparks divine,
> And all my heather-couch was wreathed
> By that celestial shine!
>
> (ln. 45–48)[33]

The speaker goes on to observe that "the wide earth echoing rung / To their strange minstrelsy," which involves the earth in the general sound (ln. 49–50). However, because of the word "echoing," this line explicitly identifies the source as somewhere other than earth. Moreover, the spirits are not described as manifestations of nature in the way that the spirits are in "The night was dark yet winter breathed" and "Shall Earth no more inspire thee?" Evidence that the spirits originate in the speaker's own mind exists in the word "Methought" that opens the stanza above about the air and earth, as well as the repeated use of the word "seem"—for example, the speaker stops herself when she introduces the spirits' song: "The little glittering spirits sung, / Or seemed to sing, to me" (ln. 51–52). The words "dream," "Fancy," and "her fond creation" in the final stanza all suggest that the speaker believes she merely imagined the vision. The spirits' words, however, as well as the sharp contrast between their message and the speaker's previously despondent frame of mind, lend credence to the idea that they come from heaven, as do the terms "sparks divine" and "celestial shine."

No single correct interpretation emerges, for there can be no clear answer to the poem's major questions; "A Day Dream" ultimately expresses ambivalence as to the place of the human being in larger processes of nature, mortality, and transcendence. The poem provides an example of the tendency Elizabeth Helsinger identifies in Emily Brontë's poems to "divide the lyric speaker into competing voices that we cannot locate.... Her imagination is perpetually displaced onto mobile disembodied presences."[34] This roving imagination resists being pinned to any particular perspective. At this point, we should recall the poems of Anne Brontë with which this chapter began. For Anne, the purpose of referring to the supernatural—or to the natural, for that matter—is to better reflect upon the power of God. To some extent, Emily is doing the same thing: natural, supernatural, and divine are bound up with one another in "A Day Dream," and the poem's central question of mortality certainly has theological significance. One important effect of attributing the assurance of immortality to supernatural spirits that do not necessarily seem religious is to sustain the speaker's and reader's uncertainty. The spirits might come from God, they might materialize out of thin air, or they might be a recycled fairy tale from the speaker's own mind. No matter the answer, they provide comfort in that moment—and no matter the answer, the speaker will continue to confront doubts in the future.

Ultimately, supernatural references in the poems of both Anne and Emily Brontë permit them to better illustrate internal experience. This distinguishes them from young Charlotte, who eagerly wrote entertaining fairy tales for their own sake, and from Branwell, whose active suspicion of fantastical subject matter rendered his supernatural references generally negative and minimal. Anne and Emily deploy supernatural references in service of the most profound questions of their poetry—questions about faith, love, nature, and mortality. Although Anne uses them relatively rarely, they help her to account for the experiences of memory and love and to refine her articulation of the powers of God. Many of Emily's supernatural references, taken together, explore what nature might say to a human being if it were capable of speech. Her personified nature spirits alternately entreat human beings to come closer and to stay away, perhaps expressing the capriciousness commonly attributed to traditional supernatural creatures like fairies by human beings who do not understand their rationales. Frequently, Emily's human speakers experience pressures in their lives as though they had the force of a magic spell. This "as though" is also central to the ways all the Brontë sisters would go on to express interior experience, often that of women, in the context of essentially realist novels. Heathcliff behaves as though he were heartsick for fairyland; Arthur Huntingdon of *The Tenant of Wildfell Hall* poses so much danger to his wife that she feels as though she were married to Bluebeard; the titular heroine of *Shirley* fades away at the end of the novel as though she were a fairy departing England forever. As we will see, allusions to folk and fairy tales, in these novels as in the poetry, often emerge as an apt means of expressing the real but elusive aspects of human experience.

PART II

Happily Ever After

4 The Mysterious Realism of *Jane Eyre*

Of all the works of the Brontës, it is Charlotte Brontë's *Jane Eyre* (1847) that has received the most attention for its affinity for fairy tales. This is due to the novel's large number of overt allusions to fairy tales and supernatural creatures (far more than I can discuss in this chapter) and to the progression of its overall plot, which is frequently compared to that of "Cinderella." A novel may borrow various plot elements, themes, and character models from different folk and fairy tales; this is very much the case with *Jane Eyre*. Simultaneously, the majority of *Jane Eyre*'s narrative follows the conventions of nineteenth-century realism; with one exception, all the plot events are plausible, if in some cases unlikely. Brontë addresses topical concerns including the position of women and the role of religious institutions and social class in British society. Yet much of the book's lasting power lies in its vivid construction of the interior life of its heroine—a life that sometimes exceeds the representative powers of conventional realism. Fairy tales are crucial to this portrayal. In this chapter, I will focus on Brontë's integration of two divergent tales about monster bridegrooms, "Beauty and the Beast" and "Bluebeard," which serve as competing paradigms for the heroine to understand her possible relation to the mysterious Mr. Rochester and her role in the adult world more generally. These tales begin with many similar features but reach different endings with vastly different implications, particularly surrounding the relationship between self and other. Whereas "Bluebeard" ends when the heroine, in surviving Bluebeard, distinguishes herself from her undifferentiated predecessors in the forbidden chamber, "Beauty and the Beast" ultimately encourages seeing fundamental similarities beyond surface differences. After following the twists and turns of *Jane Eyre*'s specific plot affinities with both tales, I demonstrate how the tales' divergent portrayals of affinity and distinction inform the complex logic of Jane's relationships to Rochester and to his wife and former mistresses. Brontë's deployment of elements from these tales is central to her brand of realism. Oriented around the truth of the individual's experience, this realism is thus often but not always faithful to the laws of the everyday external world in the way we typically expect of nineteenth-century literary realism.

Scholars have discussed the relevance of many fairy tales to *Jane Eyre*; my intention in this chapter is to supplement this body of scholarship by considering a particular pair of tales whose combined role in the novel has not been adequately explored. Adrienne Rich calls *Jane Eyre* simply "a tale"; Cynthia Carlton-Ford, "a feminist fairytale"; and Kathleen Tillotson, both "a Cinderella fable [and] a Bluebeard mystery."[1] *Jane Eyre* often serves as the exemplar of Victorian novels that incorporate fairy tales; it functions this way, for instance, in the introductory pages of Nina Auerbach and U. C. Knoepflmacher's influential study of fairy tales written by later Victorian women writers.[2] Offhand comparisons to "Cinderella" in particular are ubiquitous in *Jane Eyre* criticism; indeed, Jane begins as a penniless orphan in a house with a hostile "stepmother" and equally hostile surrogate siblings, only to end as an heiress and the wife of a wealthy man.[3] Maria Tatar, Sandra Gilbert, Susan Gubar, Karen Rowe, Phyllis Ralph, Robert Martin, Heta Pyrhönen, Molly Clark Hillard, Elizabeth Imlay, Paula Sullivan, and Abigail Heiniger are a few of the critics who have probed Brontë's fairy-tale and fairy-lore intertexts; one basic aim of this chapter is to join these critics in asserting the importance of these intertexts to *Jane Eyre*. More specifically, it is Tatar, Rowe, Ralph, Pyrhönen, and Heiniger whose readings of "Beauty and the Beast" or "Bluebeard" in *Jane Eyre* have prompted my own. Rowe, Ralph, and Heiniger have identified many of the same affinities with "Beauty and the Beast" that I do, though our interpretations vary; the same is true of Pyrhönen in the case of "Bluebeard."[4] Only Maria Tatar, though, has substantially investigated the combined influence of "Beauty and the Beast" and "Bluebeard" in the mythical landscape of Brontë's novel.[5] I build on her analysis to argue that the tension between these two tale types drives *Jane Eyre*—and that it deserves to be probed in greater depth than it has been in previous scholarship.[6]

"Bluebeard" and "Beauty and the Beast" came to Victorians along with other seventeenth- and eighteenth-century French fairy tales; allusions to them appear frequently in Victorian texts. Charles Perrault's "Bluebeard" (1697) was extremely popular in England after the first English translation by Robert Samber in 1729. In the story, a young girl marries an older man who possesses great riches but sports an alarmingly blue beard. Soon after their marriage, Bluebeard tells her that he must leave for a time, handing her his ring of keys and declaring the entire house at her disposal, save one chamber. If she enters that chamber, he says while pointing out the key that unlocks it, she will suffer dire consequences. Naturally, she enters the chamber as soon as he leaves, and there she discovers the mutilated bodies of several previous wives. In her shock, she drops the key in a pool of blood and finds to her dismay that she cannot wipe it clean—for it is a magic key. The husband returns, sees the bloody key, and prepares to kill her. Fortunately, her brothers appear just in time to rescue her and kill Bluebeard. Liberated and wealthy, the heroine provides for her brothers and sister and marries herself to a nicer man. While the literal problem of the current wife in "Bluebeard" is the realization that her husband plans to murder her, the tale also speaks more generally to any anxiety on the part of a wife that women from her husband's past might continue to pose problems for her in the present; as Maria Tatar puts it, "Bluebeard" addresses "perennial anxieties about what can happen once the honeymoon is over."[7]

"Beauty and the Beast," meanwhile, has circulated in various oral and written forms for generations. It is obviously inspired by the animal bridegroom tradition of oral stories more generally, as well as the myth of Cupid and Psyche in the second-century collection *The Golden Ass* by Apuleius. Half a century after the beginning of the vogue for literary fairy tales in France, Madame Gabrielle-Suzanne Barbot Gallon de Villeneuve introduced "Beauty and the Beast" as we know it in a novel-length narrative (1740). In 1756, Madame Jeanne-Marie Leprince de Beaumont revised Villeneuve's story, retaining the title but drastically reducing the length. Most subsequent versions, including English translations, have been based on this more pointedly didactic rendition. In Beaumont's version, a girl named Beauty whose father has lost his wealth asks him to bring her a rose upon his return from a journey. He stumbles onto a mysterious mansion, sees and plucks a rose, and finds himself face to face with a furious Beast who vows to kill him unless he brings one of his daughters to live in the castle. To save her father's life, Beauty goes to live with the Beast; soon, she adjusts to the leisurely life and even to the Beast. However, he asks every night, "Will you marry me?" She always answers no, but she feels increasingly uncomfortable with her response. Eventually she asks for a temporary visit to her family, and the Beast grants her request but warns her that he will die if she does not return by the appointed day. Beauty stays away too long, however, and rushes back to the castle to find the Beast near death. Here she discovers and declares her love for him, which prompts his transformation into a handsome prince. After a brief explanation of the curse that had turned the prince into a beast, Beauty and the prince are married.

These two fairy tales address issues that were also significant for Victorians, particularly marriage, social class, the revelation of secrets, and the relationship between human beings and animals. "Beauty and the Beast" is a story about doubles and opposites, about the relationship between the self and the feared other. From the perspective of the heroine, "Beauty and the Beast" ends in the realization that the frightening, animalistic other is not actually very different from the self and can in fact be incorporated into the self through marriage. The tale's dark cousin, "Bluebeard," is about discovering the beastly other inside the new husband and ultimately expelling him. Bluebeard's darkest secret is not the chamber full of murdered wives; rather, it is the fact that he harbors a monster inside his human body.[8] In *Jane Eyre,* these two tales drive both the plot structure and the characterization of Edward Fairfax Rochester as some combination of a Beast figure and a Bluebeard figure. Whereas the Beast is a character who initially appears beastly but is ultimately desirable to the heroine, Bluebeard is a character who is less obviously menacing at the outset but ultimately beastly on the inside. Fairy-tale terms, in other words, can articulate Jane Eyre's dilemma. "Is he a Beast figure or a Bluebeard figure?" is a concrete, vivid way of asking, "Should I trust him? Should I stay with him?" These questions highlight a crucial difference between *Jane Eyre* and Anne Brontë's *The Tenant of Wildfell Hall:* whereas *Tenant* clearly follows "Bluebeard" in that Helen Huntingdon absolutely cannot trust her husband, *Jane Eyre* enacts a contest between "Bluebeard" and "Beauty and the Beast" paradigms in that Jane legitimately struggles to answer these questions about Rochester. And readers and critics are likely to answer them in conflicting ways—as, indeed, they do. The conflicting influences of these two fairy tales can account for some scholarly disagreement about the novel.

At a basic plot level, the arrival of a young woman in an imposing house with an intimidating, suspicious master is equally evocative of "Bluebeard" and "Beauty and the Beast"—and, indeed, of the Gothic novel, whose close connections to fairy tales in general and "Bluebeard" in particular have been noted by many scholars, including Maria Tatar and Victoria Anderson in the case of *Jane Eyre*.[9] It is long unclear whether Rochester will be a Bluebeard figure or a Beast figure—that is, whether he is suspicious on the outside and thoroughly bad on the inside, or repulsive on the outside and good (or at least redeemable) on the inside. Jane herself, relatively early in their acquaintance, weighs his merits and faults, concluding, "I believed he was naturally a man of better tendencies, higher principles, and purer tastes than such as circumstances had developed, education instilled, or destiny encouraged. I thought there were excellent materials in him; though for the present they hung together somewhat spoiled and tangled."[10] The final phrase indicates that Jane recognizes in Rochester a combination of what I am calling Beast and Bluebeard qualities, even as she clearly wants to favor inner goodness.

Brontë explicitly alludes to "Bluebeard" in *Jane Eyre* (as she would later do in *Shirley* and *Villette*). Just before Jane initially meets Rochester, the housekeeper takes Jane to the third story of Thornfield Hall as part of a tour of the house; peering down the corridor, Jane reflects that it "look[s], with its two rows of small black doors all shut, like a corridor in some Bluebeard's castle" (98). Then, for the first time, she hears an eerie laugh and is told that it must belong to servant Grace Poole. The allusion is apt because, as Jane will later learn, one of the closed doors hides Rochester's secret wife, Bertha Mason, who is still alive but very much like Bluebeard's former wives in that she is discarded and hidden—and in that she causes problems for Jane. As I discuss in detail later, Jane also confronts the problem of former "wives" in the form of Rochester's various European lovers, all of whom were eventually cast aside. Despite facing no literal corpses, Jane, like Bluebeard's wife, has to deal with the problem of predecessors.

But Brontë also raises the specter of "Beauty and the Beast" early on in Rochester and Jane's acquaintance. When he asks her whether she finds him handsome and she frankly replies in the negative, many nineteenth-century readers would have been reminded of the similar scene in "Beauty and the Beast." Tatar goes so far as to maintain that Brontë intended a "conscious reprise" of the fairy tale.[11] Over time, Jane and Rochester develop companionship through conversation and Jane ceases to find him intimidating; this also echoes "Beauty and the Beast." Jane has clearly learned Beauty's lesson by the time Rochester asks her to use her fairy magic to make him handsome and she responds inwardly, "A loving eye is all the charm needed: to such you are handsome enough; or rather, your sternness has a power beyond beauty."[12] The "Beauty and the Beast" narrative seems nearly concluded when Jane accepts Rochester's proposal.

On their wedding day, however, Rochester is forced to reveal that he has a wife hidden in a chamber of the house. Given this development, the novel appears to shift to the "Bluebeard" paradigm, only to bring back "Beauty and the Beast" shortly thereafter. Instead of following in Bluebeard's footsteps by threatening the new object of his desire and earning his own death at the hands of her brothers, Rochester lives, and Jane quits Thornfield Hall with mixed feelings, just as Beauty abandons the Beast in his castle. From this point on, "Beauty and the Beast" prevails. Like Beauty, Jane bides her time with her family and is nearly tempted away from Rochester forever. This happens to Jane twice: climactically, after the aborted wedding, but also before her engagement to Rochester, at the behest of the dying Aunt Reed. The earlier episode is, at least on the surface, even more evocative of "Beauty and the Beast," hinging as it does on the illness of a relative, an unexpectedly extended sojourn, and a conversation between Jane and Rochester before her departure as to how long she will stay away. The supernatural call of distress that summons Jane back to Rochester after her second departure (discussed later) has an antecedent in some versions of "Beauty and the Beast" as well. In the 1756 Madame Leprince de Beaumont version that Brontë most likely would have known, for instance, Beauty sees in a dream that the Beast is near death because of her extended absence.

Although *Jane Eyre* contains no magical transformation from inhuman to human, it does feature a highly fortuitous event—the fire at Thornfield Hall—that "transforms" Rochester from a married man and potential bigamist into an available widower and enhances any physical monstrosity he may have already possessed, hinting at the "Beauty and the Beast" narrative. Brontë establishes the idea of a transformation for Rochester in one of his earliest conversations with Jane, in which he states that he possessed human feelings in his youth but was subsequently transformed by life into something "as hard and tough as an India-rubber ball"; he asks her whether she believes there is hope for his "final re-transformation from India-rubber back to flesh" (121). This imagined change from human to inhuman and back again follows the trajectory of the transformations in "Beauty and the Beast." After the fire in *Jane Eyre,* Rochester's blindness and debilitation render him physically less attractive than before, at the same time that this humbling transformation paves the way for his marriage to the heroine. Jane observes in his face "a change: that looked desperate and brooding," and Rochester himself feels an alteration: "Of late . . . I began to experience remorse, repentance; the wish for reconcilement to my maker" (384, 397). That the inner improvement comes at the price of a battered exterior poses no problem for Jane. Rochester expects rejection: "'I thought you would be revolted, Jane, when you saw my arm and my cicatrised visage.' 'Did you? Don't tell me so—lest I should say something disparaging to your judgment'" (388). Like Beauty, Jane loves Rochester despite his physical defects. As U. C. Knoepflmacher argues, Brontë finally "revalidate[s] both a Beast who remains a beast and Beauty who was never a beauty."[13] In Brontë's version, this revalidation discards the importance of appearance altogether; Jane outdoes Beauty by marrying a "beast" whose physical beastliness has not disappeared but increased.

Although "Bluebeard" is explicitly named in *Jane Eyre* and "Beauty and the Beast" is not, for many readers it is the latter story that most prominently structures *Jane Eyre.* As Karen Rowe puts it, *Jane Eyre* "shares the same fascination with conflicts between virtue and bestiality, deceptive appearances and underlying realities, and focuses comparably on the 'release' of a bewitched hero and education of an innocent maiden."[14] But scholars disagree on the implications of the many echoes of "Beauty and the Beast" in the novel. While Phyllis Ralph sees Jane's acceptance of Rochester as evidence of her increasing maturity, some critics argue rather that "Beauty and the Beast" is a fantasy Jane must learn to transcend.[15] Rowe maintains that Brontë "tests the paradigm of fairy tale for her *Bildungsroman* and finds it lacking, precisely because it can give shape only to the child bride of Rochester, not to the substantial human being who is Jane Eyre."[16] To Rowe, the experiences of Jane and Rochester "are not awakenings in the fairy-tale sense, where instantaneous love allows one to live happily ever after; rather they are enlightened perceptions, hard-won within a real world where fallible humans must perforce exist" (87). But to equate all fairy tales with the instantaneous is to miss the integral point of "Beauty and the Beast," which champions the opposite of "instantaneous love." In fact, the paradigm of this particular fairy tale is quite apt for Jane: "Beauty and the Beast" is precisely about the realization that one's previously held perspective on the world should always be susceptible to change, which structures Jane's growth into a more mature and multifaceted understanding of Rochester and the world around her.

It is also significant that Beauty exerts more agency than many other traditional fairy-tale heroines. Cristina Bacchilega calls her "an active heroine whose physical and psychological journeys provide most of the narrative 'suspense' and whose decisions—right and wrong—advance the plot."[17] As this description emphasizes, Beauty has agency that is interesting and substantial enough to carry a narrative; thus she is better suited than many other heroines to provide the model for a complex *Bildungsroman*. Abigail Heiniger, who, like me, sees "Beauty and the Beast" as a key intertext for *Jane Eyre*, argues that Jane differs from Beauty in that while Beauty "sacrifices herself in marriage to the Beast, accepting him despite his hideous appearance," Jane "exercise[s] the full extent of her powers with Rochester."[18] To be sure, Jane explicitly rejects Rochester's concern that a "delight in sacrifice" urges her to marry him after his mutilation in the fire.[19] But I believe that Heiniger, like some other scholars, overstates the role of self-sacrifice in Beauty's acceptance of the Beast. Feminist critics have been absolutely correct to complicate the "true love" narrative by identifying elements of self-sacrifice in Beauty's behavior throughout Beaumont's story, but in my estimation we now err in the opposite direction by asserting that self-sacrifice alone motivates her decisions. On the contrary, "Beauty and the Beast" traces Beauty's complex process of making her marriage choice, clearly demonstrating that a combination of gratitude, friendship, and disgust with her sisters' horrible husbands prompts Beauty to return to the Beast, at which point she declares that she cannot live without him.[20] This is not the same combination of feelings that prompts Jane to marry Rochester, but "Beauty and the Beast" nonetheless provides a model for mixed feelings toward a potential husband that is more sophisticated than some readers acknowledge.

Tatar, responding to Rowe, attributes to Jane not so much a graduation from fairy tales as a purposeful, ongoing revision of them: by "making productive use of fairy tales by reacting to them, resisting them, and re-writing them rather than passively consuming them and internalizing their values, Brontë's *Jane Eyre* offers a map for reading our cultural stories and using them."[21] A crucial way that Brontë "makes productive use of fairy tales" is by combining them. The combination of "Beauty and the Beast" and "Bluebeard" is greater than the sum of its parts: because, as Tatar puts it, "Bluebeard" is the "troubling flip side" of "Beauty and the Beast" (55), to evoke both is to create substantial uncertainty. Above all, *Jane Eyre* offers a central male figure who embodies elements of both Beast and Bluebeard; much of the mystery of *Jane Eyre* is precisely whether Rochester will lean more toward Bluebeard or Beast, wavering as he does between the two throughout the novel. To say that Jane is "blind" to Rochester's faults, as Anderson (119) and even Tatar (74) do, and therefore participates in a reactionary "Beauty and the Beast" narrative or in a "Bluebeard" narrative with the wrong ending is unsatisfactory because it acknowledges only part of the story.[22] The point is not that Rochester *is* the Beast or *is* Bluebeard but rather that he presents a combination of two story paradigms that suggest to Jane two different responses. Her dilemma, then, is to figure out how to translate what she has learned from fairy tales into her real-life adult relationship with a complex human being. Winifred Gérin sees this process as fundamental: "Above all, what distinguished Charlotte's conception of the hero, both in her juvenilia and adult writing, was her acceptance of his moral imperfections."[23] Gérin attributes this acceptance to Brontë's early encounters with Byron's heroes and Milton's Satan and, more acutely, to her relationship with her morally imperfect brother. The dimension of moral shortcomings is what "Bluebeard" adds to the "Beauty and the Beast" lesson to love despite physical shortcomings. Because these tales are interwoven in the underlying narrative structure of *Jane Eyre*, they produce in the hero a double imperfection without providing an obvious answer as to whether that imperfection should be overlooked.

Both "Beauty and the Beast" and "Bluebeard" raise fundamental questions about when and how to distinguish between selves and others. Whereas Beauty learns to value difference less highly over the course of the story, Bluebeard's last wife can survive only by distinguishing herself from the past wives strung up along the wall of the chamber "l'une après l'autre" ("one after the other"; trans. mine).[24] The predicament of Bluebeard's last wife is integral to Brontë's portrayal of the relationship between Jane and Bertha. Numerous critics, crucially Sandra Gilbert and

Susan Gubar, have noted the strange and intimate connection between the actions of Jane and those of Bertha, though the characterizations of and explanations for this relation vary. Gilbert and Gubar's reading of *Jane Eyre* centers on the observation that Bertha acts as Jane's "ferocious secret self," always appearing in "associat[ion] with an experience (or repression) of anger on Jane's part."[25] If, as they convincingly argue, Bertha is an agent of Jane's darker desires, and if we consider Bertha the representative of Bluebeard's dead wives, then Jane's many affinities with Bertha suggest how close she comes to assimilation with the group.

Emphasizing the similarities between Jane and Bertha may seem surprising in a scholarly moment of renewed interest in racial differences between the two. Indeed, Jane is English and White, often described as pale, while Bertha is, infamously, "Creole."[26] What exactly this word, and Bertha's characterization more broadly, means has driven much scholarship in the past few decades, prompted by Gayatri Chakravorty Spivak. Although it seems to me unlikely that Brontë intended her to be read as biologically non-White (for the same reasons attested by other scholars), the Jamaican Bertha is undoubtedly "a woman whose relationship to whiteness is less secure than Jane's."[27] Negative traits attributed to Bertha, including behavioral (drunkenness, promiscuity, madness) and physical (bloodshot eyes, unkempt hair and clothing, sallowness), were associated in the periodical press at times with Black people and at times with White Creoles. This dual association itself embodies what to a Victorian constituted the threat: that the distinction between the English and everyone else would become unclear. As Jenny Sharpe, Deirdre David, and Sue Thomas argue, Bertha as a White person of presumably English blood who now looks and acts like a person of color signifies that "whiteness alone is not the sign of racial purity."[28] Rochester's confession to Jane of his marriage to Bertha and the immoral behavior it prompted in him reads as an object lesson in the potential loss of self inherent in both the colonial enterprise as a whole and the mundane fact of marriage to an unsuitable individual person. As Thomas notes, Rochester "represents his contact with Bertha's depravity as a contamination of his being, the more begriming because Bertha is 'called by law and society a part' of him."[29] Jane readily understands the potential for contamination by or assimilation with nearby others. Much of the scholarly writing on imperialism and *Jane Eyre* assumes a high level of antagonism between Jane and Bertha. But the most critical descriptions of Bertha are spoken by Rochester, not narrator-Jane; when Jane hears the story of the marriage, her response is to chide Rochester for blaming Bertha unfairly: "She cannot help being mad."[30] Rochester demurs, "It is not because she is mad I hate her. If you were mad, do you think I should hate you?" to which Jane responds, "I do indeed, sir."[31] While Rochester emphasizes the differences between Jane and Bertha, Jane immediately imagines herself in Bertha's place. When Jane learns about Bertha, she not only discovers a practical impediment to her marriage to Rochester but also recalibrates her expectations of Rochester's potential future behavior toward her by assuming that it will exactly replicate his past and present behavior toward Bertha and his (also non-English) mistresses. Rochester differs from Bluebeard in seeing Jane as significantly distinct from Bertha. But like Bluebeard's last wife, Jane knows she must actively distinguish herself in order to avoid her predecessors' fates; difference in race or nationality alone is not enough.

Viewing Bertha and Jane in the roles of Bluebeard's last two wives offers one answer to the much-debated question of exactly why Jane leaves Rochester when she discovers the existence of his wife. Early reviewers tended to applaud Jane's moral fortitude; on the other end of the spectrum, Heta Pyrhönen suggests that Jane seizes an opportunity to act on the misgivings about Rochester she already had.[32] Ruth Yeazell maintains that "Victorian sexual morality and Christian dogma certainly influence the terms in which Jane defines her conflict, but not its essential nature. At the deepest level, Jane struggles to preserve the integrity and independence of the self. . . . The identity she thought to have found as Rochester's wife has proved illusory."[33] Indeed, Jane worries above all that Rochester will eventually abandon her if she accepts him on the same terms as his mistress Céline Varens. Toward the end of the scene in which Rochester explains his marriage to Bertha and asks Jane to stay with him as his mistress, Jane arrives at "the certain inference, that if I were so far to forget myself and all the teaching that had ever been instilled into me, as . . . to become the successor of these poor girls, he would one day regard me with the same feeling which now in his mind desecrated their memory."[34] To fail to preserve the integrity of self, as Yeazell puts it, by becoming the "successor" to a long line of discarded women is precisely to find oneself in the midst of "Bluebeard." Jane refuses to do this, just as she had refused during the proposal scene to "stay and become nothing" to a Rochester married to Blanche Ingram, the woman Jane had supposed at the time to be her rival.[35] Staying and becoming nothing is ultimately what befell Bertha, though obviously her circumstances were very different. Jane prefers to be at least something to herself ("respect myself," as she says; 284) rather than nothing to Rochester. Bertha is the strongest manifestation of Jane's susceptibility to becoming a mere successor: Jane is "like" all the other women who have been romantically involved with Rochester, but she is especially like Bertha insofar as Bertha can be read as a manifestation of aspects of Jane herself. The frequently insisted-on affinity with Bertha thus emphasizes how vital it is for Jane to distinguish herself.

Any element of the novel that diminishes Jane's individuality thus contributes to Brontë's deployment of "Bluebeard." One crucial component of the linking between Bertha and Jane is the similar use of the language of supernatural beings for both of them. Although this language is applied to many characters, it is most noticeably and frequently applied to them. Critics typically emphasize the differences between the varieties of figurative language used for Jane (fairy) and for Bertha (demon). Indeed, Rochester frequently compares Jane to fairies, elves, and sprites, whereas Bertha is associated with vampires, called a "demon" and a "fearful hag," and accused of having a "goblin appearance" and a "familiar."[36] But, as I discuss throughout this book, supernatural beings were not so easily pigeonholed in the 1840s; it took much of the nineteenth century to solidify the opposition between conceptions of the fairy as good and the goblin as bad.[37] When Rochester calls Jane a fairy, he does not mean only to praise her for being adorably petite. He is testifying to her strangeness, her ability to bewitch him, her alternation between granting and withholding physical affection, her seeming to stand for something that he desperately desires but doubts he can ever truly possess.[38] Rochester tells Adèle the story of his meeting Jane as a lighthearted tale of fairy summons, but in many contemporary tales of being "pixy-led" or otherwise sojourning with fairies, the human protagonist either dies or goes insane; the moral of these stories is that human beings cannot abide in fairyland.[39] Five times, Rochester calls Jane the predominantly negative "thing," which in the mid-nineteenth century could be used not only "in contempt or reproach, usu. suggesting unworthiness to be called a person," but also, thanks to Brontë's beloved Byron, "a particular supernatural or other dreadful monster."[40] Jane, in recounting her childhood, refers to herself as a thing in relation to the Reed family: "They were not bound to regard with affection a thing that could not sympathize with one amongst them; a heterogeneous thing . . . a useless thing . . . a noxious thing."[41] She therefore welcomes Rochester's use of "thing" while she is attempting to keep him at a distance during their engagement: "I had rather be a *thing* than an angel."[42]

Many identical or similar terms are used for both Jane and Bertha and at times for Rochester as well. As Lori Pollock has pointed out, the fact that Brontë presents both Jane and Bertha as "inhuman and degraded" as various points in the novel contributes to the sense that they "operate more in tandem than opposition."[43] Rochester applies the word "creature" to Bertha and Jane two times each.[44] He uses the term "monster" for Bertha and never for Jane, but Jane applies it to herself: "Am I a monster? . . . Is it impossible that Mr. Rochester should have a sincere affection for me?" (277, 238). Similarly, Rochester frequently characterizes his own appearance as hideous and fears that Jane will be repulsed by it; he also speculates that she refuses to dine with him because she "suppose[s] I eat like an ogre, or a ghoul" (242). He may call Jane a "shadow," but he also characterizes his past wandering self as a "Will-o'-the-wisp" and his present self as a "devil" (220, 278, 261). When Rochester wakes to see Jane dousing him with water after Bertha has set his bed on fire, he asks, "In the name of all the elves in Christendom, is that Jane Eyre? . . . What have you done with me, witch, sorceress?" (136). Late in the novel, both Jane and Bertha are compared to witches by an outsider: Jane's informant on the subject of the fire at Thornfield Hall remarks that the servants claimed never to have seen anyone as much in love as Rochester had been with her, as though he had been "bewitched"; in the following paragraph, the same man deems Bertha "cunning as a witch" (380). Obviously, the speaker intends opposing connotations, but his use of the same figure for both women nearly in the same breath is telling. Imagery of the supernatural Other does not simply contrast Jane with Bertha; rather, it pervades the novel and actually muddles the distinctions among the central characters.

Jane is always in danger of becoming Bluebeard's next wife—not only because she nearly stays with Rochester after the failed wedding but also because she is the heroine of a *Bildungsroman*, which means that she is by definition still in development and thus at risk of falling into the same trap as the women before her. She models herself on the people around her; because of her desire for control and independence, however, she adopts aspects of these people only to discard many of them over time. Acknowledging the extensive critical work on this topic, Karen Chase suggests considering characters such as serene Helen Burns, violent Bertha, and self-sacrificing St. John Rivers "not as parts of, or doubles for, Jane, but as *phases*, temporary and extreme manifestations."[45] Jane's tendency for abrupt departures and her avowed trepidation about becoming a "successor" indicate a constant fear of absorbing too much from the people around her.

Ultimately, Jane decisively distinguishes herself by leaving Rochester and establishing a successful life of her own rather than becoming another mistress indistinguishable from the many unfortunate predecessors. But while she fears and neutralizes her similarity to these other women, she insists upon her similarity to Rochester himself. This is a key reason for the ascendancy of "Beauty and the Beast" as a narrative model for the novel. Whereas "Bluebeard" hinges on the heroine's discovery that the master of the castle intends to place her in a lineage of victims, "Beauty and the Beast" progresses from her initial perception of immutable difference between her and that male figure to her realization of deeper affinity between them. Although Jane and Rochester relate to one another more immediately from the beginning than Beauty and the Beast do, Jane still has reasons to feel categorically separate from Rochester. Both of them, in fact, fear that they are not physically attractive enough to appeal to the other; this problem from the fairy tale of external "beastliness" thus plagues them both (even though Jane occupies the role of the character named Beauty). Jane, however, worries more about her inferior social class, of which she is painfully aware because of both her upbringing with the supercilious Mrs. Reed and her awkward position as governess at Thornfield Hall. She commands herself to expect no love from Rochester: "Keep to your caste."[46] Before his declaration of love for her, she assumes that despite their good rapport, he does not consider her a romantic possibility because of her physical and financial liabilities: "If God had gifted me with some beauty and much wealth, I should have made it as hard for you to leave me, as it is now for me to leave you" (227). Like Beauty in the original literary version of "Beauty and the Beast" (1740) by Madame de Villeneuve, in which the transformed Beast's mother is disinclined to allow her princely son to marry a woman she believes to be a mere merchant's daughter, Jane recognizes that she lives in a society in which rank typically trumps love when it comes to matrimony.

But unlike her fairy-tale predecessor, Jane clearly resents these external social impediments to the deeper impulses that she believes deserve to be regarded more highly: "Wealth, caste, custom intervened between me and what I *naturally and inevitably* loved."[47] Jane is keenly aware of whether or not she feels such sympathy with people; she feels none with her blood relatives, the Reeds, for instance, nor does she believe Rochester feels any with his fellow aristocrats: "He is not of their kind. I believe he is of mine. . . . I feel akin to him" (158). Rochester, too, feels "akin" to Jane; "I sometimes have a queer feeling with regard to you . . . as if I had a string somewhere under my left ribs, tightly and inextricably knotted to a similar string situated in the corresponding quarter of your little frame" (226). He calls her "my equal" and "my likeness"; "I love [you] as my own flesh" (228, 229). This is strong language—and language that acts out what it declares, mirroring Jane's famous insistence earlier in the conversation that "I have as much soul as you, and full as much heart! . . . I am not talking to you now through the medium of custom, conventionalities, nor even of mortal flesh—it is my spirit that addresses your spirit'" (227). Jane goes further than Rochester in focusing on a spiritual communion, but they both grope for language to express their unconventional feelings.

"Beauty and the Beast" resolutely gives precedence to that which unexpectedly lies under the surface. The fairy tale is thus an apt intertext for *Jane Eyre* not only for its capacity to illustrate the kinship that Jane and Rochester feel but also because Brontë's narrative strategy subordinates a superficial sense of realism to a deeper psychological "nature" and "truth." Most accounts of literary realism, varied as they are, prioritize the faithful representation of external realities over that of internal realities.[48] But Brontë's work encourages us to reevaluate that hierarchy. Critics since George Henry Lewes have appreciated *Jane Eyre* for its portrayal of a "deep reality," with some particularly noting the effectiveness of the supernatural in characterizing psychological experience.[49] John Maynard, for example, holds that "Brontë discovered how to adapt romance, fairy tale, Gothic story, or mythic modes to the conscious aim of verity to inner psychology rather than fidelity to external detail and event."[50] Although the use of fairy tales in Victorian novels can seem to some readers to be an interruption of realism, for Brontë it is actually integral to her understanding of realism's most vital aspects.

Jane Eyre's most striking example of this rejection of a superficial apparent realism for a deeper sense of reality is the episode of the "mysterious summons" that finally draws Jane back to Thornfield Hall.[51] When Jane inexplicably hears Rochester calling her name across a great distance, she quickly acknowledges and dispels the possibility that "superstition" is the cause: "This is not thy deception, nor thy witchcraft: it is the work of nature. She was roused, and did—no miracle—but her best" (374). Jane later reflects that the voice "seemed in *me*—not in the external world"; it felt "like an inspiration."[52] These two remarks seem contradictory: how can the summons come from within and yet be an "inspiration," which suggests an external source? Rochester, too, in revealing later that he heard Jane's distant response, warns, "You will think me superstitious," only to insist, "nevertheless, this is true—true at least it is that I heard what I now relate" (398). Whereas Jane focuses on the "work of nature" to insist on the deep reality of the experience, Rochester uses "true," with the clarification that though he cannot account for anything outside himself, he can insist on the authenticity of his subjective experience.

Ruth Yeazell holds that *Jane Eyre* "is part fantasy," because "even the most conventionally romantic of readers could scarcely deny, of course, that midnight conversations between lovers many miles apart . . . are scarcely the stuff of which a realistic novel is made."[53] But she takes seriously Jane's and Rochester's insistence on something natural or true about the inexplicable experience. Quoting from a letter Brontë wrote to reviewer Lewes after heeding his suggestion to read Jane Austen, Yeazell writes, "If an Austen novel, in Charlotte Brontë's terms, is 'more *real* than *true*,' *Jane Eyre* can be said to be 'more true than real.' For although the miraculous events which conclude this novel are scarcely realistic, they *are* 'true'—true to the internally consistent laws by which [Brontë's] world is governed. . . . [This] truth is the truth of the psyche."[54] The word "real" here seems contingent on the external, the objectively verifiable—the drawing-room conversations and income figures that populate Jane Austen novels, for example. In faulting Austen for losing sight of what is true in her detailed treatment of what is real, Brontë seems to be identifying the true as something deeper than the real. In Yeazell's assessment, *Jane Eyre* is "part fantasy" because the mysterious summons amounts to an external event cooperating with the demands of the psyche: "The ultimate dream which *Jane Eyre* enacts is thus the dream of the harmony between the individual psyche and the world which it confronts . . . this coincidence of inner and outer reality" (252). This is the happy ending: as signaled by Jane's convoluted language, the inexplicable call comes from inside and outside at once, both an "inspiration" and the unshackling of the soul itself. This is also, of course, the kind of happy ending toward which traditional fairy tales often tend: characters like Cinderella or the Beast achieve happiness when their external appearances and circumstances match their inner worth.[55]

To do justice to the reality of interior experience, then, is Jane's goal as a person in love and as a narrator. Brontë designates "a faithful allegiance to Truth and Nature" as the primary task of an author; she aims to "study Nature herself" and "use the language of Truth in preference to the jargon of Conventionality."[56] Lewes, despite his injunction to read Austen, understood this commitment to underlying truth, as his *Fraser's Magazine* review of *Jane Eyre* demonstrates: "The book closed, the enchantment continues. . . . Reality—deep, significant reality—is the great characteristic of the book. It *is* an autobiography,—not, perhaps, in the naked facts and circumstances, but in the actual suffering and experience."[57] Lewes subordinates the "facts and circumstances"—the trappings of a realist novel—to something more "actual" and "deep." In almost the same breath, he attributes to *Jane Eyre* "enchantment" and "deep, significant reality," only two sentences apart. Like the characters in the novel, he resorts to the language of the supernatural in attempting to access an inner reality not easily articulated in everyday language.

Lewes's assessment brings us back, finally, to "Beauty and the Beast," the deep reality of which is precisely the value of accepting an improbable truth that underlies a deceptive surface. After all Jane's insistence on independence, "how is it possible for Brontë to picture the self as engaged with, but separate from, an other?"[58] The problem with the "Bluebeard" story paradigm, in addition to its violence, is that Jane would have lost any distinction from her predecessors. By slipping into a "Beauty and the Beast" story, Jane fits herself into a fairy-tale model and thus joins a long line of predecessors anyway. But this kind of succession does not seem to bother her, rather like the oddly merged selfhood she develops with Rochester that apparently affords her sufficient independence.[59] Gilbert and Gubar pose a key question: "Does Brontë's rebellious feminism . . . compromise itself" in this ending?[60] While noting that none of Brontë's later novels would feature such an optimistic finale, they conclude that in *Jane Eyre*, the "marriage of true minds" is successful precisely because Jane and Rochester have "shed" their "social disguises—master/servant, prince/Cinderella" and can now truly see each other as equals.[61] Even as Gilbert and Gubar mention Cinderella here, their language of shedding disguises hints at the revelation of inherent kinship central to "Beauty and the Beast" as well. Jane tells Rochester after their reunion that he suits her "to the finest fibre of my nature."[62] Their marriage may not fit social norms, and the mysterious summons that reunited them may not fit conventional realist narration, but Jane insists to the end on a deeper justification.

According to Karen Chase, the "governing presupposition" of Brontë's juvenilia is that "reality is tractable."[63] Clearly this presupposition extends to *Jane Eyre*. Insisting on the value of the improbable but profoundly true, "Beauty and the Beast" offers a way to consider the flexible realism Brontë uses to emphasize the experience of the psyche over the laws of the outside world. As for the content of the novel, Jane progresses from prioritizing her uniqueness (the requirement of "Bluebeard" for the heroine's self-preservation) to prioritizing her affinity with Rochester (the requirement of "Beauty and the Beast" for the same end). But Brontë's hybrid evocation of the two tales is crucial to the novel as a whole. Jane arrives at her particular happy ending only after she has learned the lessons of both and mastered their meanings sufficiently to mold them into a narrative of her own.

PART III

Farewell to the Fairies

5 *Shirley* and the Ephemerality of the Supernatural Bride

When these tales [of fairies] were first told, and folk believed in them, the north was not industrial but a remote and rather underprivileged part of the kingdom. Not the water wheel but the steam engine scared them away for "good and all."

—Jessica Lofthouse, *North-Country Folklore in Lancashire, Cumbria and the Pennine Dales*

Shirley (1849) famously begins with an injunction not to expect another *Jane Eyre*. "If you think," the narrator warns in the second paragraph, "that anything like a romance is preparing for you, reader, you never were more mistaken. Do you anticipate sentiment, poetry, and reverie? Do you expect passion, stimulus, and melodrama? Calm your expectations. . . . Something real, cool, and solid, lies before you; something unromantic as Monday morning."[1] The narrator's promise is partially fulfilled: Charlotte Brontë's longest novel often painstakingly recounts the inane actions of the local curates and the political and economic issues surrounding the textile mill run by presumptive hero Robert Moore. Yet reality and fantasy are actually much more closely aligned in the novel than the opening lines would lead the reader to believe. As I argue throughout this book, realism can incorporate the fairy tale in many different ways. *Shirley* is undeniably realist in form and content, but Brontë subtly draws on fairy-tale models for aspects of the plot and infuses the novel with allusions to enchantment and to supernatural creatures that, taken together, provide crucial commentary on the novel's events.

In some cases, these allusions simply reflect the frequent use of fairy tales as fodder for metaphors in nineteenth-century England. Yet traditional supernatural tales are also enmeshed with the central conflicts in the novel. Specifically, supernatural creatures including fairies and mermaids are aligned (via numerous direct comparisons and sometimes plot events) with women against men and with nature against industrial development.[2] But—in stark contrast to *Jane Eyre*, in which Jane's impishness is sustained and rewarded—the fairies, the women, and nature have all been subdued at the end of *Shirley*. In this conclusion, the novel's heroines, Caroline Helstone and Shirley Keeldar, have both become engaged to be married, but the narrator provides an anticlimactically businesslike report of the double wedding. The last four paragraphs of the novel say nothing about the heroines, musing instead on the fact that the fairies who used to populate the area have departed in the face of industrialization. Readers have long puzzled over this ending: Are we to celebrate the marriages, or do the concluding paragraphs point to a darker interpretation? Although stories ending in marriage tend to be likened to the continental fairy tales that end happily, Shirley and Caroline are associated not with happily wed heroines such as Cinderella but rather with supernatural creatures from folktales about failed romantic relationships. These creatures—fairies, mermaids, and beings with the supernatural ability to move between human and sea-creature forms—are known for both their attractiveness to humans and their tendency to disappear abruptly from human view. Brontë links these creatures to her heroines through a discussion between Shirley and Caroline about their degree of similarity to mermaids, through summaries of two fairy tales read by a minor character that would have been recognizable to nineteenth-century readers as versions of a fairy bride tale and a mermaid or animal bride tale, and through numerous direct comparisons of the women to supernatural creatures on the part of other characters and the narrator. To develop these associations with tragic fairy marriage tales and then to conclude the novel with a lament over the forced departure of the fairies in the face of the very industrial development being advanced by one of the heroines' new husbands, then, emphasizes what is lost in these marriages rather than what is gained. In contrast to the usual expectation that fantastical references in a novel contribute to a sense of childhood innocence or marital happiness, such references in *Shirley* actually cast doubt on the ostensibly desirable outcome.

Most existing scholarship on *Shirley* falls into two categories, corresponding to the two major themes of the novel. One focuses on the political and historical aspects of *Shirley*, which takes place during the upheaval in the manufacturing industry in the north of England in the 1810s; the fictional Robert Moore runs a textile mill with insufficient attention to his workers' objections to the installation of new machinery that could replace them, which leads to mob violence against the mill and ultimately against Robert himself.[3] While this critical approach foregrounds the function of the novel as social commentary in terms of its engagement with public events, the second major approach considers Brontë's commentary on the social role of women. These critics have used a feminist perspective to draw a variety of conclusions about the tension between female empowerment and residual patriarchal structures in the novel.[4] Such readings of *Shirley* focus on the novel's other chief subject: the experience of eighteen-year-old Caroline Helstone as she struggles with her apparently unrequited love for Robert, endures the cold practicality of the uncle with whom she lives, becomes friends with breezily independent heiress Shirley Keeldar, and rediscovers her long-lost mother. Caroline ultimately marries Robert, as Shirley marries his brother, Louis, who appears two-thirds of the way through the novel and rekindles a romance that began when Shirley was his student. Since the earliest reviews of *Shirley* were published, critics of all persuasions have grappled with the heterogeneity of the novel and a sense that its conclusion does not satisfactorily unite the various issues raised; indeed, Rosengarten begins his entry on *Shirley* for the Wiley Blackwell *A Companion to the Brontës* by noting the seemingly irresolvable nature of the critical debate over whether Brontë satisfactorily unites the "public" and "private" facets of the novel.[5] While my reading draws on both the sociopolitical and feminist approaches, it introduces another complication, as yet little discussed by other scholars: despite an ostensible focus on industry and on the lives of ordinary people, *Shirley* is bursting with references to fantasy, fairy tales, magical objects, and supernatural creatures. Paying attention to how Brontë interweaves the threads of realism and the supernatural provides new insights into the dual resolutions of the industrial and domestic plots.

The Mermaid and the Supernatural Bride

Out of the plethora of fairy and fairy-tale references in *Shirley*, this chapter focuses on the novel's references to supernatural creatures that have figured in British and other European folktales about the doomed encounters between female supernatural creatures and mortal men.[6] Because the creatures in these tales are situated as representatives of femininity and nature in opposition to masculinity and human society, these references most productively comment on *Shirley*'s central concerns about gender and industrialization. In addition to numerous brief allusions that will be considered later, *Shirley* features two substantial passages about these stories. The first has to do with mermaids, who appear in folklore all over the globe and are particularly known for using their sexual allure to lead mortal men to death at sea. The second passage draws on the related but distinct "Supernatural or Enchanted Wife" family of folktales (Aarne-Thompson-Uther tale types 400–424).[7] Common variants of this type include tales in which the potential "bride" is a fairy or other supernatural creature and tales in which she is part animal and part human (sometimes changing form with the time of day, sometimes able to do so by means of a garment or other object). In general, these tales treat a man's temporary possession of such a creature as his human bride, culminating in her return to her animal or fairy society despite his attempts to keep her. Many such tales from the British Isles feature female beings who are part human and part sea creature, often seal or fish.[8] Precise distinctions among these different supernatural sea creatures exist, but they tend to blur as tales are told and retold. The spectrum ranges, then, from murderous mermaids to abducted animal brides, with more ethically complicated tales in between. Unsurprisingly, scholars often read all these kinds of tales as reflections of the gender politics of the societies from which they come; *Shirley*'s association of the heroines with such creatures has profound implications for the interpretation of the novel's outcome.[9]

Most prominently, the novel features an extensive discussion of mermaids that has prompted debate in works of feminist criticism. In the middle of the novel, Shirley proposes to a depressed Caroline that they go "to the Isles,—the Hebrides, the Shetland, the Orkney Islands. . . . We will see seals in Suderoe, and, doubtless, mermaids in Stromoe."[10] Caroline approves, and Shirley muses that she expects indeed to see at least one mermaid:

"She is to appear in some such fashion as this. I am to be walking by myself on deck, rather late of an August evening, watching and being watched by a full harvest-moon: something is to rise white on the surface of the sea, over which that moon mounts silent, and hangs glorious: the object glitters and sinks. It rises again. I think I hear it cry with an articulate voice: I call you up from the cabin: I show you an image, fair as alabaster, emerging from the dim wave. We both see the long hair, the lifted and foam-white arm, the oval mirror brilliant as a star. It glides nearer: a human face is plainly visible; a face in the style of yours, whose straight, pure (excuse the word, it is appropriate),—whose straight, pure lineaments, paleness does not disfigure. It looks at us, but not with your eyes. I see a preternatural lure in its wily glance: it beckons. Were we men, we should spring at the sign, the cold billow would be dared for the sake of the colder enchantress; being women, we stand safe, though not dreadless. She comprehends our unmoved gaze; she feels herself powerless; anger crosses her front; she cannot charm, but she will appal us: she rises high, and glides all revealed, on the dark wave-ridge. Temptress-terror! monstrous likeness of ourselves! Are you not glad, Caroline, when at last, and with a wild shriek, she dives?"

"But, Shirley, she is not like us: we are neither temptresses, nor terrors, nor monsters."

"Some of our kind, it is said, are all three. There are men who ascribe to 'woman,' in general, such attributes."

"My dears," here interrupted Mrs. Pryor, "does it not strike you that your conversation for the last ten minutes has been rather fanciful?"

"But there is no harm in our fancies: is there, ma'am?"

"We are aware that mermaids do not exist: why speak of them as if they did? How can you find interest in speaking of a non-entity?"

"I don't know," said Shirley.[11]

This passage has provoked sharp disagreement among critics. For Sandra Gilbert and Susan Gubar, Shirley's image of an aggressive mermaid arises out of the way in which women access their anger when they are forced to succumb to the patriarchal myths of their culture.[12] Nancy

Quick Langer argues that Shirley "interrogates" the patriarchal system and "rejects identification with the mermaid," whereas Tara Moore asserts that Shirley has "bought into" the myth that all women are monstrous temptresses.[13] Shirley's language, certainly, is ambiguous: To what extent is a "monstrous likeness" a likeness? Does Shirley mention male designation of women as temptresses in order to entertain or belittle the notion? Langer rightly notes that Shirley "rewrite[es] the script" of traditional mermaid tales by placing herself and Caroline, rather than a man, in the position of those gazing at the mermaid.[14] But they occupy the position of the mermaid as well, particularly Caroline; Shirley tells her that the mermaid has "a face in the style of yours," though it gazes "not with your eyes." The narrator sets up this passage earlier in the novel by deeming Caroline's hair "as long as a mermaid's" and her reflection in the mirror both "enchanting" and "charming."[15] Altogether, the novel offers few and conflicting clues to the interpretation of this passage.

We have other sources of information, though, about what mermaids signified for Brontë. She may have been put in mind of mermaids by *Mary Barton*, the 1848 novel by Elizabeth Gaskell (Brontë's future biographer) that also portrays manufacturing in the north of England, which Brontë read while writing *Shirley*.[16] Gaskell—herself a committed realist—devotes four pages to discussion of a sailor's claim that he saw a mermaid at sea. In addition, two of *Mary Barton*'s chapters begin with epigraphs from W. S. Landor's "The Mermaid," a poem whimsically attributed to Shakespeare within his "Imaginary Conversation," "Citation and Examination of William Shakspeare" (1834). The poem offers a fairly bland portrayal of the mermaid singing a song and combing her hair. Of course, Brontë encountered mermaids much earlier as well. Shakespeare actually does mention a mermaid singing beautifully in *A Midsummer Night's Dream* (2.1 148–54). Brontë probably also read Sir Walter Scott's *The Pirate* (1822), which mentions several traditional beliefs about mermaids, including their association with combs and mirrors, their ability to prophesy, and their capacity for mischief. A more sinister "Mermaid's Song" appears in James Hogg's collection *The Queen's Wake*, which I cited in chapter 3 as a possible source for some of Emily Brontë's poetry; Hogg's mermaid taunts the lover of the man she has stolen, claiming, "long and sound shall his slumber be / In the coral bowers of the deep with me" (ln. 17–18).[17] This version of the mermaid, taking men to die in an endless watery embrace, is the one behind the dark fantasy Shirley depicts for Caroline.[18]

Brontë herself had previously mentioned mermaids in the poem "A Serenade," written in 1830 and attributed to the "Marquis of Douro," one of the many names of the hero of her juvenilia, in which the speaker imagines a nighttime walk that includes visiting the seashore and listening to the song of a green-haired mermaid. This mermaid heralds a storm: "And when her monstrous form is seen swift-gliding o'er the deep, / the blood within the sailors' veins in frozen streams doth creep. For mighty winds behind her fly and clouds are round her shed."[19] Brontë includes this note: "The appearance of the mermaid is said by sailors to be a sign of approaching tempest. I have heard many an experienced mariner confidently assert his belief in the existence of such a creature" (132). The concept of the mermaid as monstrous emerges in this poem as in *Shirley*, though the sexual element is absent from fourteen-year-old Brontë's version. Mr. Rochester compares Jane Eyre to a mermaid on a rainy night shortly before their aborted wedding; "you are dripping like a mermaid," he remarks.[20] Lucy Snowe in *Villette* observes that her guest room at the Bretton family's home in Labassecour resembles a sea cave, and that the "shining glass might have mirrored a mermaid"; significantly, she does not then consider herself as standing in for such a mermaid, though she will associate the more feminine Paulina Home with mermaids later in the novel.[21]

In fact, one clear common thread across all these versions of the mermaid is her femininity. Many other supernatural creatures, including pixies, elves, and even fairies, are less prominently gendered in traditional folklore; in contrast, the mermaid's very name identifies her as female, while a different word applies to male creatures of the same species. These, then, are the foremost characteristics of the early nineteenth-century mermaid: she is female, she is associated with nature, she often heralds something undesirable (be it tempest or willful endangerment of a man), and she is both clearly *other* and strikingly physically similar to human women. Brontë's references to mermaids throughout her extant writings suggest that her view of them, on the whole, was aligned with this contemporary perception, and clearly shaped by her reading.

Further clues to the significance of the mermaid discussion in *Shirley* can be found in another extensive passage about fairy tales that critics of the novel have rarely commented on. In this passage, fifteen-year-old Martin Yorke, a minor character who facilitates a meeting between Robert and Caroline at a time of tension between their families, slips into the woods alone one evening to read a "contraband volume of Fairy-tales"; Brontë invents and describes two of the tales, one of which features beings similar to mermaids.[22] Tara Moore suggests that Martin's reading of fairy tales, coupled with a sudden romantic interest in Caroline, spurs him to attempt to place himself at the center of a patriarchal fairy-tale narrative, with Caroline as the heroine. But the descriptions Brontë provides suggest that Martin's tales are not of the Charles Perrault-Brothers Grimm type that readers today tend to identify as patriarchal. Instead, they sound very much like supernatural bride tales. Neither of Brontë's summaries extends beyond the initial sighting of the supernatural female figure, but she offers enough material to be understood by a reader versed in this type of tale—as nineteenth-century British readers often were. In reading the first tale,

> [Martin] is led into a solitary mountain region; all around him is rude and desolate, shapeless, and almost colourless. He hears bells tinkle on the wind; forth-riding from the formless folds of the mist, dawns on him the brightest vision—a green-robed lady, on a snow-white palfrey; he sees her dress, her gems, [568] and her steed; she arrests him with some mysterious question: he is spell-bound, and must follow her into Fairy-land. (567–68)

This is the beginning of a fairy bride tale or similar tale of a human encounter with a fairy. Traditional examples abound, as I discussed in chapter 1. Brontë's fragment strongly resembles the story of Thomas the Rhymer as rendered in Scott's *Minstrelsy of the Scottish Border*. Scott recounts that Thomas of Ercildoune was a medieval poet who, according to legend, encountered a beautiful lady who bore him away to Elfland, where she was Queen. Even small details correspond: Thomas's "ladye bright" wears a "shirt . . . o' the grass-green silk" and "At ilka tett of her horse's mane, Hang fifty siller bells and nine."[23] It bodes well for Martin Yorke that Thomas was allowed to return to the human world after seven years, bearing poems and prophecies learned in Elfland (though ultimately he was summoned to return once and for all to the fairy kingdom).[24] Brontë and her readers may also have thought of Scott's *The Monastery*, in which young Halbert Glendinning encounters the White Lady of Avenel, a spirit, while alone in a ravine. Halbert sees "an appearance, as of a beautiful female, dressed in white, . . . a being in form like to ourselves, but so different in faculties and nature."[25] Just before this moment, Scott quotes from Samuel Taylor Coleridge's "Christabel" (1798, 1800), which begins with a similar encounter between young maiden Christabel and the evil fairy spirit Geraldine. Christabel is walking alone in the forest at night when she hears a moan and then

> sees a damsel bright,
> Drest in a silken robe of white . . .
> And wildly glittered here and there
> The gems entangled in her hair
>
> (ln. 58–59, 64–65)

Christabel welcomes Geraldine into her castle, where she discovers Geraldine's evil nature but is prevented by a spell from revealing it. Christabel, of course, differs from the type here in that she is female, but considering the obvious sexual overtones of her interaction with Geraldine toward the end of part 1, her situation is much the same as that of the male protagonists of other similar stories. Across all these examples, a human being alone in the wilderness encounters a fairy or spirit and is profoundly influenced in some way. Rather like the malicious mermaid, the fairy in these tales tends to be more powerful than the human being at all stages of the encounter, despite often feigning submission or affection for a time.

Brontë, however, gives Martin two tales to read; the second recalls variants featuring animal brides, in which the power balance between the genders is more complex. Given that this passage comes after the heroines' discussion of mermaids and takes place by the sea, the reader is clearly intended to recall Shirley's gaze at the mermaid in reading this summary:

> A second legend bears him to the sea-shore: there tumbles in a strong tide, boiling at the base of dizzy cliffs: it rains and blows. A reef of rocks, black and rough, stretches far into the sea; all along, and among, and above these crags, dash and flash, sweep and leap, swells, wreaths, drifts of snowy spray. Some lone wanderer is out on these rocks, treading, with cautious step, the wet, wild sea-weed; glancing down into the hollows where the brine lies fathoms deep and emerald-clear, and seeing there wilder, and stranger, and huger vegetation, than is found on land, with treasure of shells—some green, some purple, some pearly—clustered in the coils of the snaky plants. He hears a cry. Looking up,

> and forward, he sees, at the bleak point of the reef, a tall, pale thing—shaped like a man, but made of spray—transparent, tremulous, awful: it stands not alone: they are all human figures that wanton in the rocks—a crowd of foam-women—a band of white, evanescent Nereides.[26]

Brontë's tale specifically names Nereides (alternatively "Nereids"), water nymphs in Greek mythology who are the daughters of Nereus, a sea god. However, Martin's second tale does not sound quite like a Nereid encounter from Greek mythology; nor does it sound quite like a typical mermaid tale. It sounds more like a Romantic retelling of a folktale about an encounter with some other related type of humanoid sea creature. Moreover, while Shirley speaks at greater length of mermaids, she also mentions an expectation that "we will see seals in Suderoe" in her conversation with Caroline. Indeed, the Hebrides, Shetland, Orkney, and Faroe Islands she is considering visiting were (and are) particularly associated with selkies—part-human, part-seal creatures; Benwell and Waugh call these islands "strongholds of the seal-folk."[27] I suspect Brontë knew that these relatives of the mermaid appear in many British folktales, particularly from Scotland; they change between human and seal form by means of a sealskin that they can put on or take off at will. David Thomson's *The People of the Sea* gives a representative version, set in the Hebrides; although Thomson's book was published in the twentieth century, it explicitly attributes selkie ancestry to Clan MacCodrum and thus is clearly taken from the same tradition that folklorist Katharine Briggs identifies as the "most famous example" of the tale.[28] At the beginning of the story, a man walking on the shore seizes a selkie's sealskin and refuses to return it, insisting that she accompany him home and live as his wife in her human form. The selkie goes unwillingly but apparently finds happiness in her new life and bears several human children. When she eventually finds her hidden sealskin, however, she immediately puts it on and returns to the sea as a seal. She visits her children on the shore every day and gives them fish, but she evidently has no further interaction with their father.[29] Brontë's reference to seals, coupled with Martin's tale of a man's encounter with humanoid sea creatures, may well be intended to remind the reader of this story.

Even if Brontë somehow never encountered the selkie story, she could have discovered a very similar version of the animal bride tale in

Irish folklore. The second edition of Thomas Crofton Croker's *Fairy Legends and Traditions of the South of Ireland*, a collection I discussed in chapter 1 as a possible source for the Brontës, contains several tales about merrows—fish-people from Irish folklore whom Briggs calls "the Irish equivalent of mermaids."[30] One of them, "The Lady of Gollerus," is quite typical of the sea-creature version of the animal bride tale. Like Brontë's second tale, it begins with a man standing at the edge of the sea as water creatures come into view: "On the shore of Smerwick harbor, one fine summer's morning, stood Dick Fitzgerald. . . . The sun was gradually rising behind the lofty Brandon, the dark sea was getting green in the light, and the mists [were] clearing away out of the valleys."[31] The story proceeds much like the selkie story. Dick then sees "a beautiful young creature combing her hair" and recognizes her as a merrow by the "little enchanted cap" that can be used to pass between the seashore and the merrows' undersea kingdom (4). When he seizes that cap, she bursts into tears, but she welcomes his subsequent proposal of marriage. The man ignores the priest's warning against the marriage, and he and the merrow live together "in the greatest contentment" as the family grows to contain three children (11). But when the merrow eventually finds the cap where her husband has hidden it, she remembers her own family and is overcome by longing to return to the sea. Despite her initial intention to visit her husband and children periodically, she soon forgets them. The man spends the rest of his life waiting in vain for her reappearance.[32]

As the foregoing summaries suggest, these tales of relationships between human beings and sea creatures are deeply concerned with the difficulty of achieving harmony when faced with differences—and precisely the differences that come between people in *Shirley*. The animal bride's exotic allure is partly due to her association with a predominantly nonhuman space or realm. Significantly, animal brides tend to be creatures of the water or sky—spaces in which human beings generally cannot dwell. To possess an animal bride for a time is to achieve an unusual level of mastery over or access to an aspect of the natural world. The animal bride conspicuously belongs to a different species; the priest in Croker's tale repeatedly insists, "You can't marry her, she being a fish!"[33] Thomson's selkie does not hesitate to leave her children in the end because it is so obvious to her that she does not belong in human society. Even in versions like Croker's in which the fairy or animal bride follows the man willingly, she still returns eventually to her own people. The gap between nature and human civilization is shown in these tales to be unbridgeable. The same is true of mermaid tales that end in murder; these mermaids may look like beautiful women, but they evince little kinship with human beings—or at least with human men.

Indeed, scholars have often read the explicit species difference in animal bride tales as an allegory for gender difference; that is, the tales tap into male anxiety that women are so *other* that they might as well belong to a different species. Carole Silver has suggested that fairy and animal bride stories thrived in late-Victorian Britain because of the prominent discourse surrounding gender roles in that period, as evidenced by developments including the passage of the Married Woman's Property Act of 1882 and the rise of the New Woman.[34] When *Shirley* was written in 1848–49, debates over the "Woman Question" were already fervent, spurred in particular by the expansion of male enfranchisement with the Reform Bill of 1832. Although stories like Thomson's tend to strike readers today for their portrayal of marriage as kidnapping and imprisonment, it is no less significant that the fairy or animal bride almost invariably leaves this marriage; as Briggs says of seal maidens, "Here, as in other fairy bride stories, the rule is that unions between mortals and immortals are destined for breach and bereavement."[35] Ultimately, the "other" of these tales is too other to be reconciled to the human, male world.

Clearly, then, tales of encounters with various kinds of female creatures bursting out of a natural realm with preternatural abilities provided powerful metaphors for writers and readers grappling with rapid industrial development and profound changes in attitudes toward women in nineteenth-century Britain. As I will detail in the following section, Brontë draws on all the associations with fairies, mermaids, and other supernatural and animal bride types in *Shirley*. Like these creatures, Shirley and Caroline are associated with nature and come into conflict throughout the novel with men, who are associated with industrialization and other negative aspects of human civilization. Despite the distinctions among different creature types outlined above, what becomes most important for Brontë's novel is the fact that all of these creatures almost always end up vanishing from human view. The obvious difference, then, between the plot of *Shirley* and that of the traditional animal or fairy bride tale is the ending: the last we are told of Shirley and Caroline is that they marry the Moore brothers. But I propose that even as Brontë reverses the ending of the traditional tale, she retains the sense of the bride's vanishing by creating the impression that her heroines, especially Shirley, disappear abruptly from the view of the reader. The novel's final paragraphs, which discuss the departure of the fairies from the area, cast a pall over the seemingly tidy resolution.

Gender and the (Super)natural in Shirley

A straightforward indication (beyond the mermaid passage previously cited) that the reader should specifically connect the supernatural bride to Shirley and Caroline lies in the fact that the two women are frequently compared to supernatural creatures. Although Shirley seems the more unusual of the two women because of her more obvious unconventionality, Caroline attracts these comparisons somewhat more often. Sometimes, they are likened to supernatural creatures by other women. Mrs. Pryor, once she has revealed herself to be Caroline's mother, calls Caroline the "fairy-like-representative" of her father.[36] Caroline herself sees Shirley in the distance with Robert and refers to her as a "fairy shadow" (254). As in these two examples, women's comparisons of each other to supernatural creatures tend to be positive in this novel.

Not surprisingly, considering the tension between genders underlying the metaphorical uses of supernatural beings, Shirley and Caroline are often likened to fairies and similar creatures by the men who love them. "Are you fairies?" asks Robert of both women when they appear before him suddenly (316). Louis exclaims over Shirley in his diary, "Oh, my pupil! Oh, Peri!" and refers to her as a "nymph" (525, 493). Both Robert and Louis also conceive of their lovers' effects on them in supernatural terms. "Lina, you will haunt me," Robert says to Caroline, and the narrator notes that he is under a spell (255). Louis, too, deems himself under a "spell" due to the "magical energy of youth" he finds in Shirley; he tells her that she has "bewitched him" (610, 622). Unlike the exclusively complimentary comparisons made by other women, the Moores' references to the supernatural are dubious. Most often, the Moores think of magic when reflecting on their dependence on Caroline and Shirley, whose influence they desire but also fear.

Like the supernatural, the natural is also primarily associated with women in *Shirley*. A love of nature is more than once explicitly attributed to Caroline (75, 183). Moreover, as Danielle Coriale has observed, the narrator seems to share this love; "*Shirley* is replete with exuberant passages of natural description."[37] The narrator describes Caroline as a natural landscape to illustrate her depression: "Winter seemed conquering her spring: the mind's soil and its treasures were freezing gradually to barren stagnation."[38] Shirley, conversely, possesses a "still, deep, inborn delight . . . in her young veins" that is "the pure gift of God to His creature, the free dower of Nature to her child. This joy gives her experience of a genii-life. Buoyant, by green steps, by glad hills, all verdure and light, she reaches a station scarcely lower than that whence angels looked down" (387). The same characteristic is linked to God, to nature, and to the supernatural—three entities I also identified in chapter 3 as frequently blended in Emily Brontë's poetry. Precisely what Charlotte Brontë means by "genii-life" is not specified, but we can infer from the juvenilia that she is recalling the power of the Brontë children's Chief Genii.[39]

Early in their friendship, Caroline and Shirley discuss nature while venturing on the first of many walks they will take together. They clearly associate nature with women; in conceiving a plan to spend a day in the forest of Nunnwood together, they agree that the presence of men would fundamentally alter the excursion. Specifically, they anticipate that men—curates in particular—would distract them from nature with aimless but unrelenting conversation. Caroline, by contrast, knows the wood intimately and promises to guide Shirley to all of the loveliest spots; she uses the phrase "I know" four times in naming the aspects of the wood she proposes to show to Shirley.[40]

Meanwhile, as in the fairy and animal bride tales previously discussed, the conflicts between men and women in *Shirley* are unrelenting; repeatedly throughout the novel, Shirley clashes with her uncle, Caroline clashes with *her* uncle, and other men, especially the curates, clash with women in general. Both heroines are unconventional. The evidence of Shirley's unconventionality has been amply documented in scholarship: her independent habits, her tendency to refer to herself in the masculine under the name "Captain Keeldar, Esq.," her unusual bond with the dog Tartar, and her resistance to her uncle's manipulations. Shirley's uncle rules his wife with "petty tyranny" and tries to apply the same technique to Shirley (557). Predominantly concerned with the family honor, he repeatedly urges Shirley to make a "good" marriage, unwilling to listen to her explanations of her own feelings. Caroline, meanwhile, dreads entertaining, repeatedly articulates a wish for a profession, champions the social importance of "old maids," and disobeys her uncle's command to avoid Robert.[41] Caroline's uncle is simply a misogynist; he enjoys being amused by women in company but has a very low opinion of their intellect and believes they should remain within a limited sphere. Whenever Caroline expresses a wish for anything beyond marriage and domestic duties, he responds not merely with disapproval but also with ridicule. "Are you bewitched?" he replies when she proposes that she become a governess due to her need for a change (189). "'There speaks the woman!' cried he, 'the very woman! A change! a change! Always fantastical and whimsical! Well, it's in her sex'" (190). Even in Brontë's time, comments of this type, while hardly unheard of, were offensive, expressing more than an average level of contempt for women. Both of the heroines, then, though fatherless, are oppressed by patriarchal figures on the grounds of their gender.

Other men, too, undermine Caroline and Shirley. The entire first chapter of the novel, and several sections thereafter, follow the exploits of the local curates, based on Brontë's own experiences of the men who worked with her father. These curates—delightfully described by one reviewer as "a bevy of goblins in a pantomime"—are forever descending upon the women of the neighborhood to demand food and attention.[42] They, too, belittle women with their commentary. Meanwhile, Joe Scott, Robert's "overlooker" at the mill, holds "supercilious theories about women in general" and enacts them during a conversation with Shirley and Caroline.[43] He declares that women should disregard politics and take their husbands' opinions on scripture; twice he replies to trenchant ripostes of Shirley's with a maddening "I cannot argue, where I cannot be comprehended" (327, 328). Although Shirley opposes him most vocally, even Caroline enters the conversation when scripture is at issue (328–30). Throughout the novel, the misogyny is so unrelenting that Jane Eyre seems, astonishingly, to run into comparatively little male opposition despite the tyranny of John Reed, Mr. Brocklehurst, and St. John Rivers. Like animal brides, Shirley and Caroline contend with men's attempts to control them.

More generally, men in *Shirley* tend to be occupied with things that are uncharitable or contentious. Luddites break machines and attack Robert; Robert allows working conditions to erode so much that workers like William Farren cannot afford to live. Mr. Helstone's status as a rector prompts him to Christian rigidity rather than Christian kindness. Inability to reconcile political differences causes a rupture between

Mr. Helstone and Robert. When in dire financial straits, Robert proposes to the wealthy Shirley, whom he does not love. Theoretically, Robert improves over the course of the novel, partly thanks to the civilizing influence of Caroline, but he never becomes a compelling hero. On the whole, *Shirley* presents a more negative view of men than Brontë's other works.[44] To recall the options for masculinity discussed in chapter 4, these men are less flamboyantly evil than Bluebeard, but they also never reveal the hidden depths of goodness that Beauty finds in the Beast. Instead, they are like the husbands of animal or supernatural bride tales: static, selfish, and generally unable to admit fault.

The men Caroline and Shirley choose to marry, Robert and Louis Moore, do not express the blatant misogyny of Mr. Helstone and Joe Scott. Nevertheless, Robert is on the wrong side of the novel's other central conflict, between nature and industrialization. Deirdre Mikolajcik has tracked the ways in which Robert is conflated with the mill throughout the novel, via characterization (he is described as possessing "hardness" and a "regularity" in the "chiseling" of his features, for example), and plot (first the mill and then Robert himself are attacked).[45] Moreover, in his zeal to modernize the textile mill, Robert is building up the previously "wild" natural landscape, as the novel's final pages remind us.[46] In addition to interfering with the wilderness, he also imperils the natural lives of human beings: he plans to use machines for the work that had provided local men with an income. Thus, while Robert does not express hostility toward nature, his livelihood depends on its destruction and his willingness to endanger human life.

Louis Moore, meanwhile, claims to enjoy nature, feeding birds and perceiving that a September afternoon is "pleasant."[47] Yet his relationship with Shirley suggests that he most wants to harness nature for his own purposes.[48] Shirley is often compared to animals—in one scene, to both a black swan and a white crow (389)—and she relishes independence from the constraints of society. But she also resembles an animal as Louis tames her. When he refers to her as "my leopardess," Shirley replies that real leopardesses are "tameless" but does not demur when he insists, "Tame or fierce, wild or subdued, you are *mine*" (623). Shirley borrows this language in submitting to him: she calls him "my keeper" and promises "only his voice will I follow; only his hand shall manage me; only at his feet will I repose" (624). Louis's words indicate that he knows her for what she is: "Pantheress!—beautiful forest-born!—wily, tameless, peerless nature! She gnaws her chain: I see the white teeth working at the steel! She has dreams of her wild woods, and pinings after virgin freedom" (629). He does not, though, exhibit any qualms about Shirley's lingering wish for liberty; he simply expresses a fear of losing her. Although the narrator neither explicitly criticizes Louis's language nor ultimately condemns Robert for his zeal for development, the novel nonetheless frequently refers to the importance of nature and associates it almost exclusively with women.

If, overall, *Shirley* presents the natural and the feminine as interconnected and positive entities, in opposition to a masculine sphere associated with machinery and a desire for domination and profit, then what are we to make of the fact that the heroines ultimately marry? Some scholars have suggested that the difficulty of the reconciliation between male and female, industry and nature, is the point. James Buzard, for example, insists that "the heterogeneity Brontë seeks to cultivate must include the category of gender."[49] For Danielle Coriale, similarly, "the novel suggests that industrial development must take place if social peace and domestic prosperity are to persist."[50] Shawna Ross points out that "*Shirley* recognizes that human activities have long ago transformed the area; the epoch of pristine nature has already passed."[51] Both Coriale and Ross argue that the novel itself, by its lyrical descriptions of the natural setting and, specifically, of "ecological change," constitutes some measure of compensation.[52] Indeed, "pristine nature" is never really under discussion in *Shirley;* Caroline and Shirley's fantasies of forest and ocean include their own human presence, and the concluding paragraphs, discussed in more detail below, refer back nostalgically only to a preindustrial time, not to the time before humans inhabited the region at all. Some men in the novel, meanwhile, vehemently oppose Robert's push for more machinery, as it endangers their livelihoods. To range women on the side of pristine nature and men on the side of total destruction of the landscape in favor of industrial development would be an exaggeration; Brontë does not depict a world in which men and women have no common ground.

She does, though, present a society in which men and women's separate spheres make it very difficult for them to understand each other, and this is precisely the kind of society with which animal and supernatural bride folktales most resonate. Brontë's way of deploying this tale type in *Shirley* can provide some insight into her aims. It seems that, whereas animal and supernatural bride folktales begin with capture and end with escape, *Shirley* proceeds in the opposite direction: in spending hundreds of pages on headstrong heroines only to marry them to men in the end, Brontë strikingly reverses the folktale's ending. Before winning her, Louis writes of Shirley in his notebook in terms strongly evocative of the supernatural bride figure: she "darted, or melted, from my arms—and I lost her."[53] As we will see in chapter 7 regarding Anne Brontë's *The Tenant of Wildfell Hall*, though, adapting a (short) fairy tale for use in a novel tends to require adding more stages to the story. Ultimately, Louis turns up again at Fieldhead and, this time, gains permanent possession of his erstwhile fairy bride. Both Shirley and Caroline surrender their sealskins forever, as it were, and are tamed into conventional marriages.[54] It becomes clear that Shirley and Caroline more closely resemble the captive supernatural or animal bride, whatever her precise species, than they do the femme fatale of the tales in which mermaids easily exert power over the men they encounter. The remaining question, then, is how the reader is to feel about this outcome.

Happily Ever After?

The Moore brothers have provoked criticism since *Shirley*'s earliest reviews. For example, the anonymous critic for the *Westminster Review* bluntly opines that one of the brothers, presumably Robert, "only just escapes the condemnation of the reader as a bashful blockhead."[55] George Henry Lewes, in an 1850 review for the *Edinburgh Review* that Brontë would find unjust, devotes a paragraph to the Moores' flaws.[56] He argues that both brothers are too petty and fixated on money to be worthy of the heroines: "A hero may be faulty, erring, imperfect; but he must not be sordid, mean, wanting in the statelier virtues of our kind" (470).[57] But the relationship between Louis and Shirley has generated the most skepticism. Herbert Rosengarten has attributed the "frustration many readers feel with the novel" in part to the fact that by the end, "it is as if, despite all that has happened in the world of the novel . . . nothing has really changed. . . . Shirley may experience visions of an all-powerful female deity, but she herself willingly accepts the role of domestic life and maternity."[58] Indeed, considering that many of the most vivid scenes in *Shirley* feature the heroines contending with misogynistic comments from men who threaten to interfere with their freedom, it has been hard for many readers to believe that Brontë intends for us to rejoice at Shirley's submission to Louis Moore.

Moreover, it is suspicious that neither the weddings nor the marriages of the central couples are dramatized. The heroines never speak to each other of their romantic triumphs. Indeed, we hardly see the heroines do anything after accepting their marriage proposals. The only information given about the time after the weddings is that Robert builds a more "mighty" mill.[59] For a Charlotte Brontë novel, the arrival of a bigger mill is quite an anticlimactic ending.[60] The very end of the novel (after a utilitarian report of the double wedding of the central couples) is a classic English account of the "fairies' farewell" in the face of industrialization—so classic that Carole G. Silver cites it in her discussion of this tradition.[61] In this final passage, taking place years after the wedding, the narrator reports walking past the new mill and then speaks of it to his or her old housekeeper, who reminisces about a time prior to the events of the novel, before any mill at all existed on the spot:

> There was neither mill, nor cot, nor hall, except Fieldhead, within two miles of it. I can tell, one summer-evening, fifty years syne, my mother coming running in just at the edge of dark, almost fleyed out of her wits, saying, she had seen a fairish (fairy) in Fieldhead Hollow; and that was the last fairish that ever was seen on this country-side (though they've been heard within these forty years). A lonesome spot it was—and a bonnie spot—full of oak trees and nut trees. It is altered now.[62]

Strangely, instead of providing a passage assuring the couple's years of happiness as in *Jane Eyre*, Brontë concludes *Shirley* with the observation that the mill and its trappings have caused the fairies to bid farewell to the country. She clearly draws on writers like James Hogg, who published an account in *Blackwood's* in 1827 of the reputed final sighting of fairies in the Scottish border region, "on the very outskirts of the Ettrick forest, quite out of the range of social intercourse," "in the summer twilight . . . in the bottom of a deep ravine."[63] In this piece, Hogg attributes the departure of the fairies to the coming of Christianity rather than industrialization; indeed, both Bibles and machines were cited as enemies of the fairies in the writing of the day. For Brontë, fairies are specifically associated with untouched nature as opposed to a pre-Christian belief system.[64] Moreover, this prominent passage about the departure of the fairies should recall the novel's earlier passages about the return of the mermaid to the sea and Martin's fairy tales about encounters with transient supernatural creatures.

Brontë's reasons for ending the novel with a farewell to the fairies have been the subject of some critical debate. Temma Berg associates the departure of the fairies with the disappearance of a queer Shirley into a heterosexual marriage.[65] For Helene Moglen, it constitutes an "ironic commentary" on Robert's priorities and is, on the whole, melancholy: "The momentary glimmering of light is extinguished. It can only be recaptured in tales told by women to children and to one another."[66] Susan Zlotnick, on the other hand, sees irony at the expense of the housekeeper: "The passing of this country superstition . . . is best left unmourned."[67] These attributions of irony to vastly different purposes point to the ambiguity of Brontë's language. I cannot, though, agree with Zlotnick, because her assertion disregards the frequency and complexity with which Brontë avails herself of references to fantastical creatures and tales, including in her later novels. My understanding, more in line with Berg's and Moglen's readings, connects *Shirley*'s ending with other supernatural references in the novel; I suggest that this ending can be seen as a final, unhappy stage in Brontë's use of the supernatural bride tale.

Shirley's concluding passage becomes troubling precisely because of a particular connection developed throughout the novel between fairies and Shirley. While both heroines are associated with various supernatural creatures, Shirley also speaks positively of actual fairies. She declares to Caroline that she "would walk from Fieldhead [her house] to the church any fine mid-summer night . . . for the mere pleasure of seeing the stars, and the chance of meeting a fairy."[68] Another mention of fairies on Shirley's part anticipates the novel's conclusion: "When I was a very little girl, Mr. [Robert] Moore, my nurse used to tell me tales of fairies being seen in the Hollow. That was before my father built the mill, when it was a perfectly solitary ravine: you will be falling under enchantment" while walking there (237). Although Shirley attributes the manifestation of fairies to the former emptiness of the landscape, she speculates that Robert will be enchanted in the present. The conversation quickly turns, though, to a male-centered understanding of the affinity between dangerous supernatural creatures and women—a conversation Shirley may be recalling when speaking to Caroline of mermaids as temptresses. In addition to being compared to fairies by both Moore brothers, then, Shirley also evinces more interest than any other character in the possibility of fairies' presence in the real landscape in which the novel takes place.

There is another way, too, in which Shirley is more deeply connected to fairies than Caroline despite drawing fewer offhand comparisons to them from other characters. Critics have not yet discussed the fact, provided by both Shirley and the elderly housekeeper, that the only building present in the Hollow in the old days of the fairies was Fieldhead Hall: Shirley's home. Shirley herself would not have been present fifty years earlier, but I propose that the Hall stands in for her. In this reading, then, the housekeeper's words imply that Shirley, like the house, once stood alone in the Hollow with the fairies but has since been absorbed into an industrial complex. Silver has observed that in general, nineteenth-century writers who referred to the fairies' farewell presented it as a melancholy event and "utilized the reasons for the elfin migration to indict the society they left behind."[69] If this is true of Brontë, as I believe it is, then industrialization is to blame—which bodes ill for the moral status of the man who built the mill. Although Robert is more directly responsible for the expansion of the mill than the man Shirley marries, Louis's language aligns him with his brother on the side of development: "I approve nothing Utopian. Look Life in its *iron* face: stare Reality out of its brassy countenance."[70] Louis associates the reality of life with iron, the stuff of industrialization and the traditional enemy of the fairies; as we have already seen, he associates Shirley with fairies and dreams, and he uses the word "steel" in illustrating his hold over her (629). Shirley's capitulation to Louis and disappearance from the action of the novel echoes the fairies' surrendering of their territory to man and machine.

Brontë's choice to end the novel with the farewell to the fairies, then, complicates her use of the supernatural bride story. The male characters are married rather than abandoned in the end, but considered from a less literal point of view, the vanishing of the women is still happening—it simply happens to the reader rather than to the suitor. Sally Shuttleworth has astutely observed that *Shirley* "revers[es] the trajectory" of *Jane Eyre*: whereas Jane grows less spirit-like and more psychologically, economically, and romantically powerful, Shirley and Caroline "move into increasing insubstantiality. Caroline is threatened by the ultimate form of insubstantiality, death, whilst Shirley becomes, in conclusion, virtually a figment of Louis' mind: her capitulation to his control is presented entirely through Louis' eyes, in the form of his notebook entries."[71] The "insubstantiality" Shuttleworth identifies is underscored by Brontë's frequent comparisons of Caroline and Shirley to supernatural creatures:

these creatures are ephemeral. Mermaids dive back into the ocean; selkies reclaim their skins and return to their watery homes; fairies bid farewell to England when iron overpowers them. Of course, all fictional characters vanish when the story ends, but Shirley and Caroline fade prematurely from the reader's view near the close of *Shirley* in that even though the story continues to be largely about them, their presence in the narrative subsides.

To be sure, this is less true of Caroline than it is of Shirley. The romance between Caroline and Robert is set up from the first chapters of the novel. Soon after Caroline enters the novel in chapter 5, the narrator presents her daydreaming about Robert. We then watch Caroline suffer for several hundred pages from what she believes to be unrequited love. Although Caroline begins projects of philanthropy with the neighborhood's "old maids" and partially revives at the discovery that Shirley's former governess, Mrs. Pryor, is her own long-lost mother, she remains dejected, unable to forget Robert. Ultimately, Robert discovers his love for Caroline and successfully proposes marriage. This proposal is the final dramatized event in the novel, followed only by the report of the double wedding and the farewell-to-the-fairies passage discussed previously. Structurally, the romance between Caroline and Robert is clearly crucial to the novel. The part of Caroline that vanishes at the end of the novel is the independent spirit that advocated for "old maids" and wished for a profession. Caroline's own words in the final chapter, though, indicate that she is delighted to be marrying Robert. Without doubt, twenty-first century readers are much more likely than Victorian readers to object to this shift in focus.

Caroline, after all, seems better suited than Shirley to contentment within the masculine-industrial-realist realm that triumphs at the end of the novel. Caroline's dreams of possessing the love of Robert and her mother come true in a way that Shirley's fantasies of mermaids, fairy sightings, and the primordial Eve simply cannot within the confines of realism; as Tara Moore puts it, Caroline "creates more realistic myth narratives" than Shirley.[72] Accordingly, Shirley's withdrawal from the narrative is more extensive—and more conspicuous, considering the forcefulness of her presence in earlier parts of the novel. Of the fourteen chapters in volume 3, the final six do not contain a single, directly dramatized scene including Shirley. Chapter 13 describes the romantic rapprochement between Shirley and Louis but is, as Shuttleworth observes, told exclusively through Louis's narration. Chapter 14 devotes a few paragraphs to Shirley and Louis's wedding preparations, but in generalities rather than with any actual scenes; the narrator reports that Shirley would say "Go to Mr. Moore; ask Mr. Moore" whenever anyone asked her a question about the wedding, and that a year later, she explained her total capitulation by saying that "Louis would never have learned to rule, if she had not ceased to govern: the incapacity of the sovereign had developed the powers of the premier."[73] These are her only words in the chapter—the last ones she speaks in the novel. The rest of the final paragraphs about Shirley consist of such sentences as "Thus vanquished and restricted, she pined, like any other chained denizen of deserts" and "[Louis] was virtually master of Fieldhead, weeks before he became so nominally. . . . She abdicated without a word or a struggle" (637, 638). Caroline reports to Robert that Shirley "sits alone: I cannot tell whether she is melancholy or nonchalant: if you rouse her, or scold her, she gives you a look half wistful, half reckless" (639). Robert expresses confidence that Louis and Shirley suit each other well, but the reader learns nothing about either marriage after the statement "This morning there were two marriages solemnized in Briarfield church,—Louis Gérard Moore, Esq. late of Antwerp, to Shirley, daughter of the late Charles Cave Keeldar, Esq. of Fieldhead: Robert Gérard Moore, Esq. of Hollow's mill, to Caroline, niece of the Rev. Matthewson Helstone, M.A., Rector of Briarfield" (645). It is not a twenty-first-century imposition to observe that this "ironic perfunctoriness"[74] is a long way from "Reader, I married him."

This negative emphasis at the end of the novel on the departure of the fairies and the withdrawal of Shirley into a questionable marriage may well have been affected by the circumstances of the novel's composition. When Brontë began writing *Shirley*, all three of her siblings (those who survived into adulthood, that is) were alive. By the time she completed it, all three had died, within nine months of each other. Brontë worked on volume 1 between February and September 1848. Branwell died later that September, and Emily followed in December. By May 1849, she had finished volume 2; soon after, Anne died. She completed volume 3 between June and August 1849. Citing this extraordinarily tragic sequence of events, Patsy Stoneman suggests that *Shirley* is an elegy for Emily (2015). Stoneman details, too, the numerous similarities between Shirley and Emily; indeed, according to Elizabeth Gaskell, Shirley represented Emily as she "would have been, had she been placed in health and prosperity."[75]

Indisputably, Shirley shares characteristics with Emily, ranging from her general forceful manner and eccentric, independent habits to specific scenes involving the dog, Tartar, that replicate documented interactions between Emily and her dog, Keeper. Stoneman does not discuss *Shirley*'s references to ephemeral supernatural creatures, but, particularly considering what we know about Emily, their role in the novel lends further support to her interpretation.

Charlotte's personal writing about Emily after her death stresses the fact that she is "gone"; *Shirley*'s emphasis on the transience of supernatural creatures—and linking of its most vivid heroine to such creatures—reflects this sense of departure. Charlotte wrote to Ellen Nussey on December 23: "She is gone after a hard, short conflict. . . . Yes—there is no Emily in Time or on Earth now"; to William Smith Williams on January 2: "Where is she now? Out of my reach—out of my world, torn from me."[76] She uses the word "torn" in two additional letters (192, 200). Similarly, she wrote to Williams on June 13: "Branwell—Emily—Anne are gone like dreams—gone as Maria and Elizabeth went twenty years ago" (220). She recalls here her two older sisters, who both died of tuberculosis in 1825.

Charlotte clearly wished more accomplishment for Emily: "We saw her taken from life in its prime," she wrote to Nussey on December 23; to Williams two days later, Emily was "rooted up in the prime of her own days, in the promise of her powers."[77] If Shirley is indeed a reflection of Emily, the fact that Charlotte does not mention marriage as something Emily missed suggests that when Shirley's strength is vanquished by Louis, this may not be a welcome development. For Emily—as for Shirley—fortitude and independence cannot prevent the fate that befalls so many others, be it death or a dubious marriage. Emily leaves this world, as the fairies bid farewell to human lands, as Shirley's mermaid gives a "wild shriek" and dives into the obscure depths of the ocean.[78] *Shirley* may have begun with the promise of something "real, cool, and solid" (5), but by the time Brontë reached volume 2, much of what was real in her own life was solid no longer. On a literal level, Caroline nearly dies. Shirley is not actually lost or dead at the end of the novel, but through her similarities to Emily and the references to ephemeral, supernatural creatures surrounding her, her fate is haunted by the sense of the loss of her creator's loved one. For the reader, she seems to have slipped out of reach as these supernatural creatures ultimately do. Dissatisfaction with Shirley's marriage fits smoothly within a modern feminist interpretation, but from another vantage point, the fact that the bereft reader occupies the position of a selkie's husband implicates us in what may be an unfair desire to hold the departed back. This makes sense if we view the novel's ending as, in part, Brontë's critique of her own grieving; after Anne died, she reflected in a letter to Williams on June 4, 1849: "I let Anne go to God and felt He had a right to her . . . [but] I could hardly let Emily go—I wanted to hold her back then—and I want her back hourly now. . . . They are both gone."[79] From Charlotte's Christian perspective, she should not wish to reverse Emily's passage to heaven, but nevertheless she does. In this way, associating Shirley with fairies and animal brides throughout the novel facilitates both a subtle critique of nineteenth-century marriage and an expression of the complex emotions of grief. Perhaps the time has come for Shirley to marry, England to modernize, and Emily to meet God, but one need not regard these events with unadulterated joy.

* * *

Shirley certainly is a realist novel, more strictly so than any other novel Charlotte Brontë published. While *Jane Eyre* relies on a type of interior realism that foregrounds the truth of personal experience over the details of observable reality, *Shirley* has no equivalent to the "mysterious summons" of *Jane Eyre*, in which Jane and Rochester somehow hear each other speaking across a great distance. Every event that occurs in *Shirley* unquestionably could have occurred in the time and place of the novel's setting. Yet references to fairy tales and supernatural creatures pervade the text, and various elements of the "domestic" plot follow the model of supernatural or animal bride folktales. Taken together, these manifestations of the supernatural provide vital clues for interpretation. Brontë concludes the novel by saying, "I think I now see the judicious reader putting on his spectacles to look for the moral. It would be an insult to his sagacity to offer directions."[80] What she offers instead of explicit directions is a tapestry of supernatural references throughout the novel that subtly suggests an unease with the story's outcome. Lee O'Brien has suggested that the reference to "Rumpelstiltskin" in *Middlemarch* "giv[es] rise to questions the actual narration of *Middlemarch* does not explicitly allow."[81] Something similar is happening in *Shirley*: Brontë uses folk and fairy tales to provide a commentary on the novel's events that is significant in terms of both the industrial and domestic plots. Even though *Shirley* does not dwell on the plight of the workers and misdeeds of the masters to the extent of other industrial novels like *Mary Barton*, the sustained association of women, supernatural creatures, and nature makes clear that the farewell-to-the-fairies ending expresses misgivings about industrial progress. In terms of the feminist debate about the novel, my reading suggests that while Shirley ultimately succumbs to the demands of her patriarchal society, Brontë does not fully condone her submission. Caroline, though also unconventional and associated with supernatural creatures, ultimately fits comfortably in the everyday world of men; if, as some commentators have suggested, she was intended to resemble Anne Brontë, Charlotte's comment that God "had a right" to Anne but not to Emily corresponds to the final distinction between *Shirley*'s heroines. The supernatural or animal bride tale is fundamentally sad: neither the bride's captivity nor her escape comes without a cost. The idea of the passing of fairies from rural England, too, is a melancholy one, or at least bittersweet, standing in as it does for what is lost in the face of any major change. Despite their surface-level differences, realist and nonrealist stories often deal with similar concerns; these supernatural tales, instead of compromising *Shirley*'s realism, highlight the complexities of its plot and enrich the portrait of reality it can provide.

6 From Fairy Tale to Folklore in *Wuthering Heights*

Emily Brontë's *Wuthering Heights* (1847) is a notoriously complex novel. Part ghost story, part romance, part family drama, the narrative presents no clear heroes or villains; one of the most prominent characters dies halfway through, giving way to a second act featuring a less compelling group of people. Multiple characters share identical or similar names. Children resemble not only their parents but their aunts and foster fathers. Two characters insist that they quite literally are each other. Extreme behavior predominates. Complicating matters further, most of the story is filtered through two levels of narration, neither of which is authoritative. Generations of scholars have attempted to make some sense of *Wuthering Heights;* the novel resists any totalizing theory of its workings. Nearly forty years ago, J. Hillis Miller observed that though many Victorian novels have inspired a wide range of critical interpretations, the voluminous scholarship on *Wuthering Heights* is "characterized by the unusual degree of incoherence among the various explanations. . . . The essays tend not to build on one another."[1] This extreme range of disjointed readings has only widened since Miller's remark; the 2018 special issue of *Victorians: A Journal of Culture and Literature* celebrating Emily Brontë's bicentenary offers articles on necropolitics and the novel's influence on the contemporary paranormal teen romance *Twilight* as well as engagements with topics of enduring scholarly interest such as imperialism, religion, gender, and landscape.

A study of Brontë's uses of fairy tales and folklore in *Wuthering Heights* will not provide that missing key to unlocking the novel's mysteries. Instead, it emphasizes the very refusal of closure that has so bedeviled literary scholars; I agree with Miller that the best readings of *Wuthering Heights* are those that "best account for the heterogeneity of the text," and I argue that Brontë's deployments of various (and even contradictory) tropes from folklore and negative references to happily-ever-after fairy tales contribute to this heterogeneity.[2] The ending of *Jane Eyre* differs from that of *Wuthering Heights* not so much in happiness as in tidiness; major characters are settled in appropriate marriages, secrets have been revealed, families reunited, justice meted out. From the first pages of *Jane Eyre,* Jane expresses her desires to be loved and to be treated justly; the final pages show these desires fulfilled. This tidiness makes the continental literary fairy tale an obvious structural model for the novel's plot.[3] *Wuthering Heights,* on the other hand, lacks the central organizing consciousness of *Jane Eyre,* instead spreading the focus among two unreliable narrators and multiple prickly characters. Whereas Jane Eyre continually appeals to the reader to understand and identify with her, the narrators of *Wuthering Heights* are unwilling or unable to forge such a personal connection between the reader and the characters they discuss. It is difficult to imagine what a simple happily-ever-after ending to this novel would actually look like; these characters' desires and perspectives are so at odds—their relationships to each other so tangled and claustrophobic—that no fully satisfying resolution is possible.

This is partly because *Wuthering Heights* subordinates a brief fairy-tale plot to a myriad of allusions to folktales. A few critics have commented on Brontë's debt to folklore, while a few others have noted the traces of literary fairy tales in the text; I address their assertions in this chapter and echo their common underlying argument that fairy tales and folklore do important work in the novel. As several of them have noted, a "Beauty and the Beast" plot plays out for Hareton and Cathy (I follow the practice of most critics in referring to the mother as "Catherine" and the daughter as "Cathy"). However, this storyline takes up little space in the novel, and it involves secondary characters; the literary, happily-ever-after fairy tale is decidedly not the novel's chief structural model. Convoluted and dark, *Wuthering Heights* usually lingers in readers' memories as the bizarre and unhappy love story of Catherine and Heathcliff, two deeply disturbed people; critics, too, prioritize this story, often weighing Heathcliff's suffering against his cruelties. An unambiguous failure of the "Beauty and the Beast" story, this relationship is illuminated by the novel's seemingly contradictory allusions to folklore. Scholars have examined the novel's treatment of folk beliefs and possible commentary on folkloristic practices, and I will add to their arguments by highlighting Brontë's allusions to and unmarked repetitions of certain tropes from folktales—not so much imitations of specific folktale plots as references to supernatural creatures and phenomena that recur in variants of multiple tales. Most prominently, characters in *Wuthering Heights* constantly compare Heathcliff to negatively connoted supernatural creatures, even as Brontë more subtly associates his endless mourning for Catherine with the struggle of human beings in folktales who are lured away—literally or figuratively—by creatures like fairies, pixies, and will-o'-the-wisps. While the negative comparisons are often mentioned but rarely probed by critics, the folkloric undertones of Heathcliff's mourning have thus far gone virtually unnoticed; they are legitimate to consider, though, because they point back to folktale tropes also referenced in Charlotte's juvenilia and Emily's poetry. Exploring the apparently contradictory associations of Heathcliff with both ill-intended supernatural creatures and their human victims also provides another way into the complex and ultimately fundamental question of how we are to interpret Heathcliff. Finally, the alignment of Heathcliff with the haplessly wandering mortals of folklore is repeated in the realm of storytelling itself: as he is led astray by the ghost of Catherine, so, too, are narrator Lockwood and the reader, gripped by a ghostly hand in the novel's first pages and led by narrator Nelly Dean deep into a story that will have no satisfying resolution. Folklore suits the contradictions of *Wuthering Heights* precisely because such resolution is absent.

"Beauty and the Beast"

Emily Brontë does not refer by name to any continental fairy tales in *Wuthering Heights*, and as I will demonstrate later, it is folklore that drives her central characterizations. Nevertheless, as critics from Q. D. Leavis to Elliott B. Gose to Phyllis Ralph have contended, "Beauty and the Beast" is relevant enough to the novel's plot and themes that Brontë seems to have had it consciously in mind. I discussed the importance of "Beauty and the Beast" to *Jane Eyre* in chapter 4; unlike *Jane Eyre*, however, *Wuthering Heights* evokes "Beauty and the Beast" primarily in order to overturn and marginalize it. Quite early in prospective protagonist

Catherine Earnshaw's life, she is essentially cast as Beauty. Just as in the fairy tale, as several critics have observed, her father goes on a journey after asking his children to name gifts for him to bring back. And like Beauty's father, Mr. Earnshaw goes on to encounter a figure who will turn out to be something of a beast. But the fairy-tale pattern is altered early on: instead of bringing this Beast back to the home only figuratively, Mr. Earnshaw does so literally. Heathcliff meets with the suspicion and dislike to be expected for a Beast figure. Yet this potential "Beauty and the Beast" story lacks the central tension of the fairy tale: the need for the heroine to progress from initial repulsion to sympathy to love. Catherine takes to Heathcliff almost instantly and insists far more vehemently than Beauty on her kinship with him, famously going so far as to assert that Heathcliff is "more myself than I am."[4] After years of unquestioned companionship, Catherine learns to find this Beast inadequate as a (human, marriageable) man when she has her first real encounter with the glitter of more refined civilization.[5] Then comes a marriage proposal, but not from the Beast: from the ostensibly more human male rival, who inadvertently prompts Catherine to consider and reject the alternative of marriage to Heathcliff before he has even asked.[6] Consequently, Catherine marries Edgar Linton, Heathcliff "remains untransformed," and all three spend the rest of their lives in states of comparative unhappiness.[7]

But the story continues: unusually for a stand-alone Victorian novel, *Wuthering Heights* dramatizes the childhood and adulthood of two generations. In the second generation, one storyline does resemble "Beauty and the Beast": that of Cathy and Hareton. After Catherine's death, Heathcliff pursues vengeance against the remaining Earnshaws and Lintons by striving to seize control of all their property and make their children miserable. Hindley's death leaves little Hareton in Heathcliff's charge; Hareton reaches adulthood having worked the land without wages for years (as Hindley had forced Heathcliff to do) and having received virtually no education. Like the Beast, Hareton has come into a harsh exterior through someone else's agency, but evidence of gentler qualities occasionally emerges. A servant deems Hareton "not bad-natured, though he's rough."[8] Cathy does not meet him until she is thirteen; when she does, Nelly finds her "perfectly at home, laughing and chattering" to him (228). This, however, is before she knows his identity; when Nelly identifies him as her cousin, she weeps, looking at Hareton "with a glance of awe and horror" and turning her attention in the following days to the impending arrival of the presumably more refined Linton Heathcliff, whom she calls "her 'real' cousin" (231, 234). Cathy becomes repulsed by Hareton after learning her intimate connection with him. On Cathy's next visit to Wuthering Heights, Heathcliff stages a reprise of the "Beauty and the Beast" "do you find me handsome?" exchange (as we saw in *Jane Eyre*). "Is he not a handsome lad?" Heathcliff asks Cathy, at which point "the uncivil little thing stood on tiptoe, and whispered a sentence in Heathcliff's ear"; Heathcliff laughs and reports, "She says you're a—what was it? Well, something very flattering" (252).

Once Cathy comes to live at Wuthering Heights, the Beauty-and-the-Beast-style relationship between Cathy and Hareton begins in earnest. At first, Cathy screams at Hareton when he tries to touch her and mocks his attempts to learn to read, calling him a "brute" and comparing his behavior to that of a "dog" or a "cart-horse" (333, 341). But after Nelly reproaches Cathy for her rudeness, she apologizes to Hareton and makes friends with him by way of a kiss and an amicable reading lesson. As in the fairy tale, the rapprochement does not occur all at once; as Nelly recounts to Lockwood, "The intimacy thus commenced, grew rapidly; though it encountered temporary interruptions. Earnshaw was not to be civilized with a wish, and my young lady was . . . no paragon of patience"; ultimately, though, Hareton's "honest, warm, and intelligent nature shook off rapidly the clouds of ignorance and degradation in which it had been bred. . . . His brightening mind brightened his features, and added spirit and nobility to their aspect—I could hardly fancy it the same individual" as before (346, 351–2). By the final pages of the novel, Cathy and Hareton plan to marry. And so the second-generation Beast figure is transformed into a civilized man, presumably to live with the Beauty figure happily ever after.

True enough, as far as it goes, but numerous factors would stymie an argument that *Wuthering Heights*, like *Jane Eyre*, may ultimately be read as a triumphant "Beauty and the Beast" story. To begin with, happily-ever-after fairy tales are suspect in this novel: the only person to mention them explicitly is Lockwood, who muses ruefully near the novel's end, "What a realization of something more romantic than a fairy tale it would have been for Mrs. Linton Heathcliff [Cathy], had she and I struck up an attachment!" (335). By this point, the reader knows that the idea of a relationship between Cathy and Lockwood is absurd; Lockwood's associating such a relationship with fairy tales urges the reader to be skeptical of them. Moreover, despite the happy ending for Cathy and Hareton, the novel cannot be reduced to the story of their romance. Catherine and Heathcliff are simply more compelling characters, as Brontë was surely well aware. With the arguable exception of Nelly, Heathcliff is also the only character to figure prominently in both halves of the novel. Brontë is evidently most interested in Heathcliff, and he has no part in the "Beauty and the Beast" resolution. In Brontë's world, "Beauty and the Beast" is a story only available in its entirety to minor characters.

In chapter 4, I read the portrayal of Rochester in *Jane Eyre* as a tug-of-war between the models of Beast and Bluebeard; Heathcliff, too, contains elements of both fairy-tale characters. At the beginning of the novel, he certainly seems like a Beast figure—a good-hearted but unrefined boy sneered at by almost all others except for one girl who aligns herself with him. To some extent, Catherine and Heathcliff's feeling of underlying connection despite external social barriers—epitomized in Catherine's "I *am* Heathcliff" (122) and Heathcliff's "I *cannot* live without my soul" (204) after Catherine's death—resembles the relationship between Jane and Rochester and the fundamental affinity Beauty discovers with the Beast. But when his "Beauty and the Beast" plot falls through, Heathcliff begins to take after Bluebeard. After marrying Isabella Linton, he tortures her, nearly kills her dog, behaves with indifference toward his child, and later imprisons Cathy and Nelly for days, to name a few of his most egregious offenses. Isabella marries Heathcliff but rejects the Beauty role as much as Catherine had; even though she observes in his face one day "an expression of unspeakable sadness," she nevertheless insists, "I was not going to sympathise with him—the brute beast!" (215, 207). One could not ask for a statement in starker contradiction to "Beauty and the Beast": Isabella sees human feeling beneath Heathcliff's beastly exterior but has suffered too much at his hands to welcome any affinity with him.

Ultimately, neither "Beauty and the Beast" nor "Bluebeard" provides a satisfying model for the plot of *Wuthering Heights*. Despite the length and complexity of *Jane Eyre*, its structure more closely resembles that of a classic fairy tale because it focuses on the development of one character and one relationship. Even seemingly tangential episodes in *Jane Eyre* usually do fit with a "Beauty and the Beast" or "Bluebeard" plot; for example, the chapters early in the novel in which Jane suffers and grows at Lowood School are functionally related to the portion of "Beauty and the Beast" in which Beauty and her family cope with poverty, while the extensive period she spends away from Rochester with her newfound cousins mirrors the interlude Beauty spends with her family late in the fairy tale. Such comparisons are more difficult to make with large sections of *Wuthering Heights*. As discussed, "Beauty and the Beast" underlies only a limited portion of the novel. "Bluebeard," meanwhile, hinges on the heroine's marriage, discovery of Bluebeard's secret past, escape from murder at his hands, and subsequent remarriage. This structure simply does not apply to *Wuthering Heights*, even though Heathcliff does in some ways resemble Bluebeard as a character due to his cruel behavior. Here too, though, the differences are substantial. Heathcliff's marriage to Isabella is abusive but not murderous, whereas Bluebeard's marriages end almost immediately in murder. Although Heathcliff has a romance of sorts before marrying Isabella, there is only one, and it ends because Catherine rejects Heathcliff, not because he kills her.[9] Heathcliff, too, has wealth, but he acquires it late, and it functions entirely differently in the story. In the final analysis, the novel contains many traces of both fairy tales but cannot be said to depend on either.

Heathcliff and the Supernatural Creatures of Folklore

As many scholars have observed, folk superstitions reign in the world of *Wuthering Heights*. The novel abounds in references to folk customs such as placing pigeon feathers in the bedding of a dying person to prevent their soul from departing.[10] Nelly admits to being "superstitious about dreams"; Catherine in her delirium believes her room to be haunted.[11] Ghosts continually appear, or seem to appear. Even the practice of folklore study is echoed in that the novel centers on scenes of storytelling between Nelly and Lockwood. For Paula Krebs, Lockwood stands in for the new folklorists, patronizing toward the folk but ultimately reliant on his informant, Nelly, to make sense of the community. Krebs makes a compelling argument that Brontë consciously pays "tribute" to folklore—a real part of rural life that survived all the forces Lockwood represents.[12]

Accounts of the realism of *Wuthering Heights* have had to contend with this pervasive superstition. My specific argument about fairy tales and folklore in the novel builds on the assertion of various critics that *Wuthering Heights* ultimately follows the "rules" of realism, but not without recourse to other genres, including supernatural ones.[13] For example, Lyn Pykett, recalling what is often said of Charlotte Brontë's novels, suggests that *Wuthering Heights* contains both a "Gothic framework" and a "second narrative, which seems to move progressively in the direction of Victorian Domestic Realism."[14] Several scholars have persuasively argued that many of the ways in which Emily Brontë engages with the supernatural are perfectly compatible with ordinary realism. Leo Bersani observes that "there is always a realistic 'out' for the extravagances of *Wuthering Heights*"; J. Hillis Miller, that "in spite of its many peculiarities, . . . it is, in its extreme vividness of circumstantial detail, a masterwork of 'realistic' fiction."[15] Barbara Hardy, too, points out that "the supernatural . . . does not have to be accepted as part of the action. Its reality is left tentatively in doubt, within the area of folk-superstition and dreams. As in real life, the ghosts appear in dreams or abnormal states of consciousness."[16] Hardy finds Emily Brontë's use of the supernatural ultimately more realistic than Charlotte's because whereas the ending of *Jane Eyre* is facilitated by a seemingly supernatural event, "in *Wuthering Heights* none of the supernatural 'activity' has this kind of influence on the action."[17] Indeed, the reality of the supernatural in *Wuthering Heights* is not confirmed by an authoritative narrator; instead, as in *Shirley*, the supernatural is a necessary facet of Brontë's realist portrayal of subjective experience in a particular time and place.

Sheila Smith and Susan Stewart have both suggested the folk ballad as an important supernatural genre mixing with realism in *Wuthering Heights*. Smith, explicitly contesting views of supernatural elements in the novel as a sign of immaturity (Leavis) or a weakness (Eagleton), argues that "the novel's power lies in Emily Brontë's perception of the supernatural as an essential dimension of the actual" and that the ballad and folktale are central to the style and subject matter of the novel.[18] Stewart, too, calling *Wuthering Heights* "a veritable storehouse of traditional lore," shows the novel's affinities with several traditional ballads.[19] As Smith and Stewart demonstrate, viewing the folk ballad as an intertext for *Wuthering Heights* does justice to its darkness and helps account for some of its "puzzling features."[20] Both mention the folktale but focus almost exclusively on ballads; I wish to extend their arguments by pursuing the traces of folktale plots and tropes in *Wuthering Heights*.

Much of the scholarly work that has been done on supernatural elements of *Wuthering Heights* has focused on ghosts—understandably so, considering their prominence in the novel.[21] But fairies, too, are explicitly mentioned several times, and have yielded far less scholarly exploration. Lockwood participates in the trend in the period, discussed in earlier chapters, of figuratively associating fairies with women, referring to Cathy as a "beneficent fairy."[22] But most mentions of fairies in the novel are literal. Catherine in her illness half-believes herself to have been transported to the "fairy cave" under Penistone Crag and refers to "elf-bolts" there (161). This fairy cave also attracts Cathy, who forms a vehement desire to "see where the goblin hunter rises in the marsh, and to hear about the *fairishes*," Hareton's country word for them (230). Even the devout servant Joseph leaves cake and cheese "on the table all night, for the fairies" (96).[23] The landscape of *Wuthering Heights* is one in which fairies and their ilk are traditionally believed to exist; folktales about these creatures with which Brontë was familiar should be considered among possible influences on the novel.

Brontë's use of fairies and other supernatural creatures particularly underscores the impossibility of attributing a fixed moral status to Heathcliff. On the one hand, other characters' frequent comparisons of Heathcliff to various evil supernatural creatures prompt the reader to form a negative impression of him. On the other hand, Brontë more subtly portrays Heathcliff's inability to recover from the loss of Catherine as similar to the susceptibility of human beings in folklore to being led away by creatures like fairies, pixies, and will-o'-the-wisps, and the struggle of those mortals to return to their normal lives. Susan Stewart's suggestions of ballad types at work in *Wuthering Heights* include the fairy abduction ballad; she does not outline specific parallels between this story type and the plot of *Wuthering Heights*, but I will do so here.[24] Similar to Charlotte Brontë's use of folklore to undermine the ostensibly happy ending of *Shirley*, Emily Brontë's frequent references to folklore in *Wuthering Heights* have nothing to do with happy endings—and everything to do with the power of the supernatural to articulate real feelings and forces that defy ordinary description.

Since the novel's first appearance, language identifying Heathcliff as some sort of supernatural other has permeated critics' discussions of a central question: whether a reader should ultimately pity or condemn Heathcliff. Charlotte Brontë, in her 1850 preface to *Wuthering Heights*, declares Heathcliff "unredeemed, . . . a man's shape animated by demon life—a Ghoul—an Afreet," she concludes, referring to a supernatural creature she would have encountered in the *Arabian Nights' Entertainments*.[25] Early reviewers agreed; the *Atlas* review calls Heathcliff an "evil genius" and a "tyrant," while the *Eclectic Review* similarly lands on "a perfect monster, more demon than human."[26] E. P. Whipple, writing for the *North American Review*, calls Heathcliff a "brute-demon" and "deformed monster" more reprehensible than Goethe's Mephistopheles, Milton's Satan, and Dickens's Quilp and Squeers.[27] Moral condemnation and supernatural name-calling coincide.

In general, twentieth- and twenty-first-century criticism has softened this assessment, identifying Heathcliff as a composite of "hero" and "villain" qualities. Representatively, Arnold Kettle asserts that "Heathcliff becomes a monster: what he does . . . is cruel and inhuman beyond normal thought," but "despite everything he does and is, we continue to sympathize with Heathcliff—not, obviously, to admire him or defend him, but to give him our inmost sympathy," because "Brontë convinces us that what Heathcliff stands for is morally superior to what the Lintons stand for."[28] While Kettle subordinates Heathcliff's sins to those of the Lintons, it is nonetheless Heathcliff whom he calls "monster" and "inhuman." Since the advent of postcolonial theory, critics have often read Heathcliff as a racial other—an approach that foregrounds the othering of Heathcliff *within* the text and, implicitly or explicitly, shifts ultimate responsibility for Heathcliff's cruelties to those who were first cruel to him. Heathcliff's specific race is ambiguous (he is associated with gypsies, Lascars, and the royalty of India and China), but he is described as "dark" often enough that his appearance is clearly meant to be exceptional in his environment. Susan Meyer interprets *Wuthering Heights* as an indictment of British imperialism in which Brontë "explor[es] what would happen if the suppressed power of the 'savage' outsiders were unleashed."[29] Heathcliff's cruelties are, for Meyer, integral to this "reverse colonization" narrative: "as Heathcliff takes this revenge on an oppressive British society, . . . he himself becomes a subjugator of women" (112). As Meyer demonstrates, the racially inflected disdain directed at Heathcliff in his childhood gives way to his treatment of Isabella as if she herself were "a centipede from the Indies," as Nelly puts it.[30] Approaches like Meyer's lay groundwork for my analysis in that they account for the suffering Heathcliff both experiences and inflicts. Brontë does not present a world that is perfect but for the intrusion of Heathcliff; the Lintons are childish and rude, Hindley is a brute, Nelly is often insensitive, and

Catherine treats Heathcliff atrociously. It may be going too far to maintain that Heathcliff is more sinned against than sinning, but he was at any rate sinned against before sinning—and his perceived otherness has much to do with both.

Heathcliff's known otherness, though, signifies in combination with the unknowability of his individual origins. Wuthering Heights and Thrushcross Grange constitute a closed system of family history: this is a world in which Hareton Earnshaw in 1801 can read his full name along with the year 1500 carved over the door of Wuthering Heights, and one in which two structurally identical families are resolved into a third copy with a minimum of outside genetic input.[31] In this context, Heathcliff's separation from his biological family and the obscurity of that family's history stand out as much as the variously defined otherness of his race; he seems to materialize out of nowhere. Consequently, Heathcliff comes across to the Earnshaws and Lintons as not only other but otherworldly.

This impression leads Heathcliff's acquaintances to compare him to an extensive array of supernatural creatures, encompassing the religious supernatural as well as the folklore supernatural.[32] For example, Nelly insists some of the time that Heathcliff is "a human being" (209), but in the end he looks to her like a "goblin"; "Is he a ghoul, or a vampire? . . . I had read of such hideous, incarnate demons" (359). Isabella goes so far as to ask, "Is Mr Heathcliff a man? And if not, is he a devil? . . . I beseech you to explain, if you can, what I have married" (173). Soon she provides the answers herself: she calls him "incarnate goblin," a "monster," possessing a "diabolical" forehead and "basilisk" eyes, and she concludes that he is "not a human being" (208, 209, 214, 215, 209). What is astonishing here is that the scholarly focus on Heathcliff's race does not go far enough: Heathcliff's acquaintances doubt not only his race but also his species—indeed, even the very earthliness of his origins.[33] The supernatural name-calling is so frequent as to be impossible to miss; the reader absorbs a strong association of Heathcliff with supernatural evil.

Yet this association with such a wide variety of supernatural creatures is ultimately rather imprecise. Vampires drain the lifeblood from their victims and, like ghosts, were once human but cause problems for the living by outstaying their welcome on earth. Basilisks, supernatural snakes, look to kill. Ghouls, as Brontë would have known of them, tend to haunt cemeteries.[34] Goblins will do just about anything, considering the liberal use of the word "goblin" (as noun and adjective) in the period to describe various kinds of fairy beings and demons.[35] Many of these creatures have to do with death, but they have little else in common. Heathcliff might more precisely have been compared, at least early in his life, to a brownie, a creature usually described as ugly and dark who would typically belong to a household for some time performing various domestic and horticultural tasks.[36] But brownies were generally seen as helpful and lucky; in contrast, the characters around Heathcliff dislike him already and are casting about for an explanation of his cruel behavior. They and the reader learn little, however, from the disconnected assortment of supernatural villains they name. After all, despite the occasional critical argument that Heathcliff becomes a werewolf[37] or "might *really* be a demon,"[38] no evidence in the novel suggests that Heathcliff is literally anything but human. That his behavior becomes more cruel after he returns from his three-year absence requires no supernatural explanation; he learned cruelty from the example of his elders, and he returns to Wuthering Heights with a reason to fight back and the power to do so. Like the multiple possibilities considered for his race, the variety of supernatural names for Heathcliff actually reflects the unknowability of his origins and the failure of the Earnshaws and Lintons to interpret him.

Moreover, despite all these characters' attempts to distance themselves from Heathcliff by designating him a supernatural other, it is nearly impossible to identify a characteristic or an action that is entirely unique to Heathcliff. Our first clue to Heathcliff's similarity to the Earnshaws and Lintons is the fact that even the name "Heathcliff" originally belonged to someone else: an Earnshaw son who had died.[39] Surprisingly, it is not Heathcliff but Hareton, the novel's eventual gentle "hero," who one day casually hangs a litter of puppies (217). Heathcliff tortures other people; so does Hindley (who pushes a knife between Nelly's teeth and terrorizes Hareton [114]). He comes to the house as an outsider and is given a family name; so does Frances when she marries Hindley. He prefers roaming on the moors to civilized life; so does Catherine, ultimately, and to some extent Hareton and Cathy as well. He plots revenge; so does Hindley. He marries someone he does not love and causes that person unhappiness; so does Catherine. He loves Catherine; so does Edgar. Throughout the novel, Heathcliff's situation and behavior are extreme but not unique.

In the context of the novel as a whole, two things are true of characters' explicit comparisons of Heathcliff to supernatural creatures: they disproportionately isolate Heathcliff's behavior, and they reflect the strength of the earned and unearned antipathy toward him. As with every other aspect of *Wuthering Heights,* the double layer of narration and doubtful reliability of both narrators frustrate any attempt to pinpoint Brontë's attitude. Indisputably, though, the constant association of Heathcliff with the villains of both the folkloric and the religious supernatural amplifies the reader's impression of him as evil, as critics of all stripes have agreed. However, other more subtle evocations of folklore in the novel actually position Heathcliff as the human victim of the machinations of supernatural creatures. These evocations do not erase Heathcliff's sins—particularly as they appear predominantly after much of his worst behavior so have no bearing on the causes of that behavior—but they complicate both the characterization of Heathcliff and the status of folklore in the novel.

Charlotte Brontë drew on the supernatural or animal bride folktale in order to illuminate the realist novel *Shirley,* and to some extent Catherine and Heathcliff resemble the central couple in a tale of this type. Coming from different places and backgrounds, they temporarily become a pair but ultimately separate due to their fundamental difference in kind. One could argue for viewing Heathcliff as occupying the position of the supernatural bride; he enters Catherine's realm from an unknowable other place, and he is frequently associated with supernatural creatures. As individuals, she seems to be the human and he seems to be the supernatural other. But it is Catherine who behaves like a supernatural bride: she leaves her own kind—not physically but emotionally—in order to form a dyad with Heathcliff in childhood but ultimately returns to her own kind after being exposed to the Lintons' lifestyle. Heathcliff expresses the sense of abandonment common to the husbands in supernatural bride tales. Although Catherine is the more conventional human being of the two, she is structurally the fairy bride. Similarly, in comparing *Wuthering Heights* to folk ballads about demon lovers, Smith has shown that while Heathcliff behaves like a demon lover toward Catherine first, she does the same to him after her death.[40] That one could plausibly argue that either character occupies the role of the supernatural lover speaks to the intricacy of Catherine and Heathcliff's relationship.[41]

Even though Heathcliff is compared to supernatural creatures more often than Catherine is, he displays the behavior of a human being affected by a supernatural creature far more often as well. Folklorist

Katharine Briggs notes that "one of the most common traits of the fairies was their habit of leading humans astray"; eighteenth-century antiquary Joseph Ritson had, after all, stated matter-of-factly that "there are some living who were stolen away by them [fairies], and confined seven years."[42] British folklore is full of these tales of pixies, fairies, will-o'-the-wisps, and pucks; the manner of deception may differ from tale to tale and species to species, but the common denominator is that solitary walkers are liable to be led astray if they encounter these creatures, especially in dark or stormy weather. With some exceptions, those who have been led away by the fairies for any period of time seldom recover. As Carole Silver has said of these tales, "Sadly, even when rescued, a change of body or spirit usually accompanied the return to normal life by those who had been 'away.' Those who returned were often ghosts or ghostlike, in some accounts crumbling into dust, in others wasting away in sorrow for their loss of fairy bliss."[43] Young Charlotte Brontë's numerous retellings of such tales usually brightened the endings, safely depositing the human protagonists back in the everyday world with nothing worse than a sense of awe for what they had seen. Emily Brontë, by contrast, deploys this type of tale in *Wuthering Heights* complete with the traditional consequences for those who encounter fairy beings. Heathcliff—even though he initially reacts to Catherine's death with sound and fury—finally responds to an apparent encounter with Catherine's ghost years later by quite literally wasting away. Silver cites restlessness, absentmindedness, and lack of interest in normal life as common experiences in folklore of human beings who have been lured by the fairies.[44] In the final days of his life, Heathcliff displays all these conditions.

A few examples will provide a sense of the broader tradition. Thomas Crofton Croker's *Fairy Legends and Traditions of the South of Ireland*, previously discussed a possible source for the Brontës' knowledge of folklore, includes a tale called "Llewellyn's Dance" in which two servants are walking "one evening at twilight"—a typical setting for a story of distraction by fairy beings.[45] One of them, Rhys, hears music and runs after it, out of sight; the other, Llewellyn, who heard nothing, reports the incident, but the people in the area remain ignorant of what has really happened until, one year later, someone familiar with "fairy customs" suspects the truth and successfully discovers a "fairy circle" at the spot where Rhys had gone missing (217, 218). He and Llewellyn manage to get Rhys back that day; however, upon returning to his human community, Rhys is "sad, sullen, and silent," and he soon dies (219). Rhys's inability to truly return from his sojourn with the fairies is important: these tales are at least as much about explaining some individuals' failure to thrive in human society as they are about imagining life in fairyland.

In folklore, fairies may lead mortals astray in various ways, for various purposes. Consider James Hogg's tale of Mary Burnet, likely read by the Brontës as it was printed in *Blackwood's Edinburgh Magazine* in February 1828 in an installment of his long-running series *The Shepherd's Calendar* called "Fairies, Brownies, and Witches." In this tale, fairies spirit away Mary Burnet when they observe that a man named John Allanson threatens to taint her sexual purity (Christian morals are here laid over the traditional tale of fairy abduction). The effects of the fairies' interference are dispersed: while Mary lives with the fairies, albeit happily, for the rest of her life, John Allanson literally dies. He believes seven times that he has rediscovered Mary, but each time the figure turns out to be a fairy in Mary's shape. Finally, a fairy pursues him in the guise of one Lady Elizabeth Douglas and lures him to her (illusory) mansion, while in fact the fairies have enchanted the surrounding landscape so that Allanson perceives it inaccurately and takes a fatal fall from his horse. Mary's parents, meanwhile, are "disconsolate," mourning her for seven years after her disappearance until she returns to visit them for a day before departing forever.[46] Thus the sojourn with the fairies, the resulting despondency, and the literal death befall separate characters instead of the usual one (as we saw with "Llewellyn's Dance").

Fairies can lead humans to enervation and death even without physically leading them anywhere. In the story "The Fairy Prince," as recorded in Joseph Ritson's 1831 *Fairy Tales* (copied from the 1673 *Pleasant Treatise of Witches*), a seamstress encounters a fairy prince and accedes to his request that she sew splendid clothing for him and his beloved in time for their impending wedding. But she forgets her promise, and when the fairy prince and his fairy companions arrive on the appointed day, she realizes with horror that she has nothing to give them. Even though the fairy prince responds to her delinquency with a mere look of displeasure, "the lady presently fell into a fit of melancholy, and, being asked by her friends the cause of these alterations and astonishments, related the whole matter; but, notwithstanding all their consolations, pined away, and died not long after."[47] No literal abduction or punishment is needed; the interaction alone causes the human being to waste away and die.

One species of fairy being is particularly associated with the misleading of mortals: the pixy. As Anna Eliza Bray wrote in 1838, many pixies "are sent forth to lead poor travelers astray, to deceive them with those false lights called Will-o'-the-wisp, or to guide them a fine dance in trudging home through woods and water, through bogs and quagmires, and every peril."[48] Pixies are a brand of fairy particularly associated with the west of England, famous like other fairies for a love of music, dancing, and playing tricks on human beings. Bray discusses at length the phenomenon of being "pixy-led"; she cites a "popular belief still existing, not only on the moor, but throughout all this neighborhood, that whenever a person loses his way he is neither more nor less than 'Pixy-led'" (168–69). She identifies certain spots in the region as notorious for pixy-leading and provides various anecdotes, including one in which her own husband was "suddenly surprised and enveloped in such a dense mist, or rather cloud, that he literally could scarcely see" (168). This kind of experience, she says, accounts for the currency of belief in pixy-leading. Bray also observes rather slyly that the intoxicated and the elderly are particularly likely to report being pixy-led (182, 183).

Tales of pixy-leading typically unfold over a shorter time than other tales of being led away by supernatural creatures, and they tend not to dwell on the human being's return to normal consciousness. Typically, the mortal suffers no long-term effects of the experience. Pixy-leading is nonetheless pertinent to my discussion of *Wuthering Heights* for two reasons: first, because pixy-leading involves a deliberate attempt to make the human target leave his or her path in order to follow one set by the pixies, and second, because the term "pixy-led" has entered the English language as an adjective describing the experience (according to the *OED*, it dates back to 1659 spelled as "pixie-led"). Although numerous types of supernatural creatures other than pixies are traditionally believed to lead human walkers astray, no corresponding adjective applies to them. In the following paragraphs, I sometimes use the term "pixy-led" because it so aptly describes the mental and emotional state that I attribute to the novel's characters, even though tales involving other kinds of creatures are equally relevant to *Wuthering Heights*.

An episode in the middle of the novel suggests that Brontë may have had such tales consciously in mind. In this scene, which takes place shortly before Catherine's death, Catherine and Heathcliff alternately occupy the position of pixy-led traveler. Catherine is alone with Nelly in her chamber at Thrushcross Grange, her husband unaware of the severity of her illness. The setting is precisely that of folktales of travelers led astray by supernatural creatures: "There was no moon, and everything beneath lay in misty darkness; not a light gleamed from any house."[49] Nelly believes Catherine to be raving when she looks out the window and claims to see a light at her childhood home, Wuthering Heights, to which Heathcliff has recently returned. Catherine's immediate impulse is to follow this light, as though it were a will-o'-the-wisp, and lead Heathcliff with her:

> "Look!" she cried eagerly, "that's my room, with the candle in it, and the trees swaying before it. . . . It's a rough journey, and a sad heart to travel it; and we must pass by Gimmerton Kirk, to go that journey! We've braved its ghosts often together, and dared each other to stand among the graves and ask them to come. . . . But Heathcliff, if I dare you now, will you venture? If you do, I'll keep you. I'll not lie there by myself: they may bury me twelve feet deep, and throw the church down over me; but I won't rest till you are with me . . . I never will!"
>
> She paused, and resumed with a strange smile. "He's considering . . . he'd rather I'd come to him! Find a way, then! not through that Kirkyard . . . You are slow! Be content, you always followed me!" ([1847] 1985, 164)

The positions and directions of Catherine and Heathcliff seem to be in flux here; Catherine speaks at first as though they would be walking in the same direction but later, more accurately, as though they are apart. Throughout the passage, however, Catherine initiates and Heathcliff follows. She declares her intention to urge Heathcliff to follow her even to death. Even though Catherine is the one who sees the faraway, specious light in this scene, she essentially becomes a will-o'-the-wisp for Heathcliff after she dies.[50]

Of course, Heathcliff partly resembles those who have been away with the fairies in that he is, quite literally, mysteriously absent for three years. That absence, though, while it may provide a clue that Brontë intended the reader to associate Heathcliff with fairy abduction, does not itself produce the behavior in Heathcliff that resembles that of human characters in folktales who have sojourned with supernatural beings. Whatever Heathcliff does during those three years earns him the financial power to purchase Wuthering Heights and assume a position in local society.[51] Instead, Heathcliff acts like a person affected by supernatural beings later, in his inability to get over Catherine's death. The notion of being pixy-led or away in fairyland has served to explain states of being also known as intoxication, depression, mental illness, or obsession.[52] For example, Sir Walter Scott's well-known *Minstrelsy of the Scottish Border* records a belief that people suffering from consumption were the victims of the fairies' theft of their souls.[53] But the notion also provides an apt metaphor for extreme grief. To be pixy-led is to be forced to follow someone to a realm separate from human life. Heathcliff is essentially pixy-led by the ghost or memory of Catherine, which he experiences as beckoning him to follow—to seek physical proximity to Catherine's body (past or present) through sleeping in her bed, seeing traces of her everywhere, opening her grave to look at her, and undertaking fairly elaborate planning in order to be buried next to her.

Although Heathcliff explicitly desires to be haunted by Catherine, he does not really get his wish—and the pixy-leading does not really begin—until years after her death. As he tells it late in the novel, her ghost "beguile[d] me with the spectre of a hope, through eighteen years!"[54] He recalls to Nelly that over the years since Catherine's death, "when I slept in her chamber . . . the moment I closed my eyes, she was either outside the window, or sliding back the panels, or entering the room, or even resting her darling head on the same pillow as she did when a child. And I must open my lids to see. And so I opened and closed them a hundred times a night—to be always disappointed!" (321). Heathcliff continually experiences a vague sensation of Catherine's presence, without actually seeing, touching, or speaking with her. Then, in the final days of his life, Heathcliff finally seems to see Catherine's ghost; he tells Nelly that he senses a "strange change approaching," and Nelly catches him seeing something that is not there and muttering "the name of Catherine, coupled with some wild term of endearment, or suffering; and spoken as one would speak to a person present—low and earnest, and wrung from the depths of his soul" (353, 362). The "strange change" yields the complete reversal in his behavior that renders him similar to human beings led away by fairies or pixies in traditional folktales.

Brontë dramatizes this reversal in what Q. D. Leavis has called a "prolonged account of his uncanny obsession and death."[55] Most prominently, Heathcliff stops eating; Brontë details the household's repeated, unsuccessful attempts to persuade him to eat at each meal. On the first day, Heathcliff refuses breakfast; at dinner (the midday meal), he "took his knife and fork, and was going to commence eating, when the inclination appeared to become suddenly extinct. He laid them on the table, looked eagerly towards the window, then rose and went out."[56] He says he will wait to eat until supper, but at suppertime, he announces that he will eat the next morning (358, 359). At the next day's breakfast, Heathcliff again sits at the table in response to Nelly's entreaties but again loses interest in the act of reaching for his food (361). Nelly here stops trying to persuade him to eat, and he passes the few remaining days before his death largely in a bedroom, neither eating nor sleeping.

Heathcliff's seeming inability to eat is just one manifestation of the general apathy that apparently possesses him at this point. "I take so little interest in my daily life, that I hardly remember to eat, and drink," he explains (353). One day, having angrily grabbed Cathy's hair, he suddenly looks at her and relaxes his hold (350). He reflects to Nelly, "[Is this not] an absurd termination to my violent exertions? I get levers and mattocks to demolish the two houses . . . and when everything is ready, and in my power, I find the will to lift a slate off either roof has vanished! . . . I don't care for striking, I can't take the trouble to raise my hand! . . . I have lost the faculty of enjoying their destruction" (352–53).

Heathcliff's supposed purpose in life for the past eighteen years—revenge against the Earnshaws and Lintons through Cathy and Hareton—evaporates when its fruition is at hand. "I have to remind myself to breathe—almost to remind my heart to beat! . . . it is by compulsion, that I do the slightest act, not prompted by one thought, and by compulsion, that I notice anything alive or dead, which is not associated with one universal idea" (354). Heathcliff's vanished interest in eating, sleeping, or pursuing once-cherished activities is likely to remind a modern reader of clinical depression. Although Heathcliff's behavior would seem to justify this comparison, in fact he does find incentive in "one universal idea," odd though it may seem: physical reunion with Catherine's corpse through burial beside it.[57] Revenge against his enemies has no bearing on this goal, and eating actively hinders him in attaining it; hence, he abandons these pursuits.

Indeed, Nelly uses the word "monomania" to describe Heathcliff's condition (354). When Heathcliff first learns of Catherine's death, he cries, "I pray one prayer—I repeat it till my tongue stiffens—Catherine

Earnshaw, may you not rest, as long as I am living!" (204). Clearly, Heathcliff does indeed repeat this one supplication for the rest of his life. Even eighteen years after her death, everything signifies Catherine to him: "The entire world is a dreadful collection of memoranda that she did exist, and that I have lost her!" (353). As every object or person simply reminds him of the loss of Catherine, "I have a single wish, and my whole being and faculties are yearning to attain it. They have yearned towards it so long, and so unwaveringly, that I'm convinced it *will* be reached—and *soon*—because it has devoured my existence" (354, emphasis in original). He sleeps in the bed he once shared with Catherine when they were children instead of in his own room (359). Having already bribed the sexton to bury him next to Catherine and remove the adjacent sides of their coffins so that their bodies may intermingle as they decay (319), Heathcliff has no instructions regarding the words to be said at his burial; "I have nearly attained *my* heaven; and that of others is altogether unvalued, and uncoveted by me!" (363, emphasis in original). So eager is he to attain his heaven that he not only stops eating but also opens the bedroom window on a stormy night that turns out to be his last; Nelly discovers his body soaked with rain (364).

Although spurred by his experience of Catherine's ghost, Heathcliff's withdrawal and death are clearly deliberate. This makes James Hogg's poem "Kilmeny" (1813) an important intertext for *Wuthering Heights*.[58] A young girl named Kilmeny is stolen by the fairies and lives with them for one of the traditional periods of time: seven years. Although she asks to return home in order to tell others of what she had seen, she ends up largely avoiding the society of human beings; instead, "she loved to raike [wander] the lanely glen, / And keepèd afar frae the haunts of men," telling her stories to an attentive audience of animals (ln. 290–91). After a month and a day (another traditional period),

> Kilmeny sought the green-wood wene [furze or gorse];
> There laid her down on the leaves sae green,
> And Kilmeny on earth was never mair seen
>
> (ln. 321–23)

Kilmeny cannot resume her former life in human society. Realizing this, she takes control: the line beginning "Kilmeny sought" emphasizes her agency and active pursuit of a way out. The poem does not make clear whether she leaves through traditional death or an undefined form of renewed fairy abduction; the fairies are rather more similar than usual to angels in this poem, so these two possibilities amount to the same thing. Regardless, in her abandonment of ordinary pursuits and apparently intentional death, Kilmeny anticipates the behavior of Heathcliff.

Critics have offered various explanations for Heathcliff's strange behavior in his final days. Elizabeth Helsinger is right to note that Catherine's ghost apparently "prevents Heathcliff from eating" at the end of his life; she interprets this prevention, though, as "a total denial of the physical body."[59] While this is true on a literal level, the purpose of denying Heathcliff's body food (whether Catherine actively participates in the denial or not) is to get that body to the graveyard. Carol Margaret Davison has suggested that Heathcliff "undergoes a spiritual transformation" at this time, pointing especially to the evaporation of his interest in revenge.[60] Davison's points are well taken, though I believe they underestimate the importance of Catherine in Heathcliff's mental life. Catherine—or her ghost, or her memory—affects Heathcliff as powerfully as a supernatural creature like a fairy can affect a human being. To be pixy-led is not the same as to be lost; whereas a lost person wanders about in search of direction, a pixy-led person experiences a compulsion to follow the pixies' way. In his final days, Heathcliff can only bring himself to follow the path that leads to what remains of Catherine.[61]

That Heathcliff's haunting by Catherine comes after years of wishing for it suggests that some are more apt to be pixy-led than others. Both Kilmeny and Mary Burnet catch the attention of the fairies due to their sexual purity, even as Little Red Riding Hood catches the attention of the wolf, arguably, due to an aura of sexual availability. As Bray points out, the intoxicated are particularly likely to report pixy trickery—because, she implies, no pixies need even be present for a drunken man to err on the way home. Husbands in animal or fairy bride tales have often been disappointed or hurt by human women before meeting the supernatural beloved. Beauty in "Beauty and the Beast" loves her father but otherwise does not fit in at all with the family of her birth and shows no interest in marriage to any available men. To varying degrees, all these figures are led away because they are ready to be led away. There is a circularity at work here that is entirely in keeping with the pervasive circularity of *Wuthering Heights*. It is not precisely right to say that Heathcliff loses interest in revenge because he is being beckoned by Catherine-as-pixy; rather, for him to experience this haunting is identical with his realization that he never cared for revenge anywhere near as much as he cared for Catherine. It is only when he is on the brink of attaining that revenge that he can see its futility; this, perhaps, is why Heathcliff only begins to experience an overwhelming haunting by Catherine eighteen years after her death.

Thus, while nearly everyone around him sees him as a folkloric or hellish monster, Heathcliff behaves as though affected by a supernatural creature himself. Again, after all, he is human. Brontë's portrayals of both Heathcliff's effects on others and the consequences he suffers himself belong to her broader strategy in *Wuthering Heights* (as in some of her poetry) of demonstrating that real things and real people may signify as though they are supernatural in their power. To prove to Isabella that Heathcliff is merely human would be cold comfort; similarly, whether or not ghosts truly exist has no bearing on Heathcliff's final inability to focus on anything but Catherine. Ultimately, yet another way in which Heathcliff is larger than life is this: only with reference to the supernatural can the force of both his influence and his own experience be adequately conveyed.

* * *

Heathcliff does indeed attain his heaven. But the reader, too, is pixy-led by Catherine's ghost, from the moment Lockwood first hears her tapping on the window.[62] Although Lockwood seems satisfied while standing over the graves of Catherine, Edgar, and Heathcliff at the end of the novel that there will be no "unquiet slumbers, for the sleepers in that quiet earth," many readers do not share his feeling that all has now been adequately explained.[63] Critics, certainly, do not, as evidenced by the extensive array of attempts to provide an explanatory key in the form of everything from Marxism (Terry Eagleton) to Brontë's supposed unconscious sexual desire for her dead sister (Camille Paglia). J. Hillis Miller has suggested that *Wuthering Heights*, even more than most realist fiction, positions the reader as a detective: "The reader of *Wuthering Heights*, like the narrator, is led deeper and deeper into the text by the expectation that sooner or later the last veil will be removed."[64] The raison d'être of the narrative is to account for the strange behavior that Lockwood and the reader observe in the novel's first pages—what accounts for the odd dynamic among Heathcliff, Cathy, and Hareton, and who was Catherine Earnshaw/Linton/Heathcliff?

Yet however eagerly the reader seeks an explanation, multiple features of the text thwart the attempt. Like the landscape shrouded in mist or darkness that sets the stage for a tale of a traveler led away by the fairies, the narration of *Wuthering Heights* is on many levels obscure and disorienting. The bulk of the story is filtered through not one but two narrators, neither of whom is fully reliable. Many of the primary characters have identical or similar names. With good reason has Nancy Armstrong called the world of this novel a "historical cul-de-sac."[65] Heathcliff's activities during his three-year absence are never revealed, nor is the source of his income. The character who seems like she ought to be the heroine, Catherine, dies halfway through the book, giving way to a whole other phase of the story featuring the less compelling second generation of characters. Critics continue to debate whether Heathcliff is the hero or the villain, as he bears strong traces of both. Ultimately, though readers may start by assuming that they know the way through a seemingly realist Victorian novel, in *Wuthering Heights* there is no "secret explanation which will allow [the reader] to understand the novel wholly," no "head referent which would still the wandering movement from emblem to emblem, from story to story, from generation to generation, from Catherine to Catherine, from Hareton to Hareton, from narrator to narrator."[66]

To identify *Wuthering Heights* as an anti–fairy tale, then, is more or less right, though not for precisely the reasons typically adduced. *Wuthering Heights* chiefly differs from classic literary fairy tales not in that it lacks a happy ending but in that its resolution is complicated and unsatisfying. It overlays a comic ending (the impending marriage of Cathy and Hareton) with a tragic ending (the fall of Heathcliff). Brontë teases the reader with numerous indications that the novel will turn out, like *Jane Eyre,* to resolve itself into "Beauty and the Beast," only to starkly undermine the tale's role in the narrative by refusing Beast status to Heathcliff and passing it off to a more minor character. What is consistent throughout the novel is its frequent reference to folklore. From ghosts to pigeon feathers to "fairishes," the figures and beliefs of folklore pervade the narrative. Instead of selecting one or even two fairy-tale plots around which to structure the novel, Brontë draws liberally from the folktales of the British Isles in such a way as to underscore the heterogeneity and unruliness of the story. Heathcliff, in particular, is made to seem both more cruel and more sympathetic by the folklore allusions in different parts of the novel. Emily Brontë clearly intended for readers to be unable to settle into any definitive interpretation of the story; like mortals led away by the fairies, readers are not quite sure where they have been, and equally unsure that they will ever fully find their way back.

PART IV

What Is Real?

7 Anne Brontë's Fairy-Tale Realism

An entry in Kate Beaton's *Hark! A Vagrant* comic sums up the long-prevalent attitude toward Anne Brontë's role in her family: while Charlotte and Emily ogle scowling men and imagine fantastic stories for them, Anne points out their rudeness and their liquor bottles. Her sisters demur, but she insists, "I'm just telling the truth!"[1] Although the amount of scholarship on the youngest Brontë's work remains dwarfed by the writing published every year on Charlotte and Emily, interest in Anne has increased in recent years. Unchanged, however, is the consensus that Anne is the most realist of the Brontës: indeed, neither *Agnes Grey* (1847) nor *The Tenant of Wildfell Hall* (1848) contains anything like Rochester's miraculously transmitted call to Jane Eyre or the ghosts of *Wuthering Heights*. Consequently, scholarly attention to the role of fairy tales in the works of the Brontës has never extended to Anne.[2] But she was as aware of fairy tales as her siblings. As discussed in chapters 1 and 3, young Anne, too, heard beloved servant Tabitha Aykroyd's stories from local fairy lore, read issues of *Blackwood's Edinburgh Magazine* containing fairy poems and fairy-tale allusions, and participated in the group construction of the fictional worlds of Glass Town and, later, Gondal; as late as 1840, she compares the title flowers in her poem "The Bluebell" to fairy gifts.[3] Even though Anne Brontë's adult writing carries few obvious traces of fairy tales, understanding her work in its own right requires serious consideration of the possibility that the nonrealist reading and writing of the Brontë siblings' youth produced a meaningful effect on Anne's adult work as well.

In this chapter, I suggest, first, that *Agnes Grey*, despite its prosaic style and subject matter, builds its message of perseverance around a core "Cinderella" story. Second, I argue that *The Tenant of Wildfell Hall* shares with Charles Perrault's "Bluebeard" (1697) a fundamental kinship that does not conflict with the novel's unusual structure and unflinchingly realist aims. Rather, the classic fairy-tale portrayal of a disastrous marriage to and escape from a villain provides an ideal foundation for this complex and topical novel. The parallels are subtle; unlike Charlotte, Anne does not explicitly name any fairy tales in her novels. Yet *The Tenant of Wildfell Hall*, even as it plainly "tells the truth" about marriage to Byronic alcoholics, strikingly resembles "Bluebeard." As I noted in the introduction, my project in this book is to explore not only overt fairy-tale allusions but also the less obvious ways that fairy tales influence novels and poetry for adults. Recognizing the relevance of fairy tales to the structure and themes of Anne Brontë's novels constitutes a new approach to the ongoing scholarly effort to enrich our understanding of the youngest Brontë's work; it also indicates that fairy tales so deeply penetrated nineteenth-century British culture as to shape not only the works of fantasy aficionados like Charlotte but even novels ostensibly free of all enchantment.

Agnes Grey: The Cinderella Governess

Anne Brontë spent several unhappy years working as a governess for two wealthy families; all the Brontë siblings chafed against the need to live away from home and minister to others rather than working on their own reading and writing. While she disliked the first family for whom she worked, the Inghams, she particularly disapproved of the fashionable Robinsons at Thorp Green. In her diary paper of July 31, 1845, Anne recalls the diary paper she had written four years earlier: "I was then at Thorp Green and now I am only just escaped from it—I was wishing to leave [it?] then and if I had known that I had four years longer to stay how wretched I would have been . . . but during my stay I have had some very unpleasant and undreamt experience of human nature."[4] Evidently she was never happy in this position. But the situation deteriorated further when Branwell joined the household in January 1843 in order to tutor the family's son. For some time, Branwell carried on an affair with his pupil's mother, Lydia Robinson. Anne seems to have been aware of this affair by the time she handed in her resignation in June 1845; only in

July did it become public, causing Branwell to resign as well. Very little of Anne's personal writing from this time survives; we can infer, however, that Anne's horror at Branwell's actions contributed both to the strong language in the 1845 diary paper and to the vehemence with which she criticizes immorality in general in both her novels.

In Anne Brontë's first novel, *Agnes Grey* (1847), she fictionalizes her experiences working for both the Inghams and the Robinsons (called the Bloomfields and the Murrays in the novel). In addition to omitting the Branwell episode, she also invents a romance plot for her heroine. As would be the case in *The Tenant of Wildfell Hall*, Brontë strives for unadorned realism in her portrayal of the lives of the landed gentry, the clergy, and the working-class inhabitants of the north of England.[5] Much of the novel conveys Brontë's convictions about religion and the way it should be practiced; the hero is curate Edward Weston, who clashes with his superior, the rector, apparently due to his modest style and his insistence on treating the poor with kindness rather than reproaching them for their lowly status. Accordingly, many critics, including Jennifer M. Stolpa, Elizabeth Leaver, and Mary Summers, have read *Agnes Grey* as primarily a religious text.[6]

Another strand of criticism—not incompatible with religious readings—concerns *Agnes Grey*'s relationship to education. Sandro Jung maintains that the narrator advocates an education informed by Christian principles.[7] For Elizabeth Langland, similarly, *Agnes Grey* "is foremost a novel dealing with education; it is a novel *of* education (Agnes's) and *about* education (her attempts as governess to educate her charges) whose goal is to bring about an education in the reader."[8] As Langland's language indicates, many scholars have also discussed *Agnes Grey*'s relationship to the *Bildungsroman*. Most, including Langland, either argue or take it to be obvious that *Agnes Grey* is indeed a *Bildungsroman*. Meanwhile, Cates Baldridge and Amanda Claybaugh suggest that the *Bildungsroman* gives way to other structures as the novel progresses, while Philippa Janu argues against using the *Bildungsroman* as a hermeneutic for understanding the governess novel more generally, finding the narrator's work as a governess to be precisely the impediment to her own education and development.[9] Many of Janu's examples of obstacles to Agnes's development seem to me simply to provide more evidence that her story *is* a *Bildungsroman*, since the presence of such obstacles is already built into the genre (and since none of those obstacles ultimately prevents Agnes from replacing youth and instability with marriage and financial security: the crucial outcomes of the English *Bildungsroman*). On the most basic structural level, Agnes's status at the end of the novel as compared to the beginning links the novel to the *Bildungsroman*—and to a certain form of traditional fairy tale. Franco Moretti has said of *Bildungsromane* that "deep down, these novels are fairy tales."[10] There is indeed, "deep down," a kinship among *Agnes Grey*, the *Bildungsroman*, and the traditional fairy tale that focuses on a youthful protagonist who must leave home and achieve maturation alone because of a disturbance in the stable family.

However, specific characteristics of *Agnes Grey* call for a more specific parallel. To begin with, the critics skeptical of the *Bildungsroman* label are right to note that Agnes is a little old at the beginning of the novel ("above eighteen") and that she already possesses the qualities she needs to succeed in life, including piety, determination, and work ethic.[11] Moreover, Janu is correct that a major concern of Agnes's is to encourage education and development not so much in herself as in the reader.[12] In addition, as Janu, Claybaugh, Drew Lamonica Arms, Robert Butterworth, and Robin L. Inboden have discussed, *Agnes Grey* often focuses on the governess's work.[13] This work poses two major problems for Agnes: it is repetitive, frustrating, and largely unavailing, and it threatens Agnes's own integrity.[14] Overall, *Agnes Grey*'s instructive presentation of the toils of a worthy but underappreciated heroine links it very precisely to classic continental versions of "Cinderella."

Although fairy tales are often associated with their supernatural elements, Perrault's and the Grimms' versions of "Cinderella"—the ones Anne Brontë was most likely to have known—are particularly well suited to Brontë's didactic purposes. Both explicitly foreground morality, offering a clear message that goodness will be rewarded; for example, we are told at the end of Perrault's version that Cinderella "était aussi bonne que belle" ("was as good as she was beautiful"; trans. mine).[15] The final sentence before the moral recounts that Cinderella forgave her cruel stepsisters and arranged advantageous marriages for both of them (262). The Grimms' version, though more interested in punishing the stepsisters than demonstrating Cinderella's forgiveness, is explicitly Christian: in the first sentence, Cinderella's dying mother enjoins her to "be good and pious, and then the good God will always protect you."[16] In this version, Cinderella's ball dresses come not from a fairy godmother but from the little tree beneath which she "wept and prayed" "thrice a day" (122). Both versions emphasize Cinderella's characteristics—patience, hard work, perseverance, generosity, and piety—that are entirely in keeping with the lessons, informed by Christianity, that Brontë teaches in *Agnes Grey*.

Importantly, Brontë's novel and these versions of "Cinderella" feature heroines who seem born with these characteristics already but find themselves in situations in which they are not appreciated. Cinderella does not learn to be good over the course of the story; as Perrault puts it, she already possessed a peerless goodness inherited from her mother, who was nothing less than "la meilleure personne du monde" ("the best person in the world"; trans. mine; 259). Brontë does not use such hyperbolic language, but Agnes reveals herself in the first chapter to be as generous and helpful to her parents and older sister as they will allow the baby of the family to be. Although Agnes certainly acquires wisdom about the state of human behavior and the outside world over the course of the novel, her personality does not substantially change. Agnes's challenge, like Cinderella's, is not so much to develop as to persevere: rather than stories "of development," we might characterize *Agnes Grey* and "Cinderella" as stories of waiting for acknowledgment that one has sufficiently developed already. Crucially, "Cinderella" comes very close to being not a "rise tale" but a "restoration tale"—that is, one in which the protagonist begins in a comparatively high status, falls, and is restored to approximately the original position at the end of the tale.[17] Despite popular perception, the classic continental Cinderella story is not one of "rags to riches"; rather, Cinderella begins as the daughter of a "Gentleman" (Perrault) or a "rich man" (Grimm and Grimm) and then falls to a lower position when her stepmother takes over the household.[18] Cinderella suffers not only because she is a mistreated servant but also because she should not be a servant in the first place. Cinderella is in fact situated much like the Victorian governess, not quite belonging either to the servant class or to the wealthy family. Agnes "falls" to the position of governess when her father loses money on an investment.[19] One reason she feels uncomfortable in the Bloomfield and Murray households is that she is treated as a menial but does not believe herself to be one; if anything, she feels superior to her employers on the grounds of morality. Agnes dislikes walking with the two Murray sisters to and from church, for example, because she receives harsh looks from their genteel companions if she walks alongside them but hates to walk behind "and thus appear to acknowledge my own inferiority; for in truth, I considered myself pretty nearly as good as the best of them, and wished them to know that I did so, and not to imagine that I looked upon myself as a mere domestic."[20] As with many governesses, Agnes's class background barely differs from that of her employers: her mother was a squire's daughter, disinherited for marrying a poor clergyman, Agnes's father. Perhaps more importantly, though, Agnes believes that she and her family deserve respect for their principles and their abilities.

What both Cinderella and Agnes must do, then, is work and wait. Their work responsibilities differ, of course; Cinderella, famously, must do rough household chores, while Agnes works as a governess. Still, both young women must complete difficult and tedious tasks while remaining polite to their often-unreasonable employers. The second family to employ Agnes includes two teenaged daughters not much younger than she; these girls, Rosalie and Matilda, resemble Cinderella's stepsisters. They are less unruly than the younger children Agnes had attempted to manage in her first position, but they are nonetheless careless, frivolous, and heedless of their studies. In addition to teaching lessons, Agnes often must assume other tasks to make the girls' lives easier—completing the more difficult and less ostentatious aspects of a painting, for example, which Rosalie then displays to others as entirely her own work. Mrs. Murray occupies the role of the evil stepmother in this scenario. "Evil" is likely too strong a term for her (and not one that Brontë would have employed), but she certainly mistreats Agnes. She is often exacting, unfair, and unreasonable, scrutinizing Agnes's behavior and blaming her for the shortcomings of her daughters. Mrs. Murray evokes the Grimms' evil stepmother, who more than once dumps lentils into ashes and instructs Cinderella to separate them. Like the Bloomfields, the Murrays never believe Agnes when her statements contradict those of her charges; when they make arrangements, they never consider her comfort. "Cinderella" is also evoked in that Rosalie attends a ball—before which she asks Agnes to postpone her Christmas visit to her family. "Why so?" Agnes asks, "I shall not be present at the ball" (72). Rosalie simply, ludicrously, wishes Agnes to admire her finery before she sets off for the festivities. Of course, unlike Cinderella, Agnes does not particularly want to attend the ball herself, and Rosalie's younger sister does not attend either. Nevertheless, Brontë does entitle the chapter "The Ball" even though the ball itself occupies little space in the narrative, and a scenario in which one girl attends a ball and another does not will inevitably evoke "Cinderella" for many readers.

Agnes Grey also follows "Cinderella" in using a romance plot to facilitate the heroine's reward: it will be a suitor who discovers her worth.[21] One of Rosalie and Matilda's most dangerous similarities to Cinderella's stepsisters is that they interfere with Agnes's growing intimacy with Mr. Weston. Rosalie would never "stoop" to marry a curate (she even rejects the advances of the rector she appears to love due to the belief that he is beneath her socially), but she nevertheless campaigns for Mr. Weston's affections as soon as she perceives his interest in Agnes. Despite this attempt to usurp Agnes's position, though, Mr. Weston obviously prefers the governess and seeks out her company frequently. Upon the death of her father, Agnes leaves the Murray household to establish a school with her mother. Instead of a glass slipper, Agnes is forced to leave a dog, Snap, whom Matilda had demanded as a pet and then rejected, at which point he had become a pet of Agnes's. Nevertheless, the Murrays had sent the dog to work for the village rat-catcher, "a man notorious for his brutal treatment of his canine slaves."[22] Mr. Weston, having rescued Snap, seeks Agnes for some time at the seaside town to which she has moved with her mother; he finds her at last when Snap runs up to her on the beach. As Cinderella's shoe fits, Agnes's dog sniffs out his true mistress. Mr. Weston soon declares his love for Agnes, and they are married. Mr. Weston is no prince; while Cinderella does rise from gentleman's daughter to royalty, Agnes marries a man who replicates her family's original status by providing an income "amply sufficient for our requirements" (194). This modest version of the "restoration"-fairy-tale ending clearly renders the heroine content.

Although many would assume that Brontë's realist motives differ starkly from those of a magical tale, the affinities between "Cinderella" and *Agnes Grey* surpass the vague resemblance to "Cinderella" that can be identified in any story of a woman who achieves financial stability through marriage—and they do so not despite but because of Brontë's aim to educate.

Marrying Bluebeard: *The Tenant of Wildfell Hall*

Like *Agnes Grey*, *The Tenant of Wildfell Hall* is insistently realist, and no explicit allusions to fairy tales appear. In one of the few critical mentions of fairy tales in relation to Anne Brontë, Elizabeth Langland contrasts *The Tenant of Wildfell Hall* with *Jane Eyre* and "fairy tale romance" by noting that the heroine's development continues after she marries.[23] This statement encapsulates many nonspecialists' view of fairy tales as effectively monolithic in content and structure. Yet one dark fairy tale that we know to have been a favorite in Victorian culture in general and the Brontë household in particular—"Bluebeard"—is remarkably similar to *Wildfell Hall* in structure and themes, not least in that it dramatizes the continuing development of the heroine after her wedding. A basic summary that characterizes both "Bluebeard" and *The Tenant of Wildfell Hall* is easy to write. The heroine marries a rich man she does not know very well, suspecting that he has a checkered past but not knowing the extent of his faults until it is too late. These faults include inappropriate behavior with women from his past. Feeling increasingly threatened the more she understands the man she has married, the heroine turns to her family for assistance. Ultimately, she survives, her husband dies, and she marries a nicer man. In what follows, I argue that this parallel is not only extensive but also significant: likening an outwardly respectable English marriage to a horrifying fairy-tale union underscores Brontë's exposé of the danger real women face at the hands of their husbands. In other words, subtle evocations of "Bluebeard" throughout the novel, without compromising Brontë's realism, remind the reader that an abusive, alcoholic husband, however aristocratic he may be, is not so different from the murderous fairy-tale husband.

"Bluebeard" was everywhere in Victorian print culture. Word searches in early nineteenth-century issues of *Blackwood's Edinburgh Magazine* tend to yield more results for "Bluebeard" than for any other individual continental fairy tale. Sometimes these are offhand comparisons; more substantial discussions include the February 1833 issue's eighteen-page review of Ludwig Tieck's theatrical version of "Bluebeard," including extensive excerpts from the play.[24] Although the Brontës' guaranteed access to *Blackwood's* lapsed after December 1831, we know they continued to see it as often as they could in subsequent years. This is therefore one of many places Anne Brontë may have encountered "Bluebeard"; she certainly encountered it in her siblings' works, especially *Jane Eyre* (see chapter 4). In fact, deploying the same fairy tale in *The Tenant of Wildfell Hall* may have been among the ways Anne used this novel to respond to *Jane Eyre* and, perhaps, *Wuthering Heights*.

To be sure, representing prosaic, unpolished reality was crucial to Brontë, who all but borrowed Charles Dickens's defiant "IT IS TRUE" from the 1841 preface to *Oliver Twist*. Little of Brontë's personal writing remains,[25] but, fortunately for scholars, she laid out her intentions in a forceful preface to *Wildfell Hall*'s second edition, prompted by the virulent reviews of the first edition. The word "coarse," representatively, appears in at least four reviews from 1848 and 1849, twice paired with "brutal."[26] Brontë's preface to the novel retorts, in the familiar language of nineteenth-century realism, "my object in writing the following pages, was . . . to tell the truth, for truth always conveys its own moral to those who are able to receive it. . . . When we have to do with vice and vicious characters, I maintain it is better to depict them as they really are than as they would wish to appear."[27] Brontë's language brooks little doubt: whatever her other motives, one was to reveal the evils of substance abuse and the inordinate power men held in marriage.

Wildfell Hall begins with familiar markers of a realist novel: a specific time ("autumn of 1827") and the noncommittal but decidedly English setting of "—shire." Already we are not in the world of "once upon a time," as the rest of the novel confirms. Although the story ends with marriage, another significant wedding occurs in the middle. Structurally, *Wildfell Hall* differs from most fairy tales (and from most contemporary novels, for that matter).[28] The first and third sections of the novel purport to be a long letter Gilbert Markham writes to a friend on the subject of the mysterious new tenant at Wildfell Hall, Helen, with whom Gilbert quickly falls in love. The second section goes back in time, consisting of a lengthy excerpt from Helen's diary which she gives to Gilbert in order to explain that she has fled to Wildfell Hall with her young son in order to avoid her alcoholic, abusive husband, Arthur Huntingdon. During the third section, Huntingdon dies, freeing Helen to marry Gilbert.

All these events are presented in an unimpeachably realist manner. A few supernatural references appear, but almost all are both figurative and religious, including the words "demon," "witch," and "fiend."[29] Even a realist novel, however, may draw on other genres. The very title, *The Tenant of Wildfell Hall*, clearly draws on the Gothic tradition, leaving the "tenant" unnamed and evoking a "wild" and "fell" edifice. Scholars such as N. M. Jacobs and Jan B. Gordon have discussed the key role of the Gothic mode in this novel, noting in particular the similarity between the common Gothic frame tale and the novel's otherwise puzzling structure. Within the story itself, however, Brontë overturns many of the expectations of readers familiar with the Gothic. The mysterious tenant is an ordinary young woman with an ordinary name, albeit a temporary alias. Nor does the edifice prove to be the Gothic mansion its name suggests. Gilbert Markham describes his first approach to Wildfell Hall by using the novel's only extensive supernatural imagery: "The gigantic warrior that stood on one side of the gateway, and the lion that guarded the other, were sprouted into such fantastic shapes as resembled nothing either in heaven or earth; but, to my young imagination, they presented all of them a goblinish appearance, that harmonized well with the ghostly legends and dark traditions our old nurse had told us respecting the haunted hall and its departed occupants."[30]

While Gilbert projects Gothic ideas onto Wildfell Hall's outward appearance, however, in fact it is Helen's safe haven from the true place of danger, the ordinary and innocuously named Grassdale. Brontë's sole portrayal of an otherworldly atmosphere is deliberately misleading. While the important Gothic trope of male violence against women is central to *Wildfell Hall*, most other tropes of the genre—exotic setting, cruel patriarchs, sensationalist subject matter on the level of incest or necrophilia, and supernatural events, for example—are nowhere to be seen.

One might expect fairy tales to be useful to Brontë chiefly to facilitate a similar disrupting of assumptions; however, fairy tales are not all the same, and "Bluebeard" is unusual in ways particularly suited to Brontë's novel. The typical fairy-tale cast of characters is askew, for one thing: the title character begins as the husband of the heroine but turns out to be the villain. The story commences with a marriage instead of leading toward one (though there is a modest recuperation of marriage when the heroine weds a second time). It does not feature any magic except for the key that, inexplicably, cannot be wiped clean of blood. Pinpointing the moral is difficult; Perrault's tongue-in-cheek "moralités" are not intended as moral lessons at all, and the heroine ultimately marries a man who "lui fit oublier le mauvais temps qu'elle avait passé avec la Barbe-bleue" ("made her forget the terrible time she spent with Bluebeard"; trans. mine).[31] If she forgets, she cannot gain any wisdom from the experience. Perhaps the best clue to a moral of "Bluebeard" is the correspondence between Bluebeard's behavior and inner qualities and his threatening appearance. Supposedly, his blue beard "le rendait si laid & si terrible, qu'il n'était ni femme ni fille qui ne s'enfuit de devant lui" ("made him so ugly and so terrifying that there was not a single woman or girl who did not flee from him"; trans. mine).[32] Not a single woman or girl, that is, except the many who have already married him, like the wife in the story, for his riches. Although initially repulsed, she reflects after enjoying his lavish festivities that perhaps he "n'avait plus la barbe si bleue" ("did not have such a very blue beard after all"; trans. mine; 220). Like the debonair manners of the wolf in Perrault's "Little Red Riding Hood," Bluebeard's civilized accoutrements deflect attention from both his menacing-looking body and his beastly impulses long enough to entrap women. Although "Bluebeard" begins with "Once upon a time . . ." and reaches a happy ending, its otherwise unusual structure and dark content suit Brontë's cautionary novel very well.

As I discussed while arguing that *Jane Eyre* vacillates between "Beauty and the Beast" and "Bluebeard" models, "Bluebeard" offers an extreme illustration of how any young woman could feel when married to a man with a dark and mysterious past, specifically involving sexual relationships with other women. On a fundamental level, Helen's predicament is that of Bluebeard's wife: she naïvely marries a man whose past becomes her problem in the present. Although Helen, already possessing a fortune, lacks the fairy-tale heroine's explicitly mercenary motivation, her uncle nonetheless notes Arthur Huntingdon's fortune as a point in his favor.[33] The two women's feelings toward their prospective husbands are quite different: Helen marries Huntingdon primarily because she is attracted to him. But they possess comparable amounts of knowledge about these men. Bluebeard's wife knows only that he has had several wives and that they have disappeared. Helen knows slightly more; her aunt constantly reminds her of Huntingdon's reputation as a "profligate."[34] Unlike Perrault's heroine, Helen discovers some of Huntingdon's callousness during their engagement. "My cup of sweets is not unmingled," she writes in her journal. "It is dashed with a bitterness that I cannot hide from myself, disguise it as I will. . . . I cannot shut my eyes to Arthur's faults. . . . His very heart . . . is, I fear, less warm and generous than I thought" (186). Helen cringes at Huntingdon's irreverent accounts of dissipation but insists on assuming the role of his moral guide.

Helen admits in the second paragraph of her first diary entry as Mrs. Huntingdon that "Arthur is not what I thought him at first. . . . If I had loved him first, and then made the discovery [of his true character], I fear I should have thought it my duty not to have married him. To be sure, I might have known him, for everyone was willing enough to tell me about him, and he himself was no accomplished hypocrite, but I was wilfully blind" (202). Huntingdon is less secretive than Bluebeard; Helen could have learned much more before marrying him. But she holds herself back from knowledge, as Perrault's heroine ludicrously decides that the wealthy man's beard is not *so* blue after all and asks nothing about the fate of her predecessors. Knowing just enough to fear that the full story would scare them away from what they want, both brides-to-be decline to pursue suspicious information about their prospective husbands.

After the weddings, the wives learn the husbands' most damning secrets—in both cases, because the husbands choose to reveal them. Huntingdon's early transgressions against Helen are abandonment and betrayal—sins he has already committed against other women. Helen, calling these women his "victims," writes that he frequently "tell[s] me stories of his former amours, always turning upon the ruin of some confiding girl or the cozening of some unsuspecting husband; and when I express my horror and indignation, he lays it all to the charge of jealousy, and laughs" (208). Although Huntingdon has not literally killed these women like Bluebeard, he still marries Helen with a past full of women he has ruined and discarded. Soon, he treats Helen as he treated them, having extramarital sex and habitually lying to Helen about when he plans to return from sojourns in London. As the years of marriage pass, Huntingdon's excessive drinking and subsequent misbehavior worsen.

Strangely, neither Bluebeard nor Huntingdon is actually as secretive as his behaviors warrant. Huntingdon is generally known to be a rake, and the inhabitants of Bluebeard's neighborhood know that he has married several times and that those wives are unaccounted for. Moreover, Bluebeard's elaborate ritual of giving the new wife the key, pointing out the chamber, and going on a journey suggests that the serial marriages are designed as much to exhibit the corpses as to generate a new one. Perrault offers no indication that Bluebeard is surprised or even particularly angry to come home to a bloody key; he raises his voice only from impatience, once his wife exceeds the fifteen minutes allotted to her to say her prayers. Huntingdon, meanwhile, laughs while telling Helen of his former conquests, carries on with Annabella in Helen's home, and finally brings mistress Miss Myers to live there under the flimsy pretense of working as a governess to little Arthur. Both men abandon secrecy almost entirely once they are married, satisfied that their wives lack the physical and legal power to act on their fear or disapproval.

It may be objected to this parallel that "Bluebeard," a two-thousand-word fairy tale, flames out in a burst of violence quite quickly after the heroine's discovery of the corpses, whereas in Anne Brontë's realist novel, the disastrous marriage dies a longer and less dramatic death. But comparing the novel to "Bluebeard" helps emphasize just how serious Huntingdon's treatment of Helen is. Although Huntingdon does not threaten to kill Helen, his repeated assaults on her property, her morals, and her very identity are best described as sustained violence. Technically, the first of those is no violation at all, because Huntingdon legally owns his wife's property. But the scene in question is striking for the scholar of "Bluebeard" and could be taken as evidence that Brontë intended to evoke the tale. Having seized Helen's diary and discovered her scheme for escape with little Arthur, Huntingdon demands her keys. "What keys?" Helen replies. "'The keys of your cabinet, desk, drawers, and whatever else you possess,' said he, rising and holding out his hand."[35] He wrests the keys from her despite her refusal and confiscates the money, jewels, and painting materials on which she had planned to live after escaping. Although Helen's "transgression" is quite unlike that of Bluebeard's wife, both wives come to mirror their husbands' secretive behaviors and are forced literally to hand over the keys to those secrets. The violation of Helen's secret plan and goods leads not to a literal death sentence but to another nine months of life with her husband. Helen is virtually trapped with her husband despite possessing resources that many women at the time did not—upper-class status, profitable artistic skills, a sympathetic family member, and even access to another house.[36]

Worse is the moral violence done to Helen throughout the novel, primarily at the hands of Huntingdon. Both Gilbert and Huntingdon's friend Hargrave bear some guilt for trying to persuade her into adultery before her husband's death—Helen refers to Hargrave in her diary as "the enemy" when she realizes his intentions, long before he seizes her physically.[37] Huntingdon effectively entraps her in a corrupting environment, one she feels "turning [her] nature into gall" (313). After Huntingdon, suspecting intrigue between Helen and Hargrave, subjects her to "a volley of the vilest and the grossest abuse it was possible for the imagination to conceive or the tongue to utter," she reflects, "Could I ever have imagined that I should be doomed to hear . . . such things spoken . . . by those who arrogated to themselves the name of gentlemen? And could I have imagined that I should have been able to endure it as calmly . . . as

I had done? A hardness such as this is taught by rough experience and despair alone" (359, 361).

Helen's shock is partly due to the disconnect between gentlemanly social rank and gracious behavior. The mid-nineteenth century saw much debate over whether economic status or chivalry mattered more to the definition of "gentleman"; as the century progressed, the scales tipped in favor of the latter.[38] Meanwhile, cultural discussions about marital violence and divorce increasingly reflected awareness that working-class men were not the only ones who beat their wives.[39] For Helen, though, even graver than the so-called gentlemen's misbehavior is her own diminishing sensitivity to it. Her diary entries before her marriage indicate that she recognizes the challenge of reforming Huntingdon, but not the possibility of his negatively influencing her. Bluebeard, in threatening the heroine with murder, seeks to make her into a corpse similar to those of his previous wives; the danger Huntingdon poses to Helen is that he might make her—ever so slightly—more similar to himself.

Helen fears only one thing more than the flagging of her moral fortitude: her "greatest source of uneasiness" is the danger Huntingdon poses to little Arthur.[40] She flees Huntingdon fearing not murder, but something worse from a Christian perspective: Huntingdon, by pointing his son toward alcoholism, irreverence, and general misbehavior, threatens the boy's immortal soul. The mid-Victorian debates surrounding child-rearing are crucial to the novel, though outside the scope of my discussion.[41] Adding a child exacerbates the immediacy of the problem in "Bluebeard" stories: the danger is not that the husband has dreadful secrets in his past, but that the character traits that led to those secrets remain a problem for the current wife in the present. Bluebeard cannot keep his secret from his current wife because it involves her. As Jane Eyre realizes, the condition of the past wives—murdered, replaced, turned into trophies—is always about to become the condition of the present wife. Helen, though, tolerates her husband's affair with Annabella but walks out when Huntingdon brings subsequent mistress Miss Myers into their home as governess to their child. *Wildfell Hall* amplifies the encroachment of the husband's past sins into the present by focusing the anxiety on the child, a representative of the future. In other words, Huntingdon's disruption could exceed Bluebeard's by outlasting his own life. The "Bluebeard" problem of the current wife's excessive proximity to her predecessors thus folds into Anne Brontë's concern about poor child-rearing.

Helen agonizes partly because she takes seriously the nineteenth-century moral association between spouses. She feels implicated in the very sins she has endeavored to prevent Arthur from committing: "I so identify myself with him, . . . feel for him as for myself; but I cannot act for him; and hence, I must be and am debased, contaminated by the union."[42] An Englishwoman in the middle of the nineteenth century had no legal identity separate from that of her husband. Moral equivalence is more complicated, as the nearly contradictory statements on the subject in Sarah Stickney Ellis's 1843 *The Wives of England* indicate. Early in this advice manual for women considering marriage, Ellis asserts, "human sympathy may do much to comfort, human advice to guide, and human example to encourage; but whether married or single . . . we must all bear our own burdens . . . and receive our own sentence at the bar of eternal judgment."[43] This view is more forgiving than Helen's, emphasizing the predominance of individual responsibility. But Ellis advises later, "And now, having thus loved your husband, and cast in your lot with his . . . it is meet that you should love him to the last. . . . If others turn away repelled, there is the more need for such a man, that his wife should love him still."[44] "Cast in your lot" echoes Helen's attitude; although Ellis does not say that the husband's faults are equally the wife's, she insists on the wife's responsibility to meet them with unconditional love. Graver faults, in Ellis's estimation, require her not to distance herself from an immoral influence but to minister even more closely to the man who has driven away all other acquaintances. Ultimately, Helen subscribes to a slightly more severe version of Ellis's approach. The problem of Bluebeard's wife—how to distance herself physically from her husband to avoid being murdered—becomes a nineteenth-century wife's complex dilemma of establishing the proper physical and moral distance from a contaminating husband.

What does this dilemma mean for Helen's second marriage? Critics disagree about Gilbert's worthiness; some emphasize his similarities to Huntingdon, others his gradual improvement. Since the 1840s, discussions weighing multiple Brontë novels have often boiled down to comparative analyses of their distinctive male characters.[45] Gilbert frequently appears in arguments about whether Anne Brontë intended *Wildfell Hall* as a mocking response to *Wuthering Heights* and *Jane Eyre*, of whose dangerously captivating Byronic heroes she presumably disapproved.[46] Priti Joshi and Catherine Quirk find Gilbert unsatisfying as a husband for

Helen; Claybaugh finds "no change at all" from Huntingdon to Gilbert.[47] Langland and Chitham agree that Huntingdon is designed to expose the unattractiveness of marriage to a Byronic hero in real life. As for Gilbert, Chitham argues that his many everyday faults (he is "petty, self-centered, impulsive, short-sighted and insensitive") make him ultimately unlovable and not sufficiently distinguished from Huntingdon.[48] Langland sees *Wildfell Hall* rather as "a cautionary tale that exposes the foolish romance in the attraction of a Byronic hero like Huntingdon and finally rewards the heroine with a very ordinary gentleman farmer who has had the grace to learn humility."[49] For her, Gilbert is imperfect enough to suit Brontë's realism but a desirable choice because, unlike Huntingdon, he improves under Helen's influence. Hornosty, Morse, and Pregent emphasize that despite initial similarities to Huntingdon, Gilbert lets himself be taught.[50] For both Pike and Butterworth, the crucial factor is obvious from the beginning: Gilbert's superiority to Huntingdon as a paternal figure for little Arthur.[51]

How we interpret the comparative worthiness of Gilbert depends not only on his and Huntingdon's traits but also on whether we believe that Helen's judgment has improved—a question that is difficult resolve because Gilbert, not Helen, narrates the section of the novel in which he and Helen become engaged. The "Bluebeard" reading of the novel, though, can help us by offering a tentatively optimistic answer. Perrault deems the second husband "fort honnête," which is usually translated into English as "very honest" but originally signified something closer to "very accomplished"; either way, this is a positive description.[52] As noted above, he helps the heroine "forget" her troubles with Bluebeard.[53] While this situation appears desirable (and is certainly preferable to the heroine's first marriage), it effaces the classic fairy-tale payoff of learning a lesson from misfortune. Like the second husband in "Bluebeard," Gilbert is undoubtedly a better choice than Huntingdon. But though there is no suggestion that Helen literally forgets her first marriage, embarking on a second one under identical legal conditions is risky, especially given the similarities that do exist between Huntingdon and Gilbert. As Thierauf has persuasively argued, *Tenant* indicts an entire society, not simply one fictional character, for facilitating violent misogyny (and Bluebeard's crimes, too, are enabled by his neighbors' willingness to exonerate him for his wives' disappearances as they enjoy his fabulous parties).[54] Ultimately, this ending is happy, but not wildly so; Helen's ending is milder than Jane Eyre's, for example. *The Tenant of Wildfell Hall* as a whole follows the basics of the fairy-tale model, but in a toned-down and realist fashion; the same is true of its ending. Helen marries a better man, but we are not assured that they live happily ever after.

* * *

To assert that *Agnes Grey* and *The Tenant of Wildfell Hall* are intimately linked to fairy tales is not to diminish their realism. Rather, Anne Brontë repackages the core plot and concerns of the fairy tales using a style, scope, setting, and topic appropriate to the Victorian realist novel. In arguing that *Agnes Grey* is built around "Cinderella" and *The Tenant of Wildfell Hall* is built around "Bluebeard," I cannot definitively say whether the author intended this. But something interesting is happening either way. If she did not, then the centrality of those fairy-tale plots to the novels reflects the centrality of fairy-tale narratives to nineteenth-century English culture more generally. "Cinderella" is the narrative par excellence of female advancement; "Bluebeard" is the ultimate narrative of the danger that young women face in marriage. Branwell Brontë, as I discussed in chapter 2, sometimes appears to have drawn on fantastical texts without even realizing he was doing so; it is possible that this was also true of Anne, and if so, this is a testament to the ubiquity of fairy tales in their world.

I suspect, however, that Anne Brontë did engage deliberately with fairy tales, particularly those classic continental versions that foreground their didactic potential. "I wished to tell the truth," Anne Brontë wrote in the Preface to *The Tenant of Wildfell Hall*, "for truth always conveys its own moral to those who are able to receive it."[55] Brontë's ultimate purpose, always, was to draw closer to God and assist others in doing the same. We saw this in chapter 3, in which I demonstrated that she referred to the nonreligious supernatural forces of magic and enchantment most often in an attempt to convey more vividly the experience of faith in God. Despite folk traditions that place fairies and Christianity in opposition, the fairy *tales* that underlie Brontë's novels were written in harmony with Christian belief; moreover, the lessons of these tales are easily expressed in Christian terms. "Cinderella" advocates for piety, goodness, patience, and hard work; "Bluebeard," though certainly more ambiguous, can be read as a cautionary tale that warns against marrying a man for the wrong reason, specifically greed. Although the reinforcement of

Christian values was not the primary Victorian association with fairy tales, fairy tales are useful to writers precisely because of their flexibility: they can serve any number of ends. Anne Brontë was able to use fairy tales to help her construct compelling narratives that revealed the real social problems in Victorian England and advocated Christian responses to those problems. Her use of fairy tales reminds us, too, that lived experience often carries the intensity of a fairy tale on the inside, as ordinary as it may appear from the outside. A girl forced to do demeaning work may feel like Cinderella, however commonplace that work may be; a young woman discovering the horrible secrets of a man she has just married—in a society where divorce is a near impossibility—may feel as frightened as a wife of Bluebeard, even if her husband is guilty of something less than murder. Recognizing the fairy tales inside Anne Brontë's novels allows us to appreciate on another level the Brontë sister who is still too often simply known, as the title of Elizabeth Langland's 1989 monograph indicates, as "the other one."[56]

8 A Personage in Disguise

Villette and the Narrative of Enchantment

At one point in Charlotte Brontë's *Villette,* a character asks heroine Lucy Snowe in exasperation, "Who *are* you, Miss Snowe?"[1] Lucy replies calmly, "Perhaps a personage in disguise."[2] The question and Lucy's evasive response to it anticipate decades of frustrated readerly engagement with Brontë's last heroine. Brontë strove in *Villette,* as in *Shirley,* to emerge from the shadow of *Jane Eyre;* she wrote to Ellen Nussey that Lucy Snowe "should not occupy the pedestal to which 'Jane Eyre' was raised by some injudicious admirers."[3] If anything, Brontë succeeded too well; Lucy is a decidedly strange person and a first-person narrator who seems not to confide in her readers. In fact, many aspects of *Villette* feel larger than life or simply off: the language of the narration, many of the events, most of the characters. Both the opening and the closing passages of the novel are unusual and inconclusive. The characters are extreme, ranging from the exceptionally perfect to the theatrically sinister. Critics, as I will show, have dealt with the unconventionality of *Villette* in various ways; I will argue that Lucy's narration causes readers to perceive her past life as though they are under an enchantment. In other words, much of what she reports in her retrospective narrative is perfectly realistic, but some details are hidden from view and replaced with fantastical or highly metaphorical passages that nonetheless convey information about Lucy's interior experience.

To be sure, Lucy spends much of her time dealing with everyday reality: "daily," "hourly" its rewards and demands operate on her.[4]

Accordingly, a good deal of *Villette* is narrated in a straightforward, traditionally realist manner. Lucy describes typical experiences: traveling across the English Channel to Labassecour (Brontë's fictionalized Belgium), getting lost in unfamiliar streets, dealing with the unruly students she is supposed to teach, walking in gardens, and so forth. And she does so, often, in ways that fit well with typical nineteenth-century realism. "Villette owns a climate as variable, though not so humid, as that of any English town," Lucy reports blandly in introducing the town of Villette (a stand-in for Brussels).[5] Describing an ordinary evening later in the novel, she notes, "The supper, consisting of bread, and milk diluted with tepid water, was brought in" (367). Such conventionally descriptive moments underpin the novel, grounding the reader in a reality sufficiently ordinary to make clear that Brontë wished to offer, among other things, a recognizable portrait of the everyday life of a working woman.[6]

But Lucy also possesses a strange inner life. In her early days at the pensionnat in Villette where she teaches, Lucy describes herself looking out her window in apparent calm but "thinking meantime my own thoughts, living my own life in my own still, shadow-world."[7] Certainly, many heroines of Victorian fiction might be depicted this way. But Lucy's shadow-world is particularly vivid: "I seemed to hold two lives," she reflects, "the life of thought, and that of reality; and provided the former was nourished with a sufficiency of the strange necromantic joys of fancy, the privileges of the latter might remain limited to daily bread, hourly work, and a roof of shelter" (85). It is difficult to imagine, say, Charles Dickens's Amy Dorrit or George Eliot's Dorothea Brooke expressing a need for "the strange necromantic joys of fancy," even though they, too, strive to maintain a corner of life apart from external influences. Lucy's language is overdetermined: "necromantic" alone would imply "strange." She requires not only time to indulge in private thoughts but also assurance that those thoughts be far from everyday reality. Many of *Villette*'s sentences seem to come from this inner life of Lucy's.

Villette is, then, a novel filled with both descriptions of observable facts and accounts of its first-person narrator's subjective experience. The obvious label for such a novel is psychological realism. And indeed, since its publication, many critics have identified psychological realism as the organizing principle of *Villette*'s narration. The anonymous reviewer in the *Spectator*, representatively, attributes to Currer Bell "an attempt to paint by highly figurative language the violent emotions of the heart."[8]

Later critics agree, including Charise Gendron, who praises on feminist grounds Brontë's "deliberate attempt at psychological realism" in portraying the life of the "redundant woman" in *Villette*.[9] Undoubtedly, part of Brontë's project in *Villette* is to show how both of her heroine's "two lives," internal and external, contribute to her experience of the world. Much of what I will discuss in this chapter is consistent with a reading of *Villette* as psychologically realist.

However, while a goal of psychological realism certainly accounts for some of Brontë's narrative choices in *Villette*, it does not account for all of them; I agree with Heather Glen that "Lucy's narrative is by no means merely a psychological one."[10] Many other scholars, too, have anticipated me in noting and grappling with a particular strangeness about *Villette*. Penny Boumelha, for example, asserts that *Villette* is "among the strangest of nineteenth-century novels."[11] More recently, Ezra Dan Feldman insists that we need strategies to "help rearticulate and reevaluate *Villette*'s narrative peculiarities."[12] Feldman resorts to using the word "weird" multiple times in his discussion of the novel; he identifies "weird weather," "weird perspectives of the nonhuman and cosmic," and "weird narration," leading him to argue for a "new and weird model for how to understand the narrator's most significant disruptions."[13]

Of course, one could argue for the adequacy of psychological realism as a framework for a novel narrated in a weird way by a weird first-person narrator. But Feldman's call for a new model is valid. For one thing, narrator-Lucy sometimes deliberately and explicitly bars the reader from understanding character-Lucy's thoughts, including on topics that are central to her life. Instead of simply revealing her past self, she prefers to construct a stranger and more controlled impression of her past self for the reader.[14] I suggest we try to view narrator-Lucy's narrative techniques as an enchantment that she performs on the reader. The word "enchant" comes from the French "enchanter," meaning to bewitch or charm, originally from the Latin to "sing into"—"in-cantāre," as a chant or incantation.[15] In other words, enchantment amounts to an effect produced by spoken words. All narrators, then, could be said to work enchantments upon their readers. Yet the Latin term specifies "sing" rather than "speak"; singing, of course, is a particular and heightened form of speaking. How, and for what purpose, might we delineate singing in narrative? I propose that the heightened moments in Lucy's narrative are those in which she infuses her more typically realist reporting with highly metaphorical or fantastical language.[16] This particular combination of narrative styles—by turns reporting observable facts, revealing inner thoughts, and painting abstract scenes—always conveys important information about character-Lucy, but in both direct and indirect ways. While psychological realism is an important part of this combination, it is only part. Narrator-Lucy's enchantment of the reader selectively transmits character-Lucy's experiences and thoughts, masking some of the most important with a kind of dazzling narrative cloak that conveys information in a form that better holds the reader at bay.[17]

Lucy tips her hand by portraying her former self as the occasional victim of enchantment. While on the boat from England, Lucy gazes ahead to Labassecour: "In my reverie, methought I saw the continent of Europe, like a wide dreamland, far away . . . soft with tints of enchantment."[18] But almost immediately, she changes her mind: "Cancel the whole of that, if you please, reader—or rather let it stand, and draw thence a moral . . . 'Day-dreams are delusions of the demon.'"[19] Character-Lucy briefly succumbed to an enchantment apparently because she was not paying sufficient attention to the source of her perceptions: narrator-Lucy tells us about this experience but hastens to counter it with the kind of moral one would use to chastise a schoolchild. Later, summing up the account of the pensionnat where she has taken a teaching job, narrator-Lucy concludes, "Thus did the view appear, seen through the enchantment of distance" (83). This statement provides a clear warning to the reader that the enchantment of distance is about to give way to the harsh reality of proximity. In Lucy's final direct reference to enchantment, she reports being drugged by the pensionnat headmistress, Madame Beck, the night of a festival in Villette but rising and venturing outside nonetheless. In her altered state, she feels herself to be "in a land of enchantment, a garden most gorgeous, a plain sprinkled with colored meteors . . . the wonders and the symbols of Egypt teemed throughout the park of Villette" (500). But of course, Villette is not a land of enchantment, as is harshly demonstrated by conversations Lucy overhears that night in which the sinister "secret junta" (discussed below) plots against her. In all these instances, narrator-Lucy reports on her own former hopes and disappointments by using the language of enchantment and disenchantment. For narrator-Lucy to use this language, particularly early in the novel, is perhaps a hint to the reader to beware.

Importantly, though, manifestations of enchantment in traditional folk and fairy tales are various: though enchantments are sometimes intended to distort or mislead, other times they actually reveal a more fundamental truth. Precedents for enchantment revealing inner truth are abundant in the fairy-tale tradition. At the end of Jeanne-Marie Leprince de Beaumont's definitive version of "Beauty and the Beast," Beauty's spiteful sisters are turned to stone and placed outside Beauty's palace, where they will be forced to watch her happiness until they recognize the error of their ways; their stony hearts are manifested in the stony physical form imposed on them by the good fairy. The ending of this fairy tale also features the Prince's release from the enchantment that had turned him into a Beast—for, unlike the Disney film, the Beaumont story attributes the Prince's curse not to any inner "beastliness" but to the sheer wickedness of the fairy who cursed him. In other words, then, the happy ending of "Beauty and the Beast" overturns the enchantment that masked inner truth and institutes a new one that reveals inner truth. Another fairy tale evoked in *Villette*, "Bluebeard," features one magical element: the key that cannot be cleaned once it has been soiled. The magic of this key is that it persistently displays the fact that it was dropped in a pool of blood—persistently displays, in other words, the guilt that the heroine vainly wishes to conceal. Other tales known to Brontë feature this literalizing enchantment as well. In Charles Perrault's "The Fairies," one girl's kind words are transformed into lovely jewels falling out of her mouth whenever she speaks, whereas her sister's cruel words turn into a nasty stream of toads and vipers. Sleeping Beauty's sleep is extended by a magic spell but stands in for the waiting period of adolescence. Hansel and Gretel find a house made of food because they are starving and searching for plenitude. Cinderella, in perhaps the most striking instance, is supernaturally provided with magnificent dresses and accessories that accentuate the inner and outer beauty she possesses naturally. Fairy tales in general tend toward a match between inside and outside; often this reconciliation occurs by way of an external transformation or exaggeration.[20]

For the remainder of this chapter, I will discuss the ways that three elements of *Villette* contribute to narrator-Lucy's enchantment of the reader: the references to fairy tales and the supernatural, the storyline of the mysterious nun, and the highly metaphorical sections that replace several crucial facts in the narrative. The first two sections are consistent with readings of *Villette* as psychologically realist; the third addresses aspects of the novel that seem to me to require a different explanation.

Once Upon a Time in Villette

Like *Jane Eyre, Villette* is bursting with references to fairy tales, supernatural creatures, and magic. It simply is not true, as Heiniger has asserted, that Brontë "excises the fairytale allusions" from *Villette.*[21] On the contrary, *Villette* contains more such allusions than *Shirley.* Why did Brontë increase her use of fairy tales and magical creatures in her most mature and most cynical novel? I suggest that unlike in *Jane Eyre,* where they are a natural part of Jane's world, the fairies and fairy tales in *Villette* contribute to the broader otherworldly feeling of the story. In *Jane Eyre,* they blend in with the English countryside, a confiding narrator-heroine, and the triumph of true love. In *Villette,* they exist alongside a harsh European city, an evasive narrator, a difficult heroine, and an ending that is at best ambivalent. In both novels, Brontë uses fairies and fairy tales to enhance the atmosphere she most wants to create. Whereas in *Jane Eyre* they contribute to the novel's personalized, triumphant realism, in *Villette* they reinforce the feeling of enchantment, unreality, and sadness in the narrative. *Villette*'s references to supernatural creatures and to continental and Middle Eastern tales have almost nothing to do with either childhood or romantic happy endings—on the contrary, many of them reinforce Lucy's romantic disappointments.

Numerous characters in in the novel are compared to supernatural creatures. In *Villette,* these comparisons are distributed among a larger number of characters than in any of Brontë's other novels: M. Paul, Paulina, Madame Beck, Ginevra, Madame Walravens, the nun, the student Zélie, the students as a group, the actress Vashti, and even Lucy. The notable absence is Dr. John Graham Bretton (referred to variously throughout the novel, and henceforth as Graham or Dr. John), whom Lucy seems to see as unattainably real. But narrator-Lucy refers to her second romantic interest, literature professor M. Paul Emanuel, as a brownie three times in chapter 29, just as Jane calls Rochester a brownie late in *Jane Eyre.*[22] Brownies are small, brown, shaggy creatures—after all, neither M. Paul nor Rochester is described as handsome. When it comes to women, though, there is a clear correlation between fairy comparisons and attractiveness (as was often the case in nineteenth-century writing, including other writing of the Brontës, as I discussed in earlier chapters). Beautiful Paulina Home de Bassompierre (who wins Graham) is compared to fairies, elves, nymphs, and so forth over a dozen times in the novel; flighty student Ginevra Fanshawe is a "fairy," a "Peri," or a "goblin" to her lovers, depending on how she is treating them.[23] Graham compares even his mother, Mrs. Bretton, to a fairy—he terms her daytime doze a "fairy's dream."[24] Lucy, on the other hand, is referred to once, in a letter by Ginevra's lover Alfred de Hamal, not as a fairy but as "un espèce de monstre" ("a type of monster," 123). The mysterious nun is an "incubus" and a "goblin," pensionnat headmistress Madame Beck a "dragon," Madame Walravens a "witch" and a "basilisk" (519, 519, 159, 508, 509). Vashti, modeled on the actress Rachel, whom Brontë saw perform in London, is primarily described with the religious supernatural ("demon," "fiend," and so on), but Lucy also comments on the "frenzy" of her "mænad movements" (287). As in *Jane Eyre* and *Shirley*, these comparisons of characters to supernatural creatures largely serve to emphasize characteristics: M. Paul's strangeness, Paulina's daintiness, and Madame Beck's and Madame Walravens's tyranny, for example. Almost every character in the novel has a supernatural sheen that tells us something important about how Lucy views that person.

While I do not believe that any fairy-tale plots underpin *Villette* as profoundly as some of the Brontës' other novels, the "Bluebeard" / "Beauty and the Beast" question that drives *Jane Eyre* does influence *Villette* as well. Katherine J. Kim considers "Bluebeard" central to *Villette* in various ways, both underlying the relationship between Lucy and Paul and inspiring the novel's treatment of scopophilia and the female body.[25] As Kim points out, an explicit mention of "Bluebeard" indicates that Brontë is using it intentionally. In this episode early in the novel, M. Paul enjoins Lucy to serve as a last-minute replacement for one of the students in a school play. He locks her in an attic to learn her part, then is horrified to discover hours later that she is hungry. "You will set me down as a species of tyrant and Bluebeard, starving women in a garret; whereas, after all I am no such thing."[26] Although starvation is not among Bluebeard's reported approaches to murder, M. Paul does bear a couple of slight resemblances to Bluebeard; he can indeed be tyrannical, and he has had a past romantic relationship that causes continuing problems for Lucy in the present. Ultimately, though, *Villette* draws more from "Beauty and the Beast": the initial beastliness of the man, the surface-level differences but fundamental affinity between the two romantic leads, the preternatural transformation that affinity engenders, and the gradual change in the heroine's feelings. M. Paul calls himself a "monster and a ruffian," while Lucy observes that he is "dreadful: a mere sprite of caprice and ubiquity."[27] As M. Paul observes to Lucy, "You are patient and I am choleric; you are quiet and pale, and I am tanned and fiery; you are a strict Protestant, and I am a sort of lay Jesuit; but we are alike—there is affinity" (407). These binary oppositions resemble even the title "Beauty and the Beast." The transformation comes earlier in the story: when Lucy agrees to call M. Paul "my friend," she notes a substantial change in his appearance: "You should have seen him smile, reader; and you should have marked the difference between his countenance now, and that he wore half an hour ago. I cannot affirm that I had ever witnessed the smile of pleasure, or content, or kindness round M. Paul's lips, or in his eyes before. . . . It changed as from a mask to a face. . . . I know not that I have ever seen in any other human face an equal metamorphosis from a similar cause" (355).

The transition "from a mask to a face" corresponds to the change from beast to human being in the fairy tale. Lucy specifies the extraordinary nature of M. Paul's transformation: a metamorphosis wrought by emotion that she has never seen elsewhere. Lucy's own feelings, too, resemble those of Beauty. When she and M. Paul bid goodbye before his journey to the West Indies near the end of the novel, Lucy reflects, "Once—unknown, and unloved, I held him harsh and strange; the low stature, the wiry make, the angles, the darkness, the manner, displeased me. Now, penetrated with his influence, and living by his affection, having his worth by intellect, and his goodness by heart—I preferred him before all humanity" (542). Like Beauty, she was initially put off by his harsh appearance and manner but changes her mind over time, discovering his value and coming to love him. What is missing, as I will discuss below, is the happy ending; M. Paul's presumable death indicates again that Lucy is not telling a conventional story. Both "Bluebeard" and "Beauty and the Beast," then, provide only partial models for *Villette;* in both cases, the romantic happy ending is missing. Narrator-Lucy thus raises the specter of fantastical stories but abandons them in a way that is destabilizing and disappointing for any readers who recognize the early similarities.

As we have seen, when the Victorians in general and Brontë in particular wanted to convey or produce enchantment, they often turned to the *Arabian Nights' Entertainments;* accordingly, the collection makes numerous appearances in Brontë's last novel. Again, the references serve both as "exotic" rhetorical flourishes and as serious expressions of Lucy's internal experience. Like Anne in *Agnes Grey,* Charlotte refers to the tale of Bedreddin Hassan; here, though, the reference is explicit. After a strange experience of panic and sickness at the end of volume 1, Lucy wakes from a swoon to find herself surrounded by the furnishings of the Bretton family home in which she spent much of her troubled childhood in England: "I thought of Bedreddin Hasan, transported in his sleep from Cairo to the gates of Damascus. Had a Genius stooped his dark wing down the storm to whose stress I had succumbed, and gathering me from the church-steps, and 'rising high into the air,' as the eastern tale said, had he borne me over land and ocean, and laid me quietly down beside a hearth of Old England? But no; I knew the fire of that hearth burned before its Lares no more."[28]

Briefly, then, Lucy conjectures that she may have been magically transported over the English Channel, but soon she decides that this is impossible because the Brettons have left the house she knew. She wonders if the drink a maid brings her is a "Genii-elixir or Magi-distillation" (188). It turns out that the Bretton family has, coincidentally, moved to Villette.[29] This and all of Brontë's other references to the *Arabian Nights' Entertainments* in the novel have to do with Graham Bretton. Lucy compares Graham's facility in navigating the geographical and social scenes in Villette to the possession of an "Open! Sesame" like Ali Baba's; Lucy herself, of course, enjoys no such access (221). When Graham lapses in his promise to write letters to her, she rereads the few he had sent as though they were "the Barmecide's loaf" (297)—an illusory food that cannot satisfy hunger.[30] Finally, with Graham married to Paulina (another associate of their childhood who resurfaces in Villette), Lucy reports that for the rest of her life she kept a place for Graham in her heart "like the tent of Peri-Banou" in the story of Prince Ahmed that could expand or contract as the possessor required (505). Usually, she kept it tightly folded in her hand, but had she been allowed to release it, "I know not but its innate capacity for expanse might have magnified it into a tabernacle for a host" (505). Thus, though Graham himself is never compared to a supernatural creature because he seems so fully to belong to the "real" world, narrator-Lucy feels the need to explain her relationship with him by referring to supernatural tales; it is so overwhelming and alienating that the language of the *Arabian Nights' Entertainments* best expresses what character-Lucy experienced.

Although Westerners today usually associate the *Arabian Nights' Entertainments* with magic carpets and genies, the tales in the collection vary widely from fantastical yarns to quite mundane stories. *Villette* obviously differs from the *Arabian Nights' Entertainments* in significant ways; nevertheless, Lucy does travel to what is to her a very exotic land (not the Middle East but the continent) peopled by adherents to what she considers a very strange religion (not Islam but Catholicism), and she recounts both mundane and strange things that happen to her there. What if narrator-Lucy is a sort of Scheherazade, telling stories to save her life? Scheherazade must be very careful in her storytelling—she cannot tell a story so quickly that she finishes it before dawn, for example, and she cannot tell a story that might anger the murderous King Schahriar. Lucy is presumably not narrating this novel under such an immediate threat of murder, but if the novel establishes anything, it is that Lucy's physical, mental, and financial situation is always precarious.

In the least traditionally realist episode in *Villette*, Lucy continues to "sing into" the narrative. This passage deals with Madame Walravens, Madame Beck, and Père Silas—the "secret junta," as Lucy dubs them—who are sinister enough to have sprung from the pages of a fairy tale. At the behest of her employer, Madame Beck, Lucy delivers a basket to Madame Walravens, who lives in the old part of Villette; a young woman's dangerous journey to deliver a basket to an elderly woman should remind readers of "Little Red Riding Hood" (as critics including Sandra Gilbert and Susan Gubar have noted). The surroundings are Gothic, marked by a storm and by Madame Walravens's cold, stony, dark, dungeon-like house. Narrator-Lucy clearly presents the encounter as fantastical: "Hoar enchantment here prevailed; a spell had opened for me elf-land—that cell-like room, that vanishing picture, that arch and passage, and stair of stone, were all parts of a fairy tale."[31] The characters Lucy meets during the scene are caricatures: a peasant woman in traditional Labassecourian dress; the wizened Père Silas; and above all, Madame Walravens, "hunchbacked, dwarfish," and wearing extravagant clothing and jewelry (432). To Lucy, Madame Walravens is a "sorceress," or "Malevola, the evil fairy" (431). The outside world seems to accord with her feelings: "Just as she [Walravens] turned, a peal of thunder broke, and a flash of lightning blazed broad over salon and boudoir. The tale of magic seemed to proceed with due accompaniment of the elements. The wanderer, decoyed into the enchanted castle, heard rising, outside, the spell-wakened tempest" (432). As is the case elsewhere in the novel, nothing that occurs in this episode is impossible, but several elements are unlikely. The proliferating language related to fairy tales, the Gothic, and other nonrealist genres underscores the extreme nature of Lucy's experience.

This Gothic, fairy-tale scene leads into Père Silas's calculated revelation to Lucy of Paul's relationship with the now-deceased Justine Marie, during which he shows her the shrine to the girl in Madame Walravens's home. The portentously narrated passage conveys Lucy's feeling that she is dealing with enemies. To Lucy, a manipulative Catholic hunchback might as well be a sorceress, and a persuasive priest might as well be a wizard. The British Protestant association of Catholicism with magic underlies Brontë's presentation of these characters—as Sally Shuttleworth has argued, "the extreme projections of Catholic surveillance and intrigue . . . modulate into fairy tale form."[32] Importantly, narrator-Lucy does not use similes; Madame Walravens is not "like" a sorceress, she *is* a sorceress to character-Lucy. Moreover, the dramatic storm and otherwise hostile surroundings marking Lucy's discovery of Paul's personal situation convey her feeling that the whole world—past and present, near and far—stands against their relationship.

Altogether, these references to Western and Middle Eastern fairy tales and to supernatural creatures reinforce the otherworldliness of the novel. The contrast between such references in *Jane Eyre* and in *Villette* is illuminating. Whereas Jane is forever likened to imps and fairies (by herself and by others), Lucy is not. Whereas Jane's story ultimately follows the model of "Beauty and the Beast" to its conclusion, Lucy's has no happy ending. For Lucy, supernatural creatures and tales are often present but always other. Even the references to the *Arabian Nights' Entertainments* are all fundamentally negative because associated with the unattainable Graham. In *Villette,* then, explicit allusions to fairy tales and fantasy are a vital part of Lucy's attempt to enchant the reader into a true understanding of her experience—one of alienation from a world wearing a fundamentally hostile aspect.

The Nun

As Scheherazade, narrator-Lucy does more to enchant the reader than refer explicitly to fairy tales. A crucial component of her mystifying yet revealing enchantment is the series of sightings of the mysterious nun. Like the fairy-tale allusions, information about and encounters with the nun appear throughout the novel. Early in her time at Villette, Lucy hears of a legend that a certain tree on the pensionnat grounds covers the burial spot of a nun killed for a "sin against her vow," and that the nun's ghost accordingly roams the area.[33] Three times afterward, Lucy sees the figure of a nun and wonders whether to attribute the sighting to her own disturbed mind or to something as yet unexplained in the external world. Ultimately, Lucy learns that what she had seen was a man disguised as a nun to visit his lover, a student; however, this Radcliffean revelation dispels neither the haunting descriptions of the nun nor the fact that each time Lucy saw the nun was at a moment of personal significance. As Christina Crosby has argued, the nun "cannot be dissociated from Lucy Snowe."[34] Narrator-Lucy uses encounters with the ghostly nun—a figure associated with celibacy and Catholicism—as replacements for direct reporting of two important facts about her internal experience: that the specter of lifelong celibacy truly haunted her in her tentative romantic interactions, and that the specter of capitulation to Roman Catholicism was always present to her during her time in continental Europe. The question for Lucy, as Gilbert and Gubar have argued, is, "as a single woman, how can she escape the nun's fate?"[35]

The portrayal of the nun is the primary element of the novel that has prompted scholars to associate it with the Gothic mode. These scholars have come to various conclusions—Anna Neill that realist and Gothic forms of narration are in conflict in the novel but that Gothic imagination has the upper hand, Emily Heady that Brontë ultimately rejects both forms as too focused on externals, Mary Jacobus that the novel amounts to a compromise between them.[36] Critics have tended to identify the nun in particular as a Gothic representation of Lucy's inner life.[37] Certainly, the unaided heroine, the Catholic surroundings, and the possibility of haunting owe a debt to Gothic traditions, as does the portrayal of the nun. These elements are in keeping with the atmosphere of enchantment I am discussing. But Gothic tropes account for only some of the nonrealist elements of the novel in general and of the nun episodes in particular. Moreover, I do not believe that a reading of the nun should culminate in the solution to the mystery. Although critics including Robert A. Colby contend that in demystifying the nun, Lucy sheds all illusions, in fact Lucy continues to make grave errors of interpretation after learning the truth about the nun. Furthermore, the power of the nun episodes throughout the novel lasts beyond the explanation both for character-Lucy and for the reader; the enchantment is never fully dispelled. Throughout the novel, the nun is an indicator of the strength of Lucy's fears about celibacy and Catholicism during the moments at which it appears. I concur with Ezra Dan Feldman that the nun is the strangest feature of the novel and therefore crucial to understanding Brontë's narration.[38] Chiefly, Brontë portrays Lucy's internal reality via the melodramatic narration and extremely apt placement of the nun episodes; they consistently occur when Lucy is feeling particularly "haunted" by either celibacy or Catholicism.[39]

Narrator-Lucy consistently enchants the reader by describing the nun in a heightened style. In the first episode, Lucy gradually works up to the sighting of the nun with three questions about her own perception, an ellipsis, and vague words like "something," "a stealthy foot," and "a sort of gliding."[40] She describes the attic as dark and the corner as a "black recess haunted by the malefactor cloaks" before describing a "figure" (273). Finally, in a staccato sentence daring the reader to think her mad, Lucy vows, "I saw there—in that room—on that night—an image like—a NUN" (273). The word "nun" is frequently given in all capital letters for emphasis. The second time Lucy sees the nun, she is outside at night. This time, nature is apparently affected by the nun: "the moon, so dim hitherto, seemed to shine out somewhat brighter . . . a shadow became distinct and marked . . . it took shape with instantaneous transformation" (329). We then learn that the presumptive woman "had no face—no features . . . but she had eyes, and they viewed me" (329). A figure with no face places us firmly in the land of fairy tales and Gothic novels. The final sighting, again at night, includes M. Paul but reflects Lucy's fear nonetheless. Lucy describes a disturbance in a tree, compares it to a dryad (a tree spirit and the title of the chapter), and then is surprised with M. Paul by a "sudden bell" inside that causes the "instant," "angry rush" of the "NUN" "close, close past our faces"; "the wind rose sobbing; the rain poured wild and cold; the whole night seemed to feel her" (408). These descriptions exemplify the style with which narrator-Lucy enchants the reader into perceiving the nun as a supernatural threat as character-Lucy did at the time. Even the expectation of a naturalistic explanation for the apparition cannot entirely liberate the reader from the effect of these powerful melodramatic descriptions.

The placement of the nun episodes is the other feature crucial to their enchanted manifestation of Lucy's fears. What transpires immediately before the first sighting of the nun is one of Lucy's rare joyful moments related to Graham: he fulfills a promise to write to her. Lucy's initial reaction to the promise had been skepticism. Yet later in the chapter, a letter from Graham arrives. "For once a hope was realized. I held in my hand a morsel of real solid joy: not a dream, not an image of the brain, not one of those shadowy chances imagination pictures, and on which humanity starves but cannot live" (266). Lucy goes on for several phrases about the letter's substantial nature, differentiating it from the phantoms of hope. She reports "feeling as if fairy tales were true and fairy gifts no dream" but immediately adds, "Strange, sweet insanity!" and, later, "Dr John, you pained me afterwards" (267, 273). It is just after Lucy finishes reading the letter (alone in the attic due to a wish for privacy) that the nun appears for the first time. A terrified Lucy initially attributes the nun's arrival to her unwonted happiness: "Are there wicked things, not human, that envy human bliss?" (273). This question supports the reading of the nun as representative of a part of Lucy, because Lucy herself, though not "envying" her own happiness, certainly is skeptical and rather afraid of it. Literally and symbolically, the first appearance of the nun prevents Lucy from dwelling too long on the letter and conceiving unrealistic hopes. After fleeing the attic in terror, Lucy runs into Graham, who is conveniently present at the pensionnat that evening on medical business and who attributes the incident to Lucy's "highly nervous state" (277). Lucy had wanted to see this moment as the beginning of a real relationship with Graham; however, something intervened and disturbed her happiness. This "something," the nun, is both a real man in disguise and a fantastical personification of the misgivings that Lucy feels but seems not to articulate even in her own mind at this moment—hence narrator-Lucy's placement of the nun (rather than character-Lucy's thoughts) as an obstacle to the reading of the letter.

Whereas Lucy's initial sighting of the nun accompanies the beginning of her written correspondence with Graham, the second sighting comes at the end of this period; clearly, the nun here predominantly represents the specter of celibacy. For a while after the first sighting, Graham continues to write to Lucy and "sadness, for a certain space, was held at bay"; during this period, Lucy sees no sign of the nun.[41] But later, with Graham increasingly attached and likely to become engaged to Paulina, Lucy seals all of his letters in a container and buries them under the same tree said to mark the final resting place of the legendary nun. After she buries the container of letters (a metonym, of course, for her attachment to Graham), the nun seems to appear as an answer to her unspoken question about her future life: "But what road was open?—what plan available?" (329). An image of moonlight resolves itself into the image of the nun, then "five minutes passed. I neither fled nor shrieked. She was there still. I spoke" (329). Lucy attributes her calm behavior not to bravery but to desperation. Instead of bolting in terror as before, Lucy responds this time by stoically (albeit unsuccessfully) questioning the nun as to her business. If the nun represents her fear of being alone, the reader thus sees Lucy in this moment confronting that fear sadly but calmly. The fact that the first two encounters with the nun bookend Lucy's possession of letters from Graham suggests a strong connection between Lucy's romantic hopes and her experience of the nun. In placing the nun's appearances this way, narrator-Lucy reinforces the portrait of her past inner experience: juxtaposing the nun sightings with significant moments in her relationship with Graham conveys the fact that she rarely could think of Graham without recognizing how little chance she had of eliciting romantic affection from him.

The third sighting of the nun, appropriately, relates to Lucy's next romantic interest and the ambassador for Catholicism, M. Paul Emanuel. In fact, just before this sighting, Lucy pauses at the tree and recalls the night she buried the letters there. She then converses with M. Paul, who has joined her in the garden. He raises the topic of the nun, asking whether Protestants believe in the supernatural. Lucy replies that individuals vary but that she herself has had certain "impressions" at the pensionnat; hereupon M. Paul observes, as we have seen, "You are a strict Protestant, and I am a sort of lay Jesuit: but we are alike—there is affinity" (407). This conversation between Lucy and M. Paul emphasizing their general similarity but religious differences comes to an end because the nun herself appears. This time, the nun does not terrify Lucy, partly because M. Paul, too, sees the figure. It is crucial that M. Paul sees what she sees—Graham never did, in more ways than one. Moreover, this time the nun comes close enough for Lucy to see her clearly and almost surely seems to have an objective reality. Lucy describes a match between her perception and that of the rest of the environment: she observes, "Never had I seen her so clearly" and, as we have seen, attributes the increasing wind and rain to the fact that "the whole night seemed to feel her" (408). That Lucy is not alone in perceiving the nun this time obviously comforts her, even though the nun partly represents here the threat of Catholicism obstructing the progression of Lucy and Paul's romantic relationship. Again, narrator-Lucy places the final nun episode in such a way as to express information about Lucy's internal experience.

Narrator-Lucy ultimately reveals the mystery of the nun to have a rational explanation: student Ginevra Fanshawe's lover, Alfred de Hamal, has been using a nun's habit as a disguise in which to visit her. But, as Crosby has noted, "The moment of unveiling in *Villette,* the moment of truth when Lucy rends the veil of the nun is, in fact, a moment of great textual ambiguity. For the nun is an agent of indeterminacy in a text more radical than even most feminist readings have allowed."[42] The supposed solution to the mystery does not dispel the disturbance the nun has caused. On one level, the explanation is perfectly reasonable: a man dresses up as a nun (because of the nearby convent and the legend of the ghostly nun) to visit his lover clandestinely, and Lucy happens to cross paths with him three times. But on another level, the nun causes real fear (to Lucy and perhaps to the reader), the sightings occur at very significant moments for Lucy, her mental stability is somewhat in question, and she has two crucial negative associations with nuns: Catholicism and celibacy. Even as Lucy tells the realistic story by registering the facts of the nun's movements, she also conveys her emotional responses to the nun and always situates the sightings in the context of whatever activity she was engaged in beforehand. Throughout the novel, the nun appears at such implausibly apt moments that a connection to Lucy's inner reality is undeniable—even as the nun's objective reality is likewise certain.

The nun is rendered more fantastically sinister by the fact that Lucy, before and after the discovery of de Hamal's disguise, also confronts another long-dead nun: Justine Marie, who had entered a convent after her family prevented her from marrying none other than a younger Paul Emanuel. This nun is literally enshrined in the home of her grandmother, Madame Walravens. Toward the end of the novel, she becomes a tool in the hands of the "secret junta," who are now relying on Paul for financial support and see his increasingly warm friendship with Lucy as a threat to that security. Lucy takes seriously the junta's intimations to her that Paul will remain forever devoted to Justine Marie's memory. Since at this point Lucy has been seeing what looks like the ghost of a nun for months, she worries, logically enough, that she is being haunted by someone who views her as a rival. As a result, Justine Marie becomes blurred with the legendary pensionnat nun—both figures of explicable reality and of Lucy's romantic and religious fears. Moreover, like the pensionnat nun, the deceased Justine Marie seems at one point in the novel to be manifesting as a ghost but turns out to have a living counterpart: a niece named after her, who seems to represent yet another romantic threat to Lucy until Paul's assurance late in the novel that it is Lucy he loves.

Altogether, Lucy confronts four threats associated with a nun: Justine Marie the living girl, Justine Marie the deceased, Alfred de Hamal in disguise, and the legendary nun of the pensionnat. These figures proliferate toward the end of the novel—character-Lucy knows of only one (an amalgam of de Hamal and the nun of legend) until the thirty-fourth out of forty-two chapters. They overlap, as well: the problem of the two Justine Maries arises before the mystery of the pensionnat nun is explained. Concurrently, both the romantic and the religious fears the nuns represent for Lucy increase. Although she had already encountered Père Silas and felt him to be a threat to her Protestantism at the end of volume 1, that danger mounts in the final chapters; after Paul's establishment of friendship with Lucy, the secret junta launches a serious campaign to convert her. The most perilous aspect of this campaign is that Paul himself participates: he takes her to Mass, and he delivers a tract from Père Silas on the benefits of Catholicism. At that point, Lucy believes Paul to be bound romantically to one or the other of the Justine Maries; therefore, conversion to Catholicism out of only friendship could literally lead to her becoming a nun. As for the fear of celibacy, Lucy's romantic worries regarding Paul later in the novel are deeper than her previous anxieties about Graham; as she reflects upon discovering the existence of the living Justine Marie, "I think I never felt jealousy till now. This was not like enduring the endearments of Dr John and Paulina. . . . This was an outrage."[43] The profusion of nuns toward the end of the novel reinforces the intensification of Lucy's troubles.

Because of the realistic explanation Brontë provides for the nun who appears to Lucy, many critics—including Robert A. Colby and to a lesser extent Diane Long Hoeveler—have tended to view it as the emblem of fantasy and delusion, which character-Lucy sheds in favor of reality when she learns the explanation. But I believe that the situation is more complicated than this. To begin with, the mystery of the nun sightings is solved before Lucy is released from her erroneous worries about the Justine Maries. When Lucy demystifies the nun that was Alfred de Hamal, she is still laboring under a crucial misapprehension about the plans of the secret junta: while she correctly learns during the town festival discussed earlier that they intend to send Paul to the West Indies in a moneymaking endeavor, she mistakenly infers that Paul plans to marry the young Justine Marie upon his return. But what many critics seem to miss is that narrator-Lucy tells us she had been wrong to believe she had achieved perfect clarity at this point: she reports her former thoughts with "In my infatuation, I said" (516). Lucy dismantles the nun costume before she learns the truth about Paul's romantic status. "Solving" the mystery, then, does not dispel her worries (or those of the reader) about "the nun" more broadly—that is, the generalized threat that includes both Justine Maries.

The fear of the nun, then, stands in throughout the novel for Lucy's fears of celibacy and Catholicism. While it is certainly a Gothic figure, it is not only that. The multiplying of nuns as the novel draws to a close is a stroke of enchantment on narrator-Lucy's part; it is a strange development that conveys to the reader the feelings that Lucy cannot bring herself to articulate literally. Lucy does not arrive at a conventional romantic happy ending, but she does overcome the nun when Paul confesses his love for her and sets her up with a school of her own, free of the surveillance of Madame Beck and the rest of the secret junta. The threats of celibacy and Catholicism are removed, enough at least for Lucy to be free of ghostly apparitions.

Missing Pieces

The fairy-tale allusions and the storyline of the nun that I have discussed up to this point are mostly consistent with psychological realism: there is a fairly straightforward correspondence between each fairy-tale allusion or nun sighting and a specific, known fact of Lucy's interior experience. In this section, I turn to a final, more elusive aspect of Lucy's enchantment of the reader. Several times, narrator-Lucy leaves basic information out of the narrative and replaces it with odd, highly metaphorical passages. The missing facts in the narrative—of her childhood, for example—are covered by something of a threadbare invisibility cloak; we know that something occupies that space, but we cannot see what is there. As Gilbert and Gubar put it, narrator-Lucy recounts those events "in a curiously allusive way"; for Nina Auerbach, the reality of *Villette* is "ambiguous and internal."[44] Lucy does not reveal herself to the reader like Jane Eyre; rather, she casts a spell over this picture of her life that makes it better able to convey the truth about how she feels. The result is that crucial expected details are replaced by elaborate, sometimes fanciful metaphors. My argument in this section is particularly dependent on the distinction between character-Lucy and narrator-Lucy, telling the story decades later as a woman with "white" hair and the benefit of hindsight.[45] Character-Lucy often seems buffeted by the winds of fate, but I believe that narrator-Lucy is firmly in control of her narrative, making it less an expression of trauma than a constructed presentation to the reader.

An important example of this technique is the oft-quoted, bizarre narration at the beginning of chapter 4, which gives the reader sufficient information to understand the general emotional state of Lucy as a young girl but conveys very few surface-level facts of her experience. Narrator-Lucy, after having spent the first three chapters recounting her extended visit at the age of fourteen to her godmother Mrs. Bretton's house, observes that the reader will likely assume that she was happy to return home afterward. "The amiable conjecture does no harm," she remarks, "and may therefore be safely left uncontradicted"—which, of course, has the effect of contradicting the conjecture after all (39). Lucy invites the reader to picture her spending the next eight years "as a bark slumbering through halcyon weather," then as a passenger on such a vessel: "Picture me then idle, basking, plump, and happy, stretched on a cushioned deck, warmed with constant sunshine, rocked by breezes indolently soft. However, it cannot be concealed that, in that case, I must somehow have fallen over-board, or that there must have been wreck at last. I too well remember a time—a long time, of cold, of danger, of contention. . . . A heavy tempest lay on us; all hope that we should be saved was taken away. In fine, the ship was lost, the crew perished" (39).

This passage reveals nothing literal about the crisis or the domestic situation that led to it. Lucy rarely alludes to any events of her childhood; nowhere in the novel does she refer specifically to parents or siblings. This omission could simply be seen as a mark of psychological realism if taken to indicate that Lucy had repressed a traumatic experience; however, her statement that she "too well remember[s]" the past suggests that she does think about the details of her experience but does not report those thoughts to the reader. Instead, narrator-Lucy the enchantress conjures for us two images of herself, as a marine vessel and as a passenger on such a vessel, in order to conceal the objective details while still conveying something of how she felt about whatever transpired—cold, danger, contention, and loss of hope are clear enough. Lucy then states that after this experience, she wore mourning garb and learned to rely only on herself. In other words, she reveals the results (especially internal) of the event for her, which is in keeping with *Villette*'s narrative focus on internal experience over observable facts. Karen Chase cites this passage as evidence that Lucy "exists behind a thick veil of metaphor."[46] But I argue that the "thick" metaphors are precisely what reveal Lucy's existence, simply in ways that the reader does not expect. Rachel Ablow specifies that "when Lucy suffers, that suffering seems to proliferate into multiple registers and modes of representation through which that suffering is conveyed to the reader. In other words, we are made to feel something, and that feeling has some relation to whatever happened to Lucy."[47] Ablow's "something" and "some relation" are spot on: indeed, the strange passages that stand in for descriptions of some of the most painful episodes of Lucy's history produce some feeling in the reader, but a feeling whose precise connection to Lucy's experience is difficult to determine because we sometimes do not learn what that experience was.

The most striking instance of narrator-Lucy not transmitting the literal experience of character-Lucy—the greatest distortion in her enchanted narrative—is her concealment, for six chapters, of her recognition that the Dr. John she meets in Villette is the adult version of the John Graham Bretton she knew in her youth. When she finally informs the reader, she also specifies when she had made the realization herself; the reader may, then, go back to the scene in which Lucy stares fixedly at new acquaintance Dr. John because "an idea new, sudden, and startling, riveted my attention with an overmastering strength and power of attraction . . . the force of surprise, and also of conviction, made me forget myself—and I only recovered wonted consciousness when I saw that his notice was arrested."[48] The rest of this chapter, instead of disclosing what "idea" had struck Lucy, recounts Dr. John's affronted reaction to Lucy's stare and Lucy's subsequent decision not to explain herself. The passage thus carries a very different meaning when reread later than it possibly can the first time. The reader's first reading experience, therefore, certainly does not match Lucy's experience of the episode. Because Lucy does not define her realization, the passage is not quite, or not only, psychological realism. But it resembles the sea voyage metaphor discussed earlier in that Lucy omits information about the event but does explain how it affected her: she was shocked, overwhelmed, then temporarily deprived of "wonted consciousness." Again, Lucy's enchantment masks many of her thoughts yet offers a great deal of information about her emotional experience.

The novel's conclusion, too, replaces basic information with abstract, emotional metaphors. Lucy states that Paul is sailing home from the West Indies after a three-year absence, describes a storm over the ocean, and then stops herself: "Here pause . . . leave sunny imaginations hope" (546). She refuses to declare him dead outright—a choice reminiscent of her withholding of Dr. John's identity as Graham. Moreover, Lucy conveys the experience of waiting in suspense in the final scene using militaristic, highly metaphorical language. Clouds appear take "strange forms," a phrase that recalls the "strange necromantic joys" of Lucy's fancy (545). Amid these strange forms, "there rise resplendent mornings—glorious, royal, purple as monarch in his state; the heavens are one flame; so wild are they, they rival battle at its thickest—so bloody, they shame Victory in her pride" (545). The storm "did not lull till the deeps had gorged their full of sustenance. Not till the destroying angel of tempest had achieved his perfect work, would he fold the wings whose waft was thunder" (546). The clouds, ocean, and tempest are presented as monarchs, as warriors, as devourers, as sentient destroyers—as, essentially, enemies with human attributes and superhuman capabilities. Clearly, this is how Lucy perceives these forces: given that they are keeping Paul away from her, they may as well be operating in league with the secret junta. But Lucy does not employ similes or phrases such as "it seemed to me" in this conclusion; rather, she simply imparts her perception of the sea and sky as the definitive description of them. She presents what was fundamentally real to her former self as objective reality.

Rachel Ablow suggests that a major implication of narrator-Lucy's obfuscation of basic details is a critique of sympathy.[49] Lucy resists giving the reader a straightforward account of her tragic history that would call up sympathetic images of other people (or the readers themselves) suffering in similar ways. Lucy seems aware that to seek sympathy is, at least partially, to cede power. She instead retains power over readers by telling her story in a way that keeps them off balance, always conveying something about her life but often in a confusing or imprecise way. Above all, enchantment is about control: putting something or someone under an enchantment amounts to ensuring a certain behavior or perception. Although the foregoing passages represent character-Lucy overwhelmed by crisis, narrator-Lucy can recollect her emotions in tranquility, carefully controlling the information the reader receives; we can only know how her worst experiences made her feel, not what they entailed. Instead, we must infer as best we can from descriptions of shipwrecks and martial clouds that occupy the space normally devoted to basic factual information. The distortions wrought by these enchantments are a crucial contributor to the strange feeling and narrative strategy of this retrospective novel.

* * *

One final reference to supernatural creatures appears at the close of the novel. Noting a shift in the wind, Lucy implores, "Peace, peace, Banshee—'keening' at every window!"[50] In Irish folklore, the "keen" or wail of the banshee is believed to herald a death. Lucy refers to "the legend of the Banshee" at one other significant point in her narrative: the death of Miss Marchmont, Lucy's employer before she leaves for Labassecour, during a stormy night (43).[51] During this earlier scene, Miss Marchmont describes for Lucy the untimely death of her lover Frank. This description features Miss Marchmont sitting down to wait for Frank and looking out the window at the weather, prefiguring Lucy's actions in the final scene of the novel. While Miss Marchmont dies herself, the weather outside is marked by "a voice," the wind at night taking "a new tone—an accent keen, piercing, almost articulate to the ear" (42). Lucy then uses the word "keen" once more during the scene. In fact, the entire episode with Miss Marchmont turns out to prefigure Lucy's own experience. Therefore, the reader is likely intended to recall this scene at the end of the novel and compare Miss Marchmont's fateful watch out the window for her lover's return with Lucy's: if so, that would reinforce the presumption that Paul does in fact perish in a shipwreck. The reference to the banshee thus enhances the otherworldly atmosphere and connects Paul's fate to the death of Miss Marchmont's Frank. Again, then, instead of telling us what happened to Paul, Lucy mentions the banshee and otherwise echoes aspects of the story of Miss Marchmont in order to convey—indirectly—information about what actually occurred.

Narrator-Lucy's refusal to state directly what happened to Paul is her final act of enchantment: she conceals the event and even her thoughts about it but offers vivid language conveying her emotions. The idea of enchantment helps us understand *Villette* because it encompasses a number of aspects of the novel: the references to fairy tales and supernatural creatures, the gaps and distortions in the narration, and the combination of realist and fantastical elements of the plot. To enchant is to distort but also, at times, to unveil. As generations of scholars have observed, *Villette* is a distortion of typical nineteenth-century narration. All these departures from the norm are linked to crucial, sensitive topics in the mind of Lucy Snowe. Through these enchanted elements, narrator-Lucy manifests her deepest hopes and fears. Brontë thus draws not only on Gothic tropes but on a tradition even older: the fairy tale. Liberated from her past fears, narrator-Lucy acts as a sorceress or a Scheherazade to communicate precisely what she wishes to reveal, regardless of readers' expectations. Fairy tales, supernatural creatures, and magic are thus central to *Villette* in a unique way, setting the stage and inspiring the method of narration. In her final novel, Brontë brings her work with the fairy tale to a sophisticated, distinctive conclusion.

Conclusion

On December 27, 1904, a new play opened at the Duke of York's Theatre in London. Two-thirds of the way into the show, the protagonist anxiously turned to the audience to say, "She says she thinks she could get well again if children believed in fairies. Do you believe? Say quick that you believe! If you believe, clap your hands, clap, clap. Don't let Tink die."[1] The play, of course, was *Peter Pan, or The Boy Who Wouldn't Grow Up*. Author J. M. Barrie was terrified that the audience might fail to clap when prompted, but as it turned out, the spectators "responded so strongly that Nina Boucicault, playing Peter, burst into tears."[2]

This well-known image of a roomful of children ardently proclaiming their belief in fairies epitomizes the late-Victorian changes to the fairy-tale tradition as I have presented it throughout this book. Barrie's fairy, Tinker Bell, was represented onstage as a darting light instead of being played by an actress; she "spoke" only to Peter, who would sometimes pause and then report her message to the audience. This turn-of-the-century fairy, then, not only depended on children for her existence but also had nearly dwindled into insubstantiality. Fifty years later, Tinker Bell was made over as an embodied but still diminutive and wordless sprite in the Walt Disney Studios animated film version of 1953. Even today, for most Americans and others around the world, the name "Tinker Bell" conjures an image of a small (though curvy) female figure with blond hair and a short green dress, sporting wings and surrounded by glittering fairy dust. In other words, the late-Victorian fairy is the one that stuck.

With all due respect to Barrie, I have attempted in this book to conjure a different and older image of fairies and other supernatural creatures as figures of radical uncertainty, not strictly bound by any one association. It can be difficult for us in the twenty-first century to imagine what it was like to encounter fairy tales and supernatural creatures without the filter of Andrew Lang's "color" fairy books, late-Victorian fairy iconography, and Disney animation. Perhaps the most striking difference is visual: in the world of photography, film, television, and the internet, a single image may become definitive far more quickly and completely than was possible in the early nineteenth century. This is what makes the older world of fairy tales and folklore so exciting: each tale and each type of creature could and did exist in a myriad of forms. I join scholars like Jennifer Schacker and Molly Clark Hillard in challenging the reduction of the history of the fairy tale to a linear development from the "traditional" tale (pure, straight, patriarchal, and didactic) to the twentieth- and twenty-first-century "postmodern" tale (playful, sophisticated, feminist, and radical). In fact, the fairy tale has always been a remarkably elastic form, allowing all types of writers and tellers to reshape it according to their purposes. If anything, it just might have been more flexible in the Brontës' time than it is today.

In this book, I have sought to unearth the work fairy tales do that goes unnoticed by many readers. I have argued that many novels are deeply influenced by the fairy tale even when they lack a happy ending, even when they are written for adults, and even (occasionally) when fairy tales are not explicitly mentioned. Fantastical references can work in poetry in similar ways. The evolution of the fairy tale occurs not only through explicit retellings; every allusion and every use of a fairy-tale plot structure are part of the full story of the fairy tale's role in global culture. This is true even of the sometimes negative or unconscious references to fairy tales in the works of Branwell and Anne Brontë: it is because nineteenth-century England was positively saturated with fairy tales and supernatural creatures that they underlie the plot structures and metaphorical toolkits of writers with apathy or, indeed, antipathy to the fantastical.

Meanwhile, through their uses of fairy tales and folklore in particular, the Brontës—especially Charlotte and Emily—habitually conveyed a representation of reality grounded in the perspective of the individual. Throughout this book, I have sought to claim the Brontës' novels for realism. I have argued that we should attend more closely to the role of the fairy tale in shaping undoubtedly realist novels including *Agnes Grey*, *The Tenant of Wildfell Hall*, and *Shirley*. More controversially, in the cases of *Jane Eyre*, *Wuthering Heights*, and *Villette*, I have argued against the tendency of some readers to subordinate internal truth to external plausibility in making determinations about realism. Of course, most Victorian realist novelists strove to represent both internal and external realities.

But Charlotte and Emily Brontë made the individual's unique interior experience of the everyday world vivid in a way that no other novelists have ever quite replicated. They did so in part by integrating fairy tales and folklore into their work.

In any event, it is beyond doubt that fairy tales and other fantastical traditions were vital to the Brontës' oeuvre. I hope to encourage further research into their importance to other aspects of Victorian literature and culture. In contrast to a conception of fairy tales as conservative and limiting, fairy tales are sites of boundless possibility, encouraging to the imagination and adaptable to widely varying literary purposes. This, I believe, was the fairy tale as the Brontës encountered it, and it is the fairy tale at its best.

Notes

Introduction

1. Juliet Barker, *The Brontës*, 2nd ed. (New York: Pegasus Books, 2013), 115.
2. Molly Clark Hillard in *Spellbound: The Fairy Tale and the Victorians* (Columbus: Ohio State University Press, 2014) and Jennifer Schacker in *Staging Fairyland: Folklore, Children's Entertainment, and Nineteenth-Century Pantomime* (Detroit: Wayne State University Press, 2018) offer especially helpful discussions of the terminology question in the context of nineteenth-century England in particular.
3. "About the Folklore Society," *The Folklore Society*, accessed March 26, 2021, https://folklore-society.com/about/.
4. Vladimir Propp, *Morphology of the Folktale*, translated by Laurence Scott, revised and edited by Louis A. Wagner (Austin: University of Texas Press, 1968), 19.
5. Jack Zipes, *The Irresistible Fairy Tale: The Cultural and Social History of a Genre* (Princeton, NJ: Princeton University Press, 2012), 3.
6. Maria Tatar, *The Hard Facts of the Grimms' Fairy Tales*, expanded 2nd ed. (Princeton, NJ: Princeton University Press, 2003), 33.
7. *Oxford English Dictionary Online*, s.v. "fantastic (*adj.*, *n.*)," 2023, https://www.oed.com/dictionary/fantastic_adj?tab=meaning_and_use#4752657.
8. This would of course change in the twentieth century, especially with Aarne's publication of *Verzeichnis der Märchentypen* (*Tale-Type Index*) in 1910.
9. Schacker, *Staging*, 113.
10. Charlotte Brontë, *Jane Eyre*, ed. Deborah Lutz, 4th ed. (New York: W. W. Norton, 2016), 232.
11. Nicola Bown, *Fairies in Nineteenth-Century Art and Literature* (Cambridge: Cambridge University Press, 2001), 8, 1.
12. Laurence Talairach-Vielmas, *Fairy Tales, Natural History and Victorian Culture* (New York: Palgrave Macmillan, 2014), 1.
13. Hillard, *Spellbound*, 4–5.
14. Hillard, 10; Schacker, *Staging*, 229.
15. Hillard, *Spellbound*, 11.
16. See Peter Brooks, *Reading for the Plot* (New York: Alfred A. Knopf, 1984), 114; Q. D. Leavis, "How We Must Read *Great Expectations*," in *Dickens the Novelist*, by F. R. Leavis and Q. D. Leavis (London: Chatto & Windus, 1970), 278; and Julian Moynahan, "The Hero's Guilt: The Case of *Great Expectations*," in *Victorian Literature: Selected Essays*, ed. Robert O. Preyer (New York: Harper & Row, 1966), 134.

17. Q. D. Leavis, "A Fresh Approach to *Wuthering Heights*," in *Critical Essays on Emily Brontë*, ed. Thomas John Winnifrith (New York: G. K. Hall, 1997), 207.
18. Jane Sunderland, "Canine Agency and Its Mitigation in the Characterization of Dogs in the Novels by Charlotte, Emily and Anne Brontë," *Brontë Studies* 48, no. 3 (2023): 201.
19. George Levine, *The Realistic Imagination: English Fiction from Frankenstein to Lady Chatterley* (Chicago: University of Chicago Press, 1981), 57.
20. Audrey Jaffe, *The Victorian Novel Dreams of the Real* (London: Oxford University Press, 2016), 9.
21. Jay Clayton, *Romantic Vision and the Novel* (New York: Cambridge University Press, 1987), 2; David Lodge, *The Modes of Modern Writing: Metaphor, Metonymy, and the Typology of Modern Literature* (Ithaca, NY: Cornell University Press, 1977), 25.
22. See Levine, *Realistic*, 147, and Amanda Anderson, "Trollope's Modernity," *ELH* 74, no. 3 (2007): 510.
23. Anne Brontë, *The Tenant of Wildfell Hall*, ed. Stevie Davies (London: Penguin Classics, 1996), 3.
24. Juliet Barker, *The Brontës: A Life in Letters* (London: Viking, 1997), 202.

Chapter 1: From Haworth to Glass Town

Epigraph: Victor Neufeldt, ed., *The Works of Patrick Branwell Brontë* (New York: Garland, 1997), 1:225–26.

1. Juliet Barker, *The Brontës*, 2nd ed. (New York: Pegasus Books, 2013), 113.
2. Barker, 115.
3. Distinguishing between the juvenilia and the "mature" writing of any writer is a fraught enterprise. All Branwell's writing tends to be referred to as juvenilia even though he wrote nearly up to his death at age thirty-one. Practically speaking, scholars have generally treated as juvenilia the works the Brontës did not publish. I discussed my book's approach to grouping the Brontës' works in the chapter summary of the introduction.
4. See Muhsin Jassim Ali, *Scheherazade in England: A Study of Nineteenth-Century English Criticism of the Arabian Nights* (Washington, DC: Three Continents Press, 1981), for a thorough discussion of the editions of *The Thousand and One Nights* available in nineteenth-century England.
5. Barker, *The Brontës*, 194; Claire Harman, *Charlotte Brontë: A Fiery Heart* (New York: Alfred A. Knopf, 2016), 59.
6. Mary V. Jackson, *Engines of Instruction, Mischief, and Magic: Children's Literature in England from Its Beginnings to 1839* (Lincoln: University of Nebraska Press, 1989), 114.
7. Jackson, 197, 221.
8. Jackson, 221.
9. F. J. Harvey Darton, *Children's Books in England* (Cambridge: Cambridge University Press, 1958), 82.

10. M. O. Grenby, *The Child Reader, 1700–1840* (Cambridge: Cambridge University Press, 2011), 78.
11. Jackson, *Engines*, 219.
12. Elizabeth Gaskell, *The Life of Charlotte Brontë* (New York: Penguin Classics, 1987), 146.
13. Clifford Whone, "Where the Brontës Borrowed Books," *Brontë Society Transactions* 11, no. 60 (1950): 344–58.
14. Rebecca Fraser, *The Brontës: Charlotte Brontë and Her Family* (New York: Crown, 1988), 52; Bob Duckett, "The Library at Ponden Hall," *Brontë Studies* 40, no. 2 (2015): 104–49.
15. Barker, *The Brontës*.
16. Moreover, fairy tales were largely marketed as children's literature at this time, and children's literature was not often available in circulating libraries; Grenby lists several exceptions but still finds that children's literature was "largely absent from the circulating libraries" until the middle of the nineteenth century (161). Grenby observes that in addition to owning books themselves, children often borrowed them informally from friends and other members of their community (158–61). Books were also, of course, available in the libraries of schools such as those the Brontë children attended.
17. Gaskell, *Life*, 110–1.
18. That Gaskell—such a keen observer of the mundane in her own fiction—would choose to highlight the role of fairy stories in her friend's childhood may be surprising. I would suggest that Gaskell saw fairy legends as part of the rural environment in which she wished to contextualize the Brontë children. That is, considering that Gaskell's motive in the biography was to bolster Charlotte Brontë's reputation, perhaps Tabby's fairy stories could be seen as something of an excuse for the wilder episodes in Brontë's fiction.
19. Charlotte Brontë, *Jane Eyre*, ed. Deborah Lutz, 4th ed. (New York: W. W. Norton, 2016), 11.
20. Charlotte Brontë, *Shirley*, ed. Margaret Smith (Oxford: Oxford World's Classics, 1981), 237.
21. See Nicola Bown, *Fairies in Nineteenth-Century Art and Literature* (Cambridge: Cambridge University Press, 2001); Laurence Talairach-Vielmas, *Fairy Tales, Natural History and Victorian Culture* (New York: Palgrave Macmillan, 2014); and Carole Silver, *Strange and Secret Peoples: Fairies and Victorian Consciousness* (Oxford: Oxford University Press, 1999).
22. Jennifer Schacker, *National Dreams: The Remaking of Fairy Tales in Nineteenth-Century England* (Philadelphia: University of Pennsylvania Press, 2003), 4.
23. Richard Dorson, *The British Folklorists* (Chicago: University of Chicago Press, 1968), 57, 98.
24. Quoted in Barker, *The Brontës*, 2.
25. See Edward Chitham, "The Irish Heritage of the Brontës," in *A Companion to the Brontës*, ed. Diane Long Hoeveler and Deborah Denenholz Morse (Chichester, UK: Wiley Blackwell, 2016), 403–15.

26. Emma Butcher, *The Brontës and War: Fantasy and Conflict in Charlotte and Branwell Brontë's Youthful Writings* (Basingstoke, UK: Palgrave Macmillan, 2019), 57.
27. Christine Alexander, ed., *Tales of Glass Town, Angria, and Gondal* (Oxford: Oxford University Press, 2010), 4.
28. We also know that the Brontës loved the Romantic poets, in whose works they would have found numerous supernatural creatures and events. The works of Lord Byron, William Wordsworth, Samuel Taylor Coleridge, Robert Southey, and Percy Bysshe Shelley were widely available during the Brontës' childhood in various editions and anthologies; they were also frequently published in the periodical press and discussed there years after their deaths. Charlotte communicated by letter with Southey, Branwell with Coleridge's son Hartley; Anne imitated Wordsworth's "Ode on Intimations of Immortality from Recollections of Early Childhood." All four were well aware of themselves as artistic descendants of the Romantics. Charlotte and Branwell became devoted to Byron, frequently imitating his style and alluding to his works. In Byron—especially "The Giaour," "The Bride of Abydos," and "The Corsair"—the Brontës found their own early love for the orientalized supernatural tale reflected back at them. They allude less often to Coleridge, but his supernatural poems—"Kubla Khan," "The Rime of the Ancient Mariner," and "Christabel"—were thematically in keeping with other works we know they admired. Thomas Moore, a poet less well known today, enjoyed great success with the 1817 publication of *Lalla Rookh*, an oriental romance steeped in the supernatural; *Lalla Rookh* was so popular that "everything was named for it, from ships to ice cream"; Miriam Allen DeFord, *Thomas Moore* (New York: Twayne, 1967), 24. References in the Brontës' writing to Peris and to the "prophet of Khorassan" suggest familiarity with Moore's poem. Beyond these specific Romantic works containing the supernatural, the Brontës would have encountered offhand references to fairies throughout Romantic-era writing.
29. Christine Alexander, ed., *An Edition of the Early Writings of Charlotte Brontë* (Oxford: Basil Blackwell, 1987), 1:4.
30. Emily's diary paper of July 30, 1841, notes that Aunt Branwell was at that moment reading *Blackwood's* to Patrick. Charlotte and Branwell directly quote (in *Angria and the Angrians* and "Henry Hastings") a poem that was published in *Blackwood's* in 1837. Charlotte seems to spoof Thomas Aird's "Nebuchadnezzar," which appeared in *Blackwood's* in 1834. These are just a few of the indications that they did continue to see *Blackwood's* after 1831, though we cannot be sure precisely which issues or when. See Lucasta Miller, "The Brontës and the Periodicals of the 1820s and 1830s," in *A Companion to the Brontës*, ed. Diane Long Hoeveler and Deborah Denenholz Morse (Chichester, UK: Wiley Blackwell, 2016), 285–301.
31. James Hogg, *Anecdotes of Scott*, ed. Jill Rubenstein (Edinburgh: Edinburgh University Press, 1999), 9.
32. Alexander, *Edition*, 1:5.
33. The titular character of "The Brownie of the Black Haggs" (October 1828) takes a position, as brownies traditionally do, as a domestic worker for a married

couple. The arrangement ends badly: the brownie and the wife develop a highly antagonistic relationship that culminates in her death. The April 1828 installment of "The Shepherd's Calendar" included a discussion of "Fairies, Deils [Devils], and Witches," in which, among other events, a man is lured away by two fairies who muddle his wits with drink. Another of Hogg's fairy stories for *Blackwood's*, "The Origin of the Fairies" (1830), offers a peculiar account of the origin of fairies, but it contains deeply traditional notions of fairies' characteristics—their association with sexuality, their habits of justice, their nightly activities, and the inextricable allure and danger of interactions with fairies and other supernatural creatures—that would have been reinforced in other texts the Brontës encountered.

34. Charlotte Brontë, *Tales of the Islanders* (New York: Hesperus Press, 2011), 5.
35. I am aware, of course, of the ableist assumptions of the story; what is important for my purposes is that both men in the story view the removal of their humps as desirable events. Thomas Crofton Croker, *Fairy Legends and Traditions of the South of Ireland*, 2nd ed. (London: John Murray, 1828), 2:32.
36. See Silver, *Strange*, 192–203, for a discussion of the prominence of the "fairies' farewell" tradition in nineteenth-century discourse.
37. C. Brontë, *Islanders*, 27.
38. C. Brontë, 26–27.
39. Charlotte and Branwell wrote substantially similar accounts of this moment in, respectively, "The History of the Year" and "The History of the Young Men."
40. Emily and Anne seem not to have participated as actively in the writing of articles for the magazine, though it is possible that they contributed behind the scenes.
41. When James Macpherson's *The Poems of Ossian* appeared in 1760, controversy immediately arose in the face of Macpherson's claim that he had merely "edited" the poems of an ancient Gaelic figure named Ossian instead of having written them himself; in 1829, it had not yet become public knowledge that Macpherson's claims were false. See chapter 2 for a discussion of Branwell's interest in Ossian.
42. Alexander, *Tales*, xix.
43. Firdous Azim, *The Colonial Rise of the Novel* (New York: Routledge, 1993), 3.
44. Gayatri Chakravorty Spivak, "Three Women's Texts and a Critique of Imperialism," *Critical Inquiry* 12, no. 1 (Autumn 1985): 249.
45. "The British Settlements in Western Africa," *Blackwood's* 26 (September 1829): 341–50.
46. Azim, *Colonial*, 115.
47. For additional discussion of race and empire in the Brontës' juvenilia, see the following sources: Mary Jean Corbett, *Family Likeness: Sex, Marriage, and Incest from Jane Austen to Virginia Woolf* (Ithaca, NY: Cornell University Press, 2008); Azim, *Colonial*, 1993; Kristian Nicole Wilson, "Reading Charlotte and Branwell Brontë's Early Writings as Colonialist Fantasy" (master's thesis, Clemson University, 2019); Judith E. Pike, "Rochester's Bronze Scrag and Pearl

Necklace: Bronzed Masculinity in *Jane Eyre, Shirley,* and Charlotte Brontë's Juvenilia," *Victorian Literature and Culture* 41, no. 2 (2013): 261–81; Sally Shuttleworth, *Charlotte Brontë and Victorian Psychology* (Cambridge: Cambridge University Press, 1996); Sue Thomas, *Imperialism, Reform, and the Making of Englishness in "Jane Eyre"* (London: Palgrave Macmillan, 2008); and Butcher, *Brontës and War.*

48. Alexander, *Edition,* 1:351.
49. Judith E. Pike, "Disability in Charlotte Brontë's Early Novellas, *Jane Eyre* and *Villette:* The Legacy of Finic's Disabled and Racialized Body," *Brontë Studies,* 43, no. 2 (2018): 122.
50. Alexander, *Edition,* 1:376.
51. Alexander, 1:3.
52. Susan Meyer, *Imperialism at Home: Race and Victorian Women's Fiction* (Ithaca, NY: Cornell University Press, 1996), 35.
53. Edward Said, *Orientalism* (New York: Vintage Books, 1979), 2–3.
54. Said, 43.
55. Tanya Llewellyn, "'The Fiery Imagination': Charlotte Brontë, the *Arabian Nights* and Byron's Turkish Tales," *Brontë Studies* 37, no. 3 (2012): 217.
56. Jane W. Stedman, "The Genesis of the Genii," *Brontë Society Transactions* 14, no. 5 (1965): 18.
57. Alexander, *Edition,* 1:55.
58. Branwell and Charlotte both wrote frequently under the names of literary alter egos, though sometimes they used their own initials or full names at the end of Glass Town manuscripts. Charlotte first wrote as Captain Tree and then moved on to Lord Charles Wellesley, who, like Arthur Wellesley, was based on a real son of the historical Duke of Wellington. Charles Wellesley thus frequently writes about the exploits of his older brother, in ways not always flattering. Eventually, he evolved into Charles Townshend, a less active participant in the stories he tells.
59. Alexander, *Edition,* 1:232
60. Charlotte notes in the section "The Origin of the Islanders" within "The History of the Year" (1829) that the Islanders Play had been established in 1827; it was completed in 1830. Branwell continued to write stories about the inhabitants of Glass Town and Angria nearly up to his death in 1848, though Charlotte had largely abandoned these characters by the 1840s.
61. Judith E. Pike, "Redefining the Brontë Canon: A Tribute to Christine Alexander," in *Charlotte Brontë from the Beginnings: New Essays from the Juvenilia to the Major Works,* ed. Judith E. Pike and Lucy Morrison (New York: Routledge, 2017), 15.
62. Alexander, *Tales,* xxxiii.
63. Llewellyn, "Fiery," 216.
64. Diane Long Hoeveler, "The Not-So-New Gothic: Charlotte Brontë's Juvenilia and the Gothic Tradition," in Pike and Morrison, *Charlotte Brontë from the Beginnings,* 85.

65. Zak Sitter, "On Early Style: The Emergence of Realism in Charlotte Brontë's Juvenilia," in Pike and Morrison, *Charlotte Brontë from the Beginnings*, 31.
66. Tamara Silvia Wagner, "Charlotte Brontë's *Ashworth*: From Adapted Angrian Villains to Recurring Sibling Pairs," in Pike and Morrison, *Charlotte Brontë from the Beginnings*, 128.
67. Croker, *Fairy*, 219.
68. As demonstrated in Molly Clark Hillard, "Dangerous Exchange: Fairy Footsteps, Goblin Economies, and *The Old Curiosity Shop*," *Dickens Studies Annual* 35 (2005): 63–86.
69. Silver, *Strange*, 171.
70. Alexander, *Edition*, 1:178.
71. Alexander, *Edition*, 1:156.
72. Marie-Catherine d'Aulnoy, "La Biche au bois," in *Contes de Madame d'Aulnoy* (Paris: Garniers Frères, 1882), 48, Gallica.
73. Marie-Catherine d'Aulnoy, "The White Cat," in *Beauties, Beasts, and Enchantment: Classic French Fairy Tales*, trans. and ed. Jack Zipes (Maidstone, UK: Crescent Moon, 2009), 517.
74. Alexander, *Edition*, 1:164–5.
75. Katharine Briggs, *An Encyclopedia of Fairies* (New York: Pantheon, 1976), 341.
76. Alexander, *Edition*, 1:167–8.
77. Alexander, *Tales*, 303.
78. Heather Glen, ed., *Tales of Angria*, by Charlotte Brontë (London: Penguin Classics, 2006), xvii.
79. I am considering the ratio of such allusions to page numbers in each narrative.
80. Alexander, *Tales*, 314.
81. Charlotte Brontë, *The Professor*, ed. Heather Glen (London: Penguin Books, 1989), 37.
82. C. Brontë, *The Professor*, 37.

Chapter 2: Branwell Brontë, the Fantastical, and the Real

1. In my quotations from Branwell Brontë in this chapter, I have silently corrected many of Branwell's obvious errors in spelling and in the use of apostrophes. I have retained his run-on sentences in order to maintain his rushed and exuberant tone.
2. For an extensive and compelling discussion of Branwell's military writing, see Emma Butcher, *The Brontës and War: Fantasy and Conflict in Charlotte and Branwell Brontë's Youthful Writings* (Basingstoke, UK: Palgrave Macmillan, 2019).
3. Note, again, that "fantasy"/"fantastical" in this book does not refer to the specific twentieth- and twenty-first-century literary genre of fantasy as counterpart to science fiction; I intend rather the older, more general sense of "imaginary," "supernatural," or "nonrealist."
4. Victor Neufeldt, ed., *The Works of Patrick Branwell Brontë* (New York: Garland, 1997), 1:64–65, 66.

5. Branwell's discomfort at the Genii's oppression raises the possibility that he might have been more sensitive to tyranny in general and, thus, to the colonial oppression of Africans in particular. Unfortunately, though, I do not really see evidence of such a conceptual leap in Branwell's writing. See chapter 1 for further discussion of race and imperialism in the juvenilia.
6. Neufeldt, *Works*, 1:15–19.
7. There is a chance that Charlotte, not Branwell, wrote this letter, because it was signed "UT." Eleven early texts were signed "UT" or "WT"; the letters stood for "us two" and "we two," but whether the two writers in question are Charlotte and Branwell or two of Charlotte's literary alter egos has not been resolved. See Christine Alexander, ed., *An Edition of the Early Writings of Charlotte Brontë* (Oxford: Basil Blackwell, 1987), 1:xxi and 1:74; Neufeldt *Works*, 1:xxi; Christine Alexander and Margaret Smith, *The Oxford Companion to the Brontës* (Oxford: Oxford University Press, 2018), 516–17; and Laura Forsberg, "The Miniature World of Charlotte Brontë's Glass Town," in Pike and Morrison, *Charlotte Brontë from the Beginnings*, 201. Because Charlotte sometimes wrote down stories and poems that Branwell was largely responsible for composing, analysis of handwriting offers no certainty. Several disputed texts are included in both Neufeldt's edition of Branwell's juvenilia and Alexander's edition of Charlotte's. The letter to the editor is among them; Alexander does note, however, that its "tone and subject reflect his [Branwell's] early writing rather than that of Charlotte" (*Edition*, 39n1).
8. Neufeldt, *Works*, 1:140, 152. In Charlotte's version of this story, Chief Genius Brannii menaces the new arrivals, while the other Chief Genii—the girls' avatars—check his aggression and assist the Twelve Adventurers. Christine Alexander, *Tales of Glass Town, Angria, and Gondal* (Oxford: Oxford University Press, 2010), 8–9.
9. Neufeldt, *Works*, 14.
10. James Macpherson, *The Poems of Ossian* (London: J. Walker and Other Proprietors, 1819), 57.
11. Neufeldt, *Works*, 2:298.
12. Neufeldt, 1:357.
13. Neufeldt, 2:432.
14. Neufeldt, 2:243, 135.
15. Alexander, *Edition*, 1:34–6.
16. Neufeldt, *Works*, 2:287.
17. For a thorough discussion of this belief's origins and manifestations, see Edwin Sidney Hartland, *The Science of Fairy Tales: An Inquiry into Fairy Mythology* (London: W. Scott, 1891). It is, of course, also connected to the notion that the fairies left England in the face of increasing industrialization, as discussed elsewhere in this book.
18. Neufeldt, *Works*, 3:66–7.
19. Neufeldt, 3:239, 278, 382.
20. Neufeldt, 3:412. Neufeldt persuasively suggests that the Agrippa to whom Branwell refers here must be not the ancient Roman statesman but the occult

medieval polymath Heinrich Cornelius Agrippa, who is mentioned in Christopher Marlowe's *The Tragical History of Doctor Faustus;* this Agrippa supposedly possessed the ability to conjure images of the dead.

21. Neufeldt, *Works,* 3:432.
22. Neufeldt, 2:336, 354. The "Arabian Tale" in the second reference is "The Tale of the Third Calendar."
23. Neufeldt, *Works,* 2:230, 251, 360, 626.
24. Neufeldt, 3:495.
25. Neufeldt, 2:676; 3:100, 104, 203, 434.
26. Neufeldt 2:232, 233, 287, 337, 585; 3:121, 129, 136, 263, 392, 412.
27. Neufeldt, 2:149.
28. Robert L. Mack, ed., *Arabian Nights' Entertainments* (Oxford: Oxford University Press, 2009), 298–302.
29. Neufeldt, *Works,* 3:186.
30. C. Brontë, *Jane Eyre,* 103.
31. Neufeldt, *Works,* 3:187–8.
32. Jacqueline Simpson and Stephen Roud, eds., *A Dictionary of English Folklore* (Oxford: Oxford University Press, 2000), 159.
33. Winifred Gérin, *Branwell Brontë* (London: Thomas Nelson and Sons, 1961), 136. Recall from the previous chapter Charlotte's story "The Adventures of Ernest Alembert," in which the protagonist immediately suspects that the being who comes to his door may be one of those spirits from folklore "who, in various shapes, had appeared to men shortly before their deaths" (Alexander, *Edition,* 1:156).
34. Neufeldt, *Works,* 2:149.
35. Robin St. John Conover, "Creating Angria: Charlotte and Branwell Brontë's Collaboration," *Brontë Society Transactions* 24, no. 3 (1999): 28.

Chapter 3: Natural, Supernatural, and Divine in the Poetry of Anne and Emily Brontë

1. Emily refers to her own progress on "Agustus—Almeda's life 1st vol—4th page from last" in the diary paper of June 26, 1837; Anne notes that she is "engaged writing the 4th volume of Sofala Vernon's life" on July 30, 1841, and that Emily is working on "writing the Emperor Julius's life" on July 31, 1845. Christine Alexander, *Tales of Glass Town, Angria, and Gondal* (Oxford: Oxford University Press, 2010), 487, 490, 492. These varying dates demonstrate that prose writing extended throughout much, at least, of the period during which the two produced Gondal texts.
2. The Honresfeld library was renamed the Blavatnik Honresfield Library in 2021. I have retained the spelling "Honresfeld" because of its general use in Brontë studies.
3. Robert Butterworth, in *Anne Brontë and the Trials of Life* (Oxford: Peter Lang, 2017), applies the same distinction to Anne's poetry, resembling critics of Emily's work in that he insists on the superiority of the non-Gondal

verses. Citing lines from Anne's Gondal-associated "Power of Love," for example, he states, "such heightened language, however, might be said to present a heightened—and thus less true—version of life" (102). This assertion is the exact opposite of my contention throughout this book that in fact heightened language is the only tool with which one can truly describe some aspects of life.

4. See the discussion of the controversy over the categorization of Emily's poems in Christine Alexander and Margaret Smith, *The Oxford Companion to the Brontës* (Oxford: Oxford University Press, 2018), under "Poetry by Emily Brontë."
5. Alexander, *Tales*, 485.
6. Alexander, 490.
7. Critical assessments of Anne's poetry have not yet explicitly addressed the role of the nonreligious supernatural in her work.
8. Anne Brontë, *The Poems of Anne Brontë*, ed. Edward Chitham (London: Macmillan, 1979), 76.
9. Muriel Spark and Derek Stanford, *Emily Brontë: Her Life and Work* (London: Peter Owen, 1960), 88–91; A. Brontë, *Poems*, 36.
10. A. Brontë, *Poems*, 149.
11. Among others, see Chitham in A. Brontë, *Poems*, 180; and Elizabeth Langland, *Anne Brontë: The Other One* (London: Macmillan, 1989), 72.
12. Alexander, *Tales*, 468.
13. Elizabeth Hollis Berry, *Anne Brontë's Radical Vision: Structures of Consciousness* (Victoria, BC: English Literary Studies, 1994), 30.
14. For the most part, I consider ghosts to be outside the scope of this book. For discussions of ghosts in Emily Brontë's poetry, I refer readers to Elizabeth K. Helsinger, *Rural Scenes and National Representation: Britain, 1815–1850* (Princeton, NJ: Princeton University Press, 1997) and to Simon Marsden, "Ghost Writing: Emily Brontë and Spectrality," *Brontë Studies* 45, no. 2 (April 2020): 144–55.
15. Robin Grove, "'It Would Not Do': Emily Brontë as Poet," in *The Art of Emily Brontë*, ed. Anne Smith (London: Vision Critical Studies, 1976), 47.
16. Barbara Hardy, "The Lyricism of Emily Brontë," in Smith, *The Art of Emily Brontë*, 102, 115.
17. Emily Jane Brontë, *The Complete Poems*, ed. Janet Gezari (London: Penguin Books, 1992), 56.
18. Janet Gezari, *Last Things: Emily Brontë's Poems* (Oxford: Oxford University Press, 2007), 93.
19. Gezari groups the three stanzas of this poem with two other fragments, which may or may not originally have been connected to it. I am treating the three stanzas as an individual work. See E. Brontë, *Poems*, 246.
20. E. Brontë, *Poems*, 86.
21. James Hogg, *The Queen's Wake: A Legendary Poem* (Edinburgh: George Goldie, 1813), 98. HathiTrust Digital Library.
22. Hogg may have been inspired by Goethe's "Erl-King" (1782), in which a malevolent forest spirit takes the life of a little boy during a nighttime horseback ride.

23. C. W. Hatfield, *The Complete Poems of Emily Jane Brontë* (New York: Columbia University Press, 1995), 19.
24. I follow Gezari in referring to the speaker of this poem as male; see E. Brontë, *Poems*, 255.
25. As Anna Eliza Bray says in *Traditions, Legends, Superstitions, and Sketches of Devonshire on the Borders of the Tamar and the Tavy* (London: John Murray, 1838) of pixies in particular, "pixies are so poetical, they always talk in rhyme" (176).
26. Quoted in E. Brontë, *Poems*, 265n122.
27. Rosalind Miles, "A Baby God: The Creative Dynamism of Emily Brontë's Poetry," in Smith, *The Art of Emily Brontë*, 89; Margaret Homans, *Women Writers and Poetic Identity* (Princeton, NJ: Princeton University Press, 1980), 127–28; E. Brontë, *Poems*, 265n122.
28. E. Brontë, *Poems*, 130.
29. E. Brontë, 18, 19.
30. Simon Marsden, *Emily Brontë and the Religious Imagination* (London: Bloomsbury, 2014), 43.
31. Homans, *Women Writers*, 143–4.
32. E. Brontë, *Poems*, 17.
33. E. Brontë, 18.
34. Helsinger, *Rural*, 196.

Chapter 4: The Mysterious Realism of Jane Eyre

1. Adrienne Rich, "Jane Eyre: The Temptations of a Motherless Woman," in *The Brontë Sisters: Critical Assessments*, ed. Eleanor McNees, vol. 3 (Bodmin, UK: Helm Information, 1996), 227; Cynthia Carlton-Ford, "Intimacy without Immolation: Fire in *Jane Eyre*," in McNees, *The Brontë Sisters*, 350; Kathleen Tillotson, *Novels of the Eighteen-Forties* (Oxford: Clarendon Press, 1954), 258.
2. Nina Auerbach and U. C. Knoepflmacher, eds., *Forbidden Journeys: Fairy Tales and Fantasies by Victorian Women Writers* (Chicago: University of Chicago Press, 1992), 11–20.
3. See, for instance, Richard Benvenuto, "The Child of Nature, the Child of Grace, and the Unresolved Conflict of *Jane Eyre*," in McNees, *The Brontë Sisters*, 212; Sandra M. Gilbert and Susan Gubar, *The Madwoman in the Attic: The Woman Writer and the Nineteenth-Century Literary Imagination*, 2nd ed. (New Haven, CT: Yale University Press, 2000), 342; Q. D. Leavis, introduction to 1966 Penguin Classics edition of *Jane Eyre*, in McNees, *The Brontë Sisters*, 143; and Gina M. Miele, "Intertextuality," in *Marvelous Transformations: An Anthology of Fairy Tales and Contemporary Critical Perspectives*, ed. Christine A. Jones and Jennifer Schacker (Peterborough, ON: Broadview Press, 2013), 501, which also suggests the related "Donkeyskin." Strictly speaking, as I will discuss in chapter 7, the classic continental Cinderella story is not one of "rags to riches"; rather, Cinderella begins as the daughter of a "rich man" (Jacob Grimm and Wilhelm

Grimm, *The Complete Grimm's Fairy Tales* [New York: Pantheon, 1972], 121) or a "Gentilhomme" ("Gentleman," Charles Perrault, *Contes*, ed. Catherine Magnien [Paris: Librairie Générale Française, Livre de Poche Classiques, 2006], 259) and then falls to a lower position when her stepmother takes over the household. When scholars of *Jane Eyre* refer casually to "Cinderella," they generally do so with the popular perception of "Cinderella" as a "rags-to-riches" story in mind.

4. See especially Phyllis Ralph, "'Beauty and the Beast': Growing Up with Jane Eyre," in *Approaches to Teaching Brontë's "Jane Eyre,"* ed. Diane Long Hoeveler and Beth Lau (New York: MLA, 1993), 56–61. Ralph implicitly links the fairy tale to the *Bildungsroman* by pointing out that understanding the key to "Beauty and the Beast"—namely, the fact that the transformation of the Beast is less significant than the change in the young woman's perception of him—"is important in understanding the growth of Jane Eyre and her evolving relationship with Edward Rochester. As Jane moves toward emotional and psychological maturity, she sees beyond Rochester's bestial appearance and behavior to the human strengths and weaknesses beneath" (57). Ralph goes on to argue that "there are many surface references to fairies and other supernatural beings in *Jane Eyre*, but more significant is the underlying psychological meaning conveyed by the themes and patterns from the tales, especially that of the animal groom" (59).
5. John Seelye has also raised the possibility of both tales' relevance to *Jane Eyre*: "We for a time are treated to an updated version of the story about the Beauty and the Beast, resolved when the Beast at long last declares his love for the little governess. . . . Her lover in effect strips off his beastly guise, only to reveal yet another mask, a Prince Charming who is really a clean-shaven Bluebeard, who keeps his wife locked in an attic room." John Seelye, Jane Eyre's *American Daughters* (Newark: University of Delaware Press, 2005), 24. But he moves away from these fairy tales immediately and does not pursue the analysis. His assessment is, too, rather odd, as a declaration of love from the Beast comes sooner than Beauty desires it, not later. I agree with him that the two tales alternately affect the plot, but I argue that the narrative goes back and forth repeatedly between both models.
6. In *Spellbound: The Fairy Tale and the Victorians* (Columbus: Ohio State University Press, 2014), Molly Clark Hillard argues persuasively that *Jane Eyre* contains far too many references to fairy tales and legends to support critics' claims about the predominance of any single source. She suggests rather that the novel "more closely resembles the natural history in its widespread collection and interpolation of the fantastic" (55). Although I agree that no tale can be justly considered Brontë's primary model, I maintain nonetheless that the interaction between the two tales I consider in this essay warrants more examination than it has thus far received.
7. Maria Tatar, *Secrets beyond the Door: The Story of Bluebeard and His Wives* (Princeton, NJ: Princeton University Press, 2004), 56.

8. For substantial lists and discussions of the many versions of "Bluebeard" in nineteenth-century English culture, see Casie E. Hermansson, *Bluebeard: A Reader's Guide to the English Tradition* (Jackson: University Press of Mississippi, 2009); Betsy Hearne, *Beauty and the Beast: Visions and Revisions of an Old Tale* (Chicago: University of Chicago Press, 1989); and Shuli Barzilai, *Tales of Bluebeard and His Wives from Late Antiquity to Postmodern Times* (New York: Routledge, 2009).
9. I make a "yes, and" response to scholarly work on the Gothic in *Jane Eyre*, including Robert B. Heilman, "Charlotte Brontë's 'New Gothic,'" in *From Jane Austen to Joseph Conrad: Essays Collected in Memory of James T. Hillhouse*, ed. Robert C. Radiburn and Martin Steinmann Jr. (Minneapolis: University of Minnesota Press, 1958), 118–32, and Diane Long Hoeveler, *Gothic Feminisms: The Professionalization of Gender from Charlotte Smith to the Brontës* (University Park: Pennsylvania State University Press, 1998). Much in *Jane Eyre* that other scholars have identified as indebted to the Gothic can likewise be attributed to the influence of "Bluebeard"; since we know that Brontë was familiar with "Bluebeard" and with Gothic fiction, both assessments are reasonable. The Gothic mode itself, of course, grew out of preexisting supernatural genres including fairy tale and folklore—"Bluebeard," with its murderous patriarch, besieged heroine, and frightening mansion, anticipates the Gothic more than perhaps any other well-known continental fairy tale.
10. Charlotte Brontë, *Jane Eyre*, ed. Deborah Lutz, 4th ed. (New York: W. W. Norton, 2016), 134.
11. Tatar, *Secrets*, 71.
12. C. Brontë, *Jane Eyre*, 221.
13. U. C. Knoepflmacher, "Introduction: Literary Fairy Tales and the Value of Impurity," *Marvels and Tales* 17, no. 1 (2003): 24.
14. Karen E. Rowe, "'Fairy-Born and Human-Bred': Jane Eyre's Education in Romance," in *The Voyage In: Fictions of Female Development*, ed. Marianne Hirsch and Elizabeth Langland (Hanover: University Press of New England, 1983), 79.
15. Ralph, "'Beauty and the Beast,'" 57. Many critics say the same of fairy tales in general or "Cinderella" in particular. As Huang Mei representatively puts it, Jane's life "is a long search for the 'truth' beyond 'the tale.'" Huang Mei, *Transforming the Cinderella Dream* (New Brunswick, NJ: Rutgers University Press, 1990), 117. If, as is true for Huang, the fairy-tale model under consideration is "Cinderella," this makes sense: Cinderella's attainment of financial security through marriage to a prince she has just met has little to do with the third volume of *Jane Eyre*. But "Beauty and the Beast" differs from "Cinderella" in important ways, as I will discuss.
16. Rowe, "Fairy-Born," 71.
17. Cristina Bacchilega, *Postmodern Fairy Tales: Gender and Narrative Strategies* (Philadelphia: University of Pennsylvania Press, 1999), 76.
18. Abigail Heiniger, *Jane Eyre's Fairytale Legacy at Home and Abroad: Constructions and Deconstructions of National Identity* (New York: Routledge, 2016), 39, 44.

19. C. Brontë, *Jane Eyre*, 396.
20. Jeanne-Marie Leprince de Beaumont, "La Belle et la bête," in *La Belle et la bête, suivi de l'oiseau bleu* (Paris: Livres de Poche Jeunesse, 2014), 38.
21. Tatar, *Secrets*, 73.
22. Victoria Anderson, "Investigating the Third Story: 'Bluebeard' and 'Cinderella' in *Jane Eyre*," in *Horrifying Sex: Essays on Sexual Difference in Gothic Literature*, ed. Ruth Bienstock Anolik (Jefferson, NC: McFarland, 2007), 119; Tatar, *Secrets*, 74.
23. Winifred Gérin, *Charlotte Brontë* (London: Oxford University Press, 1967), 89.
24. Perrault, *Contes*, 223.
25. Gilbert and Gubar, *Madwoman*, 360.
26. For descriptions of Jane as pale, see, among others, C. Brontë, *Jane Eyre*, 91, 109, 163, 195, 204, 307.
27. Sharon Marcus, introduction to *Jane Eyre* by Charlotte Brontë (New York: Norton Library, 2022), e-book. Some scholars argue or simply state that Bertha should be read as literally a person of color; see, for example, Suvendrini Perera, *Reaches of Empire: The English Novel from Edgeworth to Dickens* (New York: Columbia University Press, 1991). This reading has become prominent in popular discourse about the novel in the twenty-first century. The word "Creole," frequently applied to Bertha in the novel, today usually involves the idea of mixing of languages or races, but in England during Brontë's time it instead meant one of four different things: "White people of Spanish descent naturalized by birth in Spanish America; people of non-aboriginal descent naturalized by birth in the West Indies; non-aboriginal people 'of different colours' (white or 'negro') born in Spanish America (Johnson and Walker); and white people of European descent naturalized by birth in the West Indies." Sue Thomas, *Imperialism, Reform, and the Making of Englishness in "Jane Eyre"* (London: Palgrave Macmillan, 2008), 32. It seems obvious to me that, as Meyer puts it, Bertha "is a woman whom the younger son of an aristocratic British family would consider marrying, and so she is clearly imagined as white." Susan Meyer, *Imperialism at Home: Race and Victorian Women's Fiction* (Ithaca, NY: Cornell University Press, 1996), 67. Even Spivak and Plasa refer to Bertha as a "white Creole"; see Gayatri Chakravorty Spivak, "Three Women's Texts and a Critique of Imperialism," *Critical Inquiry* 12, no. 1 (Autumn 1985): 247, and Carl Plasa, *Charlotte Brontë* (London: Palgrave Macmillan, 2004), xi. Bertha and her brother move freely in social circles that probably would not have been welcoming to people of color. Many scholars have argued, however, that the descriptions of Bertha link her metaphorically with non-White people or, more specifically, enslaved or newly freed Africans. See Spivak, "Three"; Plasa, *Charlotte*; Meyer, *Imperialism*; Deirdre David, *Rule Britannia: Women, Empire, and Victorian Writing* (Ithaca, NY: Cornell University Press, 1995); and Patricia McKee, "Racial Strategies in Jane Eyre," *Victorian Literature and Culture* 37, no. 1 (2009): 67–83. Others have pointed out that the same descriptions

were stereotypically applied to White Creoles in the period; see Philip Rogers, "'My Word Is Error': 'Jane Eyre' and Colonial Exculpation," *Dickens Studies Annual* 34 (2004): 329–50; Thomas, *Imperialism;* and Jenny Sharpe, *Allegories of Empire: The Figure of Woman in the Colonial Text* (Minneapolis: University of Minnesota Press, 1993). Determining whether it makes more sense to read Bertha as a figure for the colonizer or the colonized is, ultimately, outside the scope of this book; for my purposes, the fact that both readings are possible speaks to the high stakes of the period's implicit imperative to distinguish between the White English and everyone else. The sources noted throughout this endnote offer important perspectives on the novel; for a discussion of orientalism in *Jane Eyre,* see Joyce Zonana, "The Sultan and the Slave: Feminist Orientalism and the Structure of 'Jane Eyre,'" *Signs* 18, no. 3 (Spring 1993): 592–617.

28. Sharpe, *Allegories,* 46.
29. Thomas, *Imperialism,* 40.
30. C. Brontë, *Jane Eyre,* 270.
31. C. Brontë, 270.
32. Heta Pyrhönen, *Bluebeard Gothic: "Jane Eyre" and Its Progeny* (Toronto: University of Toronto Press, 2010), 5.
33. Ruth Bernard Yeazell, "More True Than Real: Jane Eyre's 'Mysterious Summons,'" in McNees, *The Brontë Sisters,* 248.
34. C. Brontë, *Jane Eyre,* 279.
35. C. Brontë, 227.
36. C. Brontë, 192, 255, 269, 256, 270. Rochester's conception of Jane as a fairy also resonates with the revelation in Madame de Villeneuve's original novel-length "Beauty and the Beast" (1740) that Beauty had a fairy mother. Although Brontë may not have encountered this version, the connection between Jane-as-fairy and Jane-as-Beauty-figure nonetheless adds helpful complexity to our conception of Jane's particular fairy status.
37. For a discussion of this shift, see Molly Clark Hillard, "Dangerous Exchange: Fairy Footsteps, Goblin Economies, and *The Old Curiosity Shop,*" *Dickens Studies Annual* 35 (2005): 63–86.
38. One could certainly argue that the fairy bride folktale type plays a role in *Jane Eyre,* considering Rochester's frequent statements that Jane seems to come from elsewhere (specifically fairyland, in some scenes). Ultimately, however, the fairy bride tale is about a failed relationship between two beings who must separate because they are not of the same kind. As I will discuss later in this chapter, Rochester and Jane consistently feel a fundamental kinship that, in contrast to the fairy bride tale, ultimately brings them together. See also Francisco José Cortés Vieco, "A Changeling Becomes Titania: The Realm of the Fairies in Charlotte Brontë's *Jane Eyre,*" *Anglia,* 138, no. 1 (2020): 20–37, which argues for reading Jane and Rochester as Titania and Oberon.
39. See chapters 1, 5, and 6 for further discussion of the role of these folktales in the Brontës' writing.

40. "Thing," senses II.10a and II.8e, *Oxford English Dictionary*. 2023.
41. C. Brontë, *Jane Eyre*, 17.
42. C. Brontë, 235; emphasis in original.
43. Lori Pollock, "(An)Other Politics of Reading *Jane Eyre*," *Journal of Narrative Technique* 26, no. 3 (Fall 1996): 266, 265.
44. C. Brontë, *Jane Eyre*, 192, 255, 280, 285.
45. Karen Chase, *Eros and Psyche: The Representation of Personality in Charlotte Brontë, Charles Dickens, and George Eliot* (New York: Methuen, 1984), 73; emphasis in original.
46. C. Brontë, *Jane Eyre*, 147.
47. C. Brontë, 226; emphasis mine.
48. See, for example, David Lodge, *The Modes of Modern Writing: Metaphor, Metonymy, and the Typology of Modern Literature* (Ithaca, NY: Cornell University Press, 1977); George Levine, *The Realistic Imagination: English Fiction from Frankenstein to Lady Chatterley* (Chicago: University of Chicago Press, 1981); Nancy Armstrong, *Fiction in the Age of Photography: The Legacy of British Realism* (Cambridge, MA: Harvard University Press, 1999); and Amanda Claybaugh, *The Novel of Purpose: Literature and Social Reform in the Anglo-American World* (Ithaca, NY: Cornell University Press, 2007).
49. George Henry Lewes, "Recent Novels: French and English," *Fraser's Magazine for Town and Country* 36 (December 1847): 691.
50. John Maynard, *Charlotte Brontë and Sexuality* (New York: Cambridge University Press, 1994), 215.
51. C. Brontë, *Jane Eyre*, 398.
52. C. Brontë, 375; emphasis in original.
53. Yeazell, "More," 251, 240.
54. Yeazell, 241.
55. Biographer Elizabeth Gaskell reports hearing a conversation in which someone objected to this episode and Brontë replied, "But it is a true thing; it really happened." *The Life of Charlotte Brontë* (New York: Penguin Classics, 1987), 401. Whatever Brontë's personal beliefs about the supernatural, she surely anticipated such objections. She needed to construct a realism that could incorporate episodes like this.
56. Juliet Barker, *The Brontës: A Life in Letters* (London: Viking, 1997), 202, 206.
57. Lewes, "Recent," 691.
58. Chase, *Eros*, 85.
59. As Adrienne Rich concludes, Jane's marriage to Rochester does not "diminish" her but rather constitutes a "continuation of this woman's creation of herself." Rich, "Jane Eyre," 239.
60. Gilbert and Gubar, *Madwoman*, 369.
61. Gilbert and Gubar, 371, 368.
62. C. Brontë, *Jane Eyre*, 397.
63. Chase, *Eros*, 11.

Chapter 5: Shirley and the Ephemerality of the Supernatural Bride

1. Charlotte Brontë, *Shirley*, ed. Margaret Smith (Oxford: Oxford World's Classics, 1981), 5.
2. I have already discussed the age-old tradition of animosity between fairies and iron, as well as its nineteenth-century manifestation in anxieties about industrialization. Katharine Briggs, *An Encyclopedia of Fairies* (New York: Pantheon, 1976), 234. As previously noted in the context of Emily Brontë's poetry, traditional tales and beliefs have long connected the natural to the supernatural. Fairies are often associated with green; nymphs are associated with the element from which they come (often water or wood).
3. See, for example, Peter J. Capuano, "Networked Manufacture in Charlotte Brontë's *Shirley*," *Victorian Studies* 55, no. 2 (Winter 2013): 231–42, which joins Terry Eagleton's interest in connecting the superfluity of Luddite workers and that of middle-class "odd women" in *Myths of Power* (London: Palgrave Macmillan, 1975). See also Albert D. Pionke, "Reframing the Luddites: Materialist and Idealist Models of Self in Charlotte Brontë's *Shirley*," *Victorian Review* 30, no. 2 (2004): 81–102, and Herbert Rosengarten, "Charlotte Brontë's *Shirley*," in *A Companion to the Brontës*, ed. Diane Long Hoeveler and Deborah Denenholz Morse (Chichester, UK: Wiley Blackwell, 2016), 167–82, as well as the Coriale, Ross, and Buzard pieces discussed later in the chapter. Catherine Gallagher's reading of *Shirley* in *The Industrial Reformation of English Fiction: Social Discourse and Narrative Form, 1832–1867* (Chicago: University of Chicago Press, 1985) was a foundational text for this critical conversation.
4. See the Berg, Gilbert and Gubar, Langer, Moglen, and Moore pieces referenced later in this chapter. Susan Zlotnick's reading, also referenced below, unites the industrial and feminist readings, as does Capuano's.
5. Rosengarten, *Shirley*, 167.
6. Such tales appear all over the world, of course, but Brontë's purview was primarily western, with the exception of the *Arabian Nights' Entertainments*.
7. I am referring to the *Verzeichnis der Märchentypen* (*Tale-Type Index*), the definitive international folklore classification first published by Antti Aarne in 1910 and updated over the next century by Stith Thompson and Hans-Jörg Uther.
8. See Katharine Briggs's *An Encyclopedia of Fairies* (1976) for details about many such creatures, including roane, part human and part seal; Gwragedd Annwn, or water fairies; and the selkies and merrows I discuss later in this section.
9. See Carole Silver, "'East of the Sun and West of the Moon': Victorians and Fairy Brides," *Tulsa Studies in Women's Literature* 6, no. 2 (Autumn 1987): 283–98.
10. C. Brontë, *Shirley*, 244.
11. C. Brontë, 245–6.
12. Sandra M. Gilbert and Susan Gubar, *The Madwoman in the Attic: The Woman Writer and the Nineteenth-Century Literary Imagination*, 2nd ed. (New Haven, CT: Yale University Press, 2000), 386–87.

13. Nancy Quick Langer, "'There Is No Such Ladies Now-a-Days': Capsizing 'The Patriarch Bull' in Charlotte Brontë's 'Shirley,'" *Journal of Narrative Technique* 27, no. 3 (Fall 1997): 285; Tara Moore, "Women and Myth Narratives in Charlotte Brontë's *Shirley*," *Women's Writing* 11, no. 3 (2004): 480.
14. Langer, "There Is," 285.
15. C. Brontë, *Shirley*, 100.
16. Margaret Smith, ed., *The Letters of Charlotte Brontë*, vol. 2 (Oxford: Clarendon Press, 2000), 174, EBSCOhost.
17. James Hogg, *The Queen's Wake: A Legendary Poem* (Edinburgh: George Goldie, 1813), 298, HathiTrust Digital Library.
18. Readers today, of course, think first of Hans Christian Andersen's "The Little Mermaid," which was first published in English translation in 1846, both in *Bentley's Miscellany* and in Caroline Peachey's *Danish Fairy Legends and Tales*. Andersen did achieve popularity in England fairly quickly, so this tale might have crossed Brontë's path. But the *Blackwood's* article on Andersen's works in 1847 does not mention "The Little Mermaid," as it reviews a collection of translations of his tales by Charles Boner that does not include the mermaid tale. More importantly, none of Brontë's own references to mermaids suggests that she was influenced by Andersen's version of the mermaid as a loving child desperate for a soul.
19. Charlotte Brontë, *The Poems of Charlotte Brontë*, ed. Tom Winnifrith (Oxford: Shakespeare Head Press, 1984), 131–2.
20. C. Brontë, *Jane Eyre*, 291.
21. Charlotte Brontë, *Villette* (New York: Penguin Classics, 2004), 203. The narrator of *Villette* also refers to Paulina Home as an "Undine" (336). "Undine" was another name for Mélusine, a popular sea creature originally from French folklore, who appears sometimes as a human woman but other times in her true form (that is, half human and half serpent). The story of Mélusine or Undine was adapted by several European Romantic writers, including Friedrich de la Motte Fouqué, who also applies the word "mermaid" to her at times in his 1811 story "Undine." Brontë may have learned of Fouqué's "Undine" from a review published in *Blackwood's* in December 1826 of the new collection *German Stories; Selected from the Works of Hoffman, De la Motte Fouqué, Pichler, Kreuse, and Others*, by R. P. Gillies (itself published by *Blackwood's* in 1826); "Undine" is not the work of Fouqué's included in this book, but the *Blackwood's* review describes the story as part of the discussion of Fouqué's work more broadly. The appellation "Undine" varied in meaning throughout nineteenth-century writing, sometimes referring to a specific character but other times used simply as a synonym for "mermaid" or "nymph."
22. C. Brontë, *Shirley*, 567.
23. Sir Walter Scott, *Minstrelsy of the Scottish Border* (Kelso, UK: Ballantyne, 1802).
24. For a modern reader, Martin's tale may also call to mind John Keats's "La Belle Dame Sans Merci," in which a man meets a fairy in the meadow and is lured

to her "elfin grot" (ln. 29). Whether Brontë would have read this poem (published in *The Indicator* in 1820 and book form in 1848) is unclear, but the strong similarities (down to the beautiful lady, the horse, and the gems) are easily explained by the fact that Keats, too, knew Scott's "Thomas the Rhymer" (see Miriam Allott, ed., *The Poems of John Keats* [London: Longman, 1970], 503). Keats was not a touchstone for the Brontës in the way that Byron was, though they would have seen him discussed in articles published in *Blackwood's* in 1828, 1830, and 1840.

25. Sir Walter Scott, *The Monastery* (Edinburgh: Longman [1820] 1910), 314–15.
26. C. Brontë, *Shirley*, 567–8.
27. Gwen Benwell and Arthur Waugh, *Sea Enchantress: The Tale of the Mermaid and Her Kin* (New York: Citadel Press, 1965), 161. Historical resources on Faroese folklore in English are difficult to come by, but Benwell and Waugh state that "the mermaid is less frequently encountered in the Faroes than is the seal-maiden" (185), and the currency of the selkie story is evidenced by its prominence on the official tourism website of the islands: "The Seal Woman," Visit Faroe Islands, accessed April 5, 2024, https://visitfaroeislands.com/en/about1/myths-legends/the-seal-woman.
28. Briggs, *Encyclopedia*, 349.
29. David Thomson, *The People of the Sea* (London: Canongate Books, 2017), 194–98.
30. Briggs, *Encyclopedia*, 290.
31. Thomas Crofton Croker, *Fairy Legends and Traditions of the South of Ireland*, 2nd ed. (London: John Murray, 1828), 3.
32. Benwell and Waugh report a tale from Skye in which a man catches a mermaid and keeps her for a year, at which point she leaves him (*Sea*, 166). This story, clearly, is an animal bride tale, even though mermaids usually do not appear in tales of extensive, marriage-like capture. Again, attempts to draw absolute distinctions among different supernatural creatures tend to fail in the face of the sheer number and variety of tales that have been told.
33. Croker, *Fairy*, 10.
34. Silver, "East," 284.
35. Briggs, *Encyclopedia*, 350.
36. C. Brontë, *Shirley*, 437.
37. Danielle Coriale, "Charlotte Brontë's 'Shirley' and the Consolations of Natural History," *Victorian Review* 36, no. 2 (Fall 2010): 118.
38. C. Brontë, *Shirley*, 184.
39. Shirley's reverence for nature is due in part to an association she makes—thanks to what Caroline calls the "hash of Scripture and mythology" in her head—between nature and Eve, who is according to Shirley the mother of the Titans as well as the first woman of Judeo-Christian scripture (321). She refers to her as "my mother Eve, in these days called Nature" (321). Critics have sometimes turned to this and other comments Shirley makes about Eve in an attempt to find something that sheds light on the novel's outcome. Some read

Shirley's interest in and portrayal of Eve as a defiance of the patriarchy; see Gilbert and Gubar, *Madwoman;* Yolanda Padilla, "Dreaming of Eve, Prometheus, and the Titans: The Romantic Vision of Shirley Keeldar," *Brontë Society Transactions* 21, issue 1–2 (1993): 9–14; and Gisela Argyle, "Gender and Generic Mixing in Charlotte Brontë's *Shirley*," *Studies in English Literature 1500–1900* 35, no. 4 (1995): 741–56. Others note that some aspects of Shirley's musings are themselves patriarchal; see Moore, "Women." In any event, Shirley's cosmology holds that the original Feminine, Eve, has now become known as ungendered Nature. This absorption of a feminine element may prefigure the vanishing of fairies, mermaids, and women at the end of the novel.

40. C. Brontë, *Shirley*, 214.
41. Several critics have suggested a queer reading of *Shirley* in which Shirley and Caroline's mutual affection takes precedence over other elements of the novel. There is undeniably something "queer," in the Victorian and twenty-first-century senses of the word, about both women, especially Shirley. My attention to the supernatural creatures and comparisons in the novel complements queer readings, as it, too, attends to the heroines' unconventionality and troubles the marriage-plot resolution.
42. "Review of *Shirley*," *Atlas*, November 3, 1849, rptd. in *The Brontës: The Critical Heritage*, ed. Miriam Allott (Routledge & Kegan Paul, 1974), 121.
43. C. Brontë, *Shirley*, 326–31.
44. Arthur Wellesley (also known as the Duke of Zamorna) and Rochester are at least magnetic while they behave badly. William Crimsworth of *The Professor* is far from perfect, but he is clearly superior to his brother and to several other characters, including some female ones. *Villette* foregrounds its evil women over its evil men, and M. Paul is clearly Lucy's truest friend despite his faults. The men of *Shirley* are uniquely both bland and blameworthy.
45. C. Brontë, *Shirley*, 51, 27; Deirdre Mikolajcik, "Mooring Points: Manly Leaders, Trade, and Charlotte Brontë's *Shirley*," *Victorians: A Journal of Culture and Literature*, no. 131 (Summer 2017): 57–67.
46. C. Brontë, *Shirley*, 645–46.
47. C. Brontë, 458–59.
48. The other adult men, too, tend to disturb or disregard nature. The curates, unsurprisingly, are oblivious to nature, as the narrator wryly observes: "Malone was not a man given to close observation of Nature. . . . He could walk miles on the most varying April day, and never see the beautiful dallying of earth and heaven" (19).
49. James Buzard, *Disorienting Fiction: The Autoethnographic Work of Nineteenth-Century British Novels* (Princeton, NJ: Princeton University Press, 2005), 238.
50. Coriale, "Charlotte Brontë's 'Shirley,'" 129.
51. Shawna Ross, *Charlotte Brontë at the Anthropocene* (Albany: SUNY Press, 2020), 219.
52. Ross, *Charlotte Brontë*, 220.
53. C. Brontë, *Shirley*, 631.

54. It is possible that Brontë intended the animal bride tale to gesture toward a subsequent phase of her story in which the heroines might leave the men they married; ultimately, though, the novel provides no evidence that Caroline would wish to do so, and it seems clear that Shirley's surrender to Louis is final. But though Brontë would scarcely condone permanent captivity of selkies or women, the ending of the folktale becomes much more complicated in the context of the Victorian realist novel: leaving one's husband means divorce, an extremely challenging proposition in and of itself, not to mention the real pain and/or stigma involved in abandoning one's children and the slim chances of being able to visit them on a daily basis as do some escaped selkie mothers.
55. "Review of *Shirley*," *Westminster Review* 52 (January 1850), rptd. in *The Brontë Sisters: Critical Assessments*, ed. Eleanor McNees, vol. 3 (Bodmin, UK: Helm Information, 1996), 475.
56. George Henry Lewes, "Currer Bell's *Shirley*," *Edinburgh Review* (1850), in McNees, *The Brontë Sisters*, 462–74. Lewes notes in his review that though women have done well in literature, the primary purpose of their lives is maternity. Brontë wrote to Lewes twice after reading his review, first simply expressing anger and then explaining that "after I had said earnestly that I wished critics to judge me as an author, not as a woman, you so roughly—I even thought—so cruelly handled the question of sex." Smith, *Letters*, 332–3.
57. Robert Moore also despises the Duke of Wellington: during a dispute with Helstone, he calls him "the most humdrum of common-place martinets." C. Brontë (1849) 1981, 38. Brontë herself, as is clear in the juvenilia, revered Wellington deeply. Is this an attempt to portray Robert's half-Belgian status realistically, or is it a hint that the reader should be skeptical of him? There is not enough discussion of international politics in the novel to resolve the question.
58. Rosengarten, *Shirley*, 178–9.
59. C. Brontë, *Shirley*, 645.
60. Moreover, the villainous Edward Crimsworth in *The Professor* owns a mill that has damaged the surrounding landscape: "Steam, trade, machinery had long banished from it all romance and seclusion." Charlotte Brontë, *The Professor*, ed. Heather Glen (London: Penguin Books, 1989), 48. There is thus a precedent in Brontë's work for associating industrial development with dubious male characters.
61. Carole Silver, *Strange and Secret Peoples: Fairies and Victorian Consciousness* (Oxford: Oxford University Press, 1999), 194.
62. C. Brontë, *Shirley*, 646.
63. James Hogg, "Shepherd's Calendar, April 1827," *Blackwood's Edinburgh Magazine* 21 (1827): 442.
64. See Silver for a discussion of the "fairies' farewell" tradition (*Strange*, 193–203).
65. Temma Berg, "Reading Amazon Fragments: Queering *Shirley*," *Brontë Studies* 41, no. 3 (September 2016): 216–28.
66. Helene Moglen, *Charlotte Brontë: The Self Conceived* (Madison: University of Wisconsin Press, 1984), 189.

67. Susan Zlotnick, "Luddism, Medievalism and Women's History in *Shirley:* Charlotte Brontë's Revisionist Tactics," *Novel* 24, no. 3 (Spring 1991): 284.
68. C. Brontë, *Shirley*, 332.
69. Silver, *Strange*, 196.
70. C. Brontë, *Shirley*, 495; emphasis mine.
71. Sally Shuttleworth, *Charlotte Brontë and Victorian Psychology* (Cambridge: Cambridge University Press, 1996), 187. See also Anna Krugovoy Silver's observation that Caroline and Shirley both refuse food at times and thus become literally lessened on the way to their final vanishing from the text; *Victorian Literature and the Anorexic Body* (Cambridge: Cambridge University Press, 2002).
72. Moore, "Women," 477. Moreover, as Heather Glen points out, "if that reference to her [Shirley's] dreams as a 'genii-life' is, for those who know Glass Town, charged with remembered excitement, it carries also a more chilling reminder of promise blasted and hopes destroyed." *Charlotte Brontë: The Imagination in History* (Oxford: Oxford University Press, 2002), 162.
73. C. Brontë, *Shirley*, 638.
74. Glen, *Imagination*, 164.
75. Gaskell, *Life*, 379.
76. Smith, *Letters*, 157, 165.
77. Smith, 157.
78. C. Brontë, *Shirley*, 246.
79. Smith, *Letters*, 216.
80. C. Brontë, *Shirley*, 646.
81. Lee O'Brien, "Letty Garth's Little Red Book: 'Rumpelstiltskin,' Realism, and *Middlemarch*," *Victorian Literature and Culture* 45 (2017): 556.

Chapter 6: From Fairy Tale to Folklore in Wuthering Heights

1. J. Hillis Miller, *Fiction and Repetition: Seven English Novels* (Cambridge, MA: Harvard University Press, 1982), 50.
2. Miller, *Fiction*, 51.
3. I refer here to both the "complex" and the "compact" continental literary fairy tales, as Elizabeth Wanning Harries defines them. Harries distinguishes between the compact tales of Perrault and the Grimms—traditional, short, simple—and the complex tales of Marie-Catherine d'Aulnoy and other French women writers—generally longer, more digressive, and intertextual. See Harries, *Twice Upon a Time: Women Writers and the History of the Fairy Tale* (Princeton, NJ: Princeton University Press, 2001), 16–17. Even the complex tales of d'Aulnoy and her fellow *conteuses*, though, tend to revolve around the desires and fortunes of a central character or central couple, and most resolve their complexities by the end of the tale.
4. Emily Brontë, *Wuthering Heights*, ed. David Daiches (London: Penguin Books, 1985), 121.

5. I say this acknowledging what several critics have pointed out: the fact that Thrushcross Grange is hardly Buckingham Palace, but at least a notch above Wuthering Heights on the scale of refinement.
6. Gose suggests that Catherine has trouble choosing "which kind of fairy tale she is participating in." After a childhood of "Beauty and the Beast," she discovers Thrushcross Grange as a palace which she could enter as queen and decides she wants to switch to a different tale. Elliott B. Gose, *Imagination Indulged: The Irrational in the Nineteenth-Century Novel* (Montreal: McGill-Queen's University Press, 1972), 65.
7. Gose, *Imagination*, 62.
8. E. Brontë, *Wuthering Heights*, 246.
9. When the dying Catherine says "You have killed me" to Heathcliff, her "you" includes Edgar; moments later, she revises, "You never harmed me in your life" ([1847] 1985, 195, 196).
10. See the entry for "pigeon" in Jacqueline Simpson and Stephen Roud, eds., *A Dictionary of English Folklore* (Oxford: Oxford University Press, 2000).
11. E. Brontë, *Wuthering Heights*, 120.
12. Paula M. Krebs, "Folklore, Fear, and the Feminine: Ghosts and Old Wives' Tales in *Wuthering Heights*," *Victorian Literature and Culture* 26, no. 1 (1998): 50. Nancy Armstrong, too, likens Nelly to the informants of folklorists. Peter Caracciolo has suggested viewing Nelly as a Scheherazade figure—an interesting idea but not as well supported as that of Armstrong and Krebs. See Armstrong, "Imperialist Nostalgia and *Wuthering Heights*," in *Wuthering Heights: Case Studies in Contemporary Criticism*, ed. Linda H. Peterson (Boston: Bedford / St. Martin's, 1992), 428–49; and Caracciolo, "Introduction: 'Such a Store House of Ingenious Fiction and of Splendid Imagery,'" in *The Arabian Nights in English Literature*, ed. Peter Caracciolo (New York: St. Martin's, 1988).
13. A few early critics, such as those writing in the *Britannia* and *Eclectic Review*, insisted that nothing natural or true could be found in the novel at all. Perhaps surprisingly for modern readers, early reviewers often doubted *Wuthering Heights*'s realism on the grounds of its portrayal of extreme brutality—whereas events in *Jane Eyre* struck some as implausibly auspicious, *Wuthering Heights* could seem implausibly sordid. See Review of *Wuthering Heights* in *Eclectic Review* (1851), in *Wuthering Heights*, ed. Alexandra Lewis, 5th ed. (New York: W. W. Norton, 2019), 346–48.
14. Lyn Pykett, *Emily Brontë* (Basingstoke, UK: Macmillan, 1989), 76.
15. Leo Bersani, *A Future for Astyanax* (Boston: Little, Brown, 1969), 210; Miller, *Fiction*, 42.
16. Barbara Hardy, *Wuthering Heights* (Oxford: Basil Blackwell and Mott, 1963), 77, 59.
17. Hardy, *Wuthering Heights*, 58.
18. Sheila Smith, "'At Once Strong and Eerie': The Supernatural in Wuthering Heights and Its Debt to the Traditional Ballad," *Review of English Studies*, n.s., 43, no. 172 (November 1992): 516.

19. Susan Stewart, "The Ballad in *Wuthering Heights*," *Representations* 86 (Spring 2004): 181.
20. Stewart, 181.
21. See Henry Staten, *Spirit Becomes Matter: The Brontës, George Eliot, Nietzsche* (Edinburgh: Edinburgh University Press, 2014); Carol Margaret Davison, "Emily Brontë's *Ars Moriendi*," *Victorians: A Journal of Culture and Literature*, no. 134 (Winter 2018): 151–65; Krebs, "Folklore"; and Peter D. Grudin, "*Wuthering Heights*: The Question of Unquiet Slumbers," *Studies in the Novel* 6, no. 4 (Winter 1974): 389–407.
22. E. Brontë, *Wuthering Heights*, 55.
23. Seemingly related to this catalog of fairies is the fact that Nelly sings a song called "Fairy Annie's Wedding" (339). But Colin Wilcockson's research turned up no existing song of that name; he found instead a song called "Fair Annie" that is thematically appropriate to the later part of the novel. Wilcockson thus suggests that "'Fairy Annie' was a misprint in the first edition" of *Wuthering Heights*. Colin Wilcockson, "'Fair(y) Annie's Wedding': A Note on Wuthering Heights," *Essays in Criticism* 33, no. 3 (July 1983): 259–61. Stewart agrees that "Fair Annie" seems to be the song Brontë meant. Stewart, "Ballad," 191.
24. Stewart, "Ballad," 178.
25. E. Brontë, *Wuthering Heights*, 40.
26. Review of *Wuthering Heights* in *Atlas* (1848), in *Wuthering Heights*, ed. Alexandra Lewis, 274; Review of *Wuthering Heights* in *Eclectic Review* (1851), in *Wuthering Heights*, ed. Alexandra Lewis, 348.
27. E. P. Whipple, "Novels of the Season" (1848), in *Wuthering Heights*, ed. Alexandra Lewis, 300–301.
28. Arnold Kettle, *An Introduction to the English Novel, Vol. 1* (New York: Harper & Row, 1951), 195–96, 194.
29. Susan Meyer, *Imperialism at Home: Race and Victorian Women's Fiction* (Ithaca, NY: Cornell University Press, 1996), 100–101.
30. E. Brontë, *Wuthering Heights*, 144; Meyer, *Imperialism*, 117.
31. E. Brontë, *Wuthering Heights*, 46. At the beginning of the novel, Thrushcross Grange and Wuthering Heights each house one boy and one girl, along with their respective parents. By the end, the two boy-girl pairs from the earlier generation have been slimmed down to one Linton and one Earnshaw, who are planning to marry and live at Thrushcross Grange.
32. The role of religion in *Wuthering Heights* is outside the scope of this chapter but well worth pursuing. See Marianne Thormählen, *The Brontës and Religion* (Cambridge: Cambridge University Press, 1999) for a good starting point, and the chapter "Looking Oppositely: Emily Brontë's Bible of Hell" in Gilbert and Gubar, *Madwoman*, for a Miltonic take.
33. In addition, Heathcliff and other characters are frequently compared to or characterized as animals, as many critics have discussed. See, for example, Ivan Kreilkamp, "Petted Things: *Wuthering Heights* and the Animal," *Yale Journal of*

Criticism 18, no. 1 (2005): 87–110; and Deborah Denenholz Morse, "'The Mark of the Beast': Animals as Sites of Imperial Encounter from Wuthering Heights to Green Mansions," in *Victorian Animal Dreams*, ed. Morse and Martin A. Danahay (London: Routledge, 2017).

34. Ahmed K. Al-Rawi points out that in old Arabic folklore, the *ghūl* was most often a shapeshifting creature who lived in the wilderness and led travelers astray; see Al-Rawi, "The Arabic Ghoul and its Western Transformation," *Folklore* 120, no. 3 (2009): 291–98. Brontë, however, would have known the description of the ghoul that entered Western culture via Antoine Galland's translation of *The Thousand and One Nights*: that of the hideous demon who dwelt in graveyards and feasted on corpses.
35. Simpson and Roud, *Dictionary*, 146; Katharine Briggs, *The Fairies in English Tradition and Literature* (Chicago: University of Chicago Press, 1967), 55–61.
36. Simpson and Roud, *Dictionary*, 36–7.
37. Pier Paolo Piciucco, "*Wuthering Heights* as a Childlike Fairy Tale," *Brontë Studies* 31, no. 3 (November 2006): 223.
38. Dorothy van Ghent, *The English Novel: Form and Function* (New York: Rinehart, 1953), 154; emphasis in original.
39. E. Brontë, *Wuthering Heights*, 78.
40. Smith, "'At Once,'" 512–13.
41. Similarly, as Susan Stewart observes, both Catherine and Heathcliff are "associated with the changeling tradition," Catherine when Lockwood explicitly suggests that the wraith who appears at his window is a changeling, and Heathcliff when he comes to Wuthering Heights as a mysterious child with unknown origins and is given the name of a dead son. "Ballad," 182.
42. Briggs, *Encyclopedia*, 330; Joseph Ritson, *Fairy Tales* (London: Thomas Davison, 1831), 33.
43. Silver, *Strange*, 168.
44. Silver, 169.
45. Thomas Crofton Croker, *Fairy Legends and Traditions of the South of Ireland*, 2nd ed. (London: John Murray, 1828), 215.
46. James Hogg, "Fairies, Brownies, and Witches," *The Shepherd's Calendar*, Class 9, *Blackwood's Edinburgh Magazine* 23 (February 1828): 224–25.
47. Ritson, *Fairy*, 121.
48. Anna Eliza Bray, *Traditions, Legends, Superstitions, and Sketches of Devonshire on the Borders of the Tamar and the Tavy* (London: John Murray, 1838), 175.
49. E. Brontë, *Wuthering Heights*, 164.
50. Complexity persists: one could also argue that Catherine is first pixy-led by the splendor of the Lintons' lifestyle and remains unhappy for the rest of her life as a result.
51. Moreover, the place to which he goes—and also the place from which he originally comes—is apparently simply the real world beyond Wuthering Heights. The realm of the Heights and the Grange functions as the fairy realm, from which Heathcliff—like Lockwood—finds he cannot stay away. Although he is

perfectly capable of taking care of himself financially and of attracting women other than Catherine (as evidenced by the fact that the one other eligible woman in the neighborhood of Wuthering Heights falls for him immediately), he is lured back.

52. Silver, *Strange*, 168–72.
53. Scott, *Minstrelsy*, 218–19.
54. E. Brontë, *Wuthering Heights*, 321.
55. Q. D. Leavis, "A Fresh Approach to *Wuthering Heights*," in *Critical Essays on Emily Brontë*, ed. Thomas John Winnifrith (New York: G. K. Hall, 1997), 207.
56. E. Brontë, *Wuthering Heights*, 357.
57. Heathcliff is not quite as badly off as the bereft human knight of John Keats's fairy bride poem, "La Belle Dame Sans Merci," for he does not despair; in both cases, though, the mortal men remain or wish to remain in a physical space associated with the beloved. Heathcliff lingers near and excavates Catherine's grave, while making plans to be buried there himself. The knight's narrative provides an explanation not only of his status as "alone and palely loitering" but also of his location: in the end, "I awoke and found me *here*, / On the cold hill's side. // And this is why I sojourn *here*" (ln. 43–45, emphasis mine). "Here" the elfin lady left him, and here he will remain. In Heathcliff's case, the goal of his final effort becomes the literal endpoint of the text of *Wuthering Heights*: the final words of the novel name the "quiet earth" of the neighboring graves of Catherine and Heathcliff ([1847] 1985, 367).
58. "Kilmeny" was included in Hogg's collection *The Queen's Wake*, which I have already discussed in chapters 3 and 5 as a possible source for Emily Brontë's poetry and for *Shirley*. The poem was not printed in *Blackwood's*, but it is mentioned there twice during the time the Brontës may have seen it: in *Noctes Ambrosianae* in 1830, vol. 27, p. 660, and quite favorably in vol. 31, 1832, pp. 981–1002, in a review of Allan Cunningham's "The Maid of Elvar" that provides a more general discussion of Scottish poetry, including Hogg's.
59. Helsinger, *Rural*, 210.
60. Davison, "*Ars Moriendi*," 155.
61. Obsession, of course, does not require a supernatural explanation, but Heathcliff's is excessive. He himself uses the word "strange" to describe the change coming over him in these final days, and Nelly applies the word to him four times in the novel's final chapter. "Wild" is applied to Heathcliff's appearance three times in this chapter as well, and once "queer."
62. On a related note, see chapter 8 on Lucy Snowe's enchantment of the reader of *Villette*.
63. E. Brontë, *Wuthering Heights*, 367.
64. Miller, *Fiction*, 60.
65. Nancy Armstrong, "Emily Brontë In and Out of Her Time," *Genre* 15, no. 3 (Fall 1982): 254.
66. Miller, *Fiction*, 42, 67. As Stoneman put it, "We cannot in fact master [*Wuthering Heights*]. It leaves us still puzzled." Patsy Stoneman, "A Peculiar Illusion:

Narrative Technique and the Lovers in *Wuthering Heights*," *Brontë Studies* 45, no. 2 (2020): 206.

Chapter 7: Anne Brontë's Fairy-Tale Realism

1. Kate Beaton, "Dude Watchin' with the Brontës," Comic 202 in *Hark! A Vagrant* (Montreal: Drawn & Quarterly, 2011).
2. On the contrary, if fairy tales are mentioned in Anne Brontë criticism, it is by way of contrast; for example, Deborah Logan's 2020 review essay of new work on Anne Brontë comments that "for Helen, as with Agnes Grey, such dramatic shifts, initiated and realized by seemingly powerless females, do not yield an uncomplicated happily-ever-after." Deborah A. Logan, "Review Essay: New Work on Anne Brontë." *Victorians: A Journal of Culture and Literature*, no. 138 (Winter 2020): 318.
3. Anne Brontë, *The Poems of Anne Brontë*, ed. Edward Chitham (London: Macmillan, 1979), 74.
4. Juliet Barker, *The Brontës*, 2nd ed. (New York: Pegasus Books, 2013), 536–37.
5. *Agnes Grey* alludes several times to magic and supernatural creatures. Interestingly, two of these allusions contribute to unfavorable descriptions of elderly women. Late in the novel, Agnes's former pupil Rosalie Murray refers to her mother-in-law as "a usurper, a tyrant, an incubus, a spy" in the house she shares with Rosalie and her husband (176). Rosalie is hardly a character to be emulated, so her strongly worded insult is unremarkable. But in one scene, pious Agnes uses similar terms in her narration. Regarding Mrs. Bloomfield, the grandmother in the first family for whom Agnes works as a governess, Agnes observes that when the woman's attitude toward her changes, her smile "gave place to a glare of gorgon ferocity" (38). Mrs. Bloomfield is also the subject of the novel's one metaphorical reference to magic: in an attempt to repair their relationship, Agnes tries flattery and finds that "the effect of this was magical" (38). Agnes rejects further use of the magic trick, however, because she opposes flattery on principle. As I have discussed in other chapters, including regarding Anne Brontë's poetry in chapter 3, such allusions to supernatural creatures and forces convey the perceived intensity of real events and experiences. Agnes also makes an unmarked reference to the *Arabian Nights' Entertainments*. After arriving at the house of the Murray family, Agnes wakes on the first morning with "a joyless kind of curiosity," "feeling like one whirled away by enchantment, and suddenly dropped from the clouds into a remote and unknown land" (58). She does not explicitly name the *Arabian Nights' Entertainments*, but the analogy is clearly taken from the popular story of Bedreddin Hassan (also referenced in the Brontë juvenilia and in *Villette*). Agnes struggles to find the words to convey her turbulent emotions in this scene; after another attempt involving a wind-blown thistle seed, she gives up with "but this gives no proper idea of my feelings at all" (59). Like the nature analogy, the fairy-tale analogy is mentioned and then dismissed as inadequate. Yet, like her siblings, Anne Brontë

resorts here to the language of magical tales when more mundane terms fail to signify.

6. See Jennifer M. Stolpa, "Preaching to the Clergy: Anne Brontë's *Agnes Grey* as a Treatise on Sermon Style and Delivery," *Victorian Literature and Culture* 31, no. 1 (2003): 225–40; Elizabeth Leaver, "The Critique of the Priest in Anne Brontë's *Agnes Grey*," *Brontë Studies* 37, no. 4 (2012): 345–51; Mary Summers, "Fact to Fiction: Anne Brontë Replicates La Trobe's Biblically Inspired Advice in Scenes from *Agnes Grey*," *Brontë Studies* 37, no. 4 (2012): 352–58.
7. Sandro Jung, "Knowledge Economies in *Agnes Grey*," *Brontë Studies* 36, no. 3 (2011): 224–34.
8. Elizabeth Langland, *Anne Brontë: The Other One* (London: Macmillan, 1989), 97; italics in original.
9. See Cates Baldridge, "*Agnes Grey*: Brontë's *Bildungsroman* That Isn't," *Journal of Narrative Technique* 23, no. 1 (Winter 1993): 31–45; Amanda Claybaugh, "Everyday Life in Anne Brontë," in *Narrative Middles: Navigating the Nineteenth-Century British Novel*, ed. Mario Ortiz-Robles and Caroline Levine (Columbus: Ohio State University Press, 2011), 109–27; and Philippa Janu, "Plotting the Governess: The Lessons of *Agnes Grey*," *Brontë Studies* 48, no. 4 (2023): 336–46. Maria Frawley, compatibly, proposes understanding *Agnes Grey* as an example of life writing. Like Janu, she is especially interested in Agnes as a writer: "Interpreted through the lens of life writing, Brontë's novel charts Agnes Grey's 'passage' from 'vacancy' to 'individual' and, in turn, to an individual more fully known by herself and others, perhaps most especially her readers, as 'Agnes Grey.'" Frawley, "'It Seemed as If They Looked on Vacancy': Life Writing in *Agnes Grey*," *Victorians: A Journal of Culture and Literature*, no. 138 (Winter 2020): 251.
10. Franco Moretti, *The Way of the World: The* Bildungsroman *in European Culture* (London: Verso, 1987), 185.
11. Anne Brontë, *Agnes Grey* (New York: Modern Library Classics, 2003), 10.
12. Janu, "Plotting," 10.
13. Janu; Claybaugh, "Everyday"; Drew Lamonica Arms, "Anne Brontë's Labors," *Victorians: A Journal of Culture and Literature*, no. 138 (Winter 2020): 169–80; Robert Butterworth, *Anne Brontë and the Trials of Life* (Oxford: Peter Lang, 2017); and Robin L. Inboden, introduction to *Agnes Grey*, by Anne Brontë (Peterborough, ON: Broadview Press, 2020).
14. On futility, see Claybaugh, "Everyday," 116; Janu, "Plotting," 2; Inboden, introduction, 27; Butterworth, *Trials*, 48. On loss of integrity, see Janu, "Plotting," 7; Arms, "Labors," 175; and Butterworth, *Trials*, 23.
15. Charles Perrault, *Contes*, ed. Catherine Magnien (Paris: Librairie Générale Française, Livre de Poche Classiques, 2006), 269.
16. Jacob Grimm and Wilhelm Grimm, *The Complete Grimm's Fairy Tales* (New York: Pantheon, 1972), 121.
17. Ruth Bottigheimer, *Fairy Tales: A New History* (Albany: SUNY Press, 2009), 10.

18. Perrault, *Contes*, 259; Grimm and Grimm, *Complete*, 121.
19. The way in which this loss occurs is in fact reminiscent of "Beauty and the Beast": like Beauty's father, Agnes's father loses his fortune because a shipwreck destroys all his cargo. A. Brontë, *Agnes Grey*, 6.
20. A. Brontë, 105.
21. Claybaugh ("Everyday") argues that *Agnes Grey* begins as a *Bildungsroman* then shifts to a courtship plot.
22. A. Brontë, *Agnes Grey*, 144.
23. Langland, *Other*, 52.
24. "Tieck's Bluebeard: A Dramatic Tale, in Five Acts," *Blackwood's Edinburgh Magazine* 33 (February 1833): 206–23.
25. Biographer Edward Chitham gives this account: "We have five of her letters, though we know she wrote hundreds. She may have kept a journal or diary, but if so, it has not survived. Two of her 'journal papers' . . . have been printed, but the manuscripts have been lost." Edward Chitham, *A Life of Anne Brontë* (Cambridge, MA: Blackwell, 1991), 5.
26. See the unsigned reviews from *Literary World*, *Spectator*, and *Sharpe's London Magazine*, all in *The Brontës: The Critical Heritage*, ed. Miriam Allott (Routledge & Kegan Paul, 1974), 249–50, 257–61, 263–65.
27. Anne Brontë, *The Tenant of Wildfell Hall*, ed. Stevie Davies (London: Penguin Classics, 1996), 3, 4.
28. For further discussion of the novel's structure, see Maggie Berg, "'Let Me Have Its Bowels Then': Violence, Sacrificial Structure, and Anne Brontë's *The Tenant of Wildfell Hall*," *Literature Interpretation Theory* 21, no. 1 (2012): 20–40; Jan B. Gordon, "Gossip, Diary, Letter, Text: Anne Brontë's Narrative Tenant and the Problematic of the Gothic Sequel," *ELH* 51, no. 4 (Winter 1984): 719–45; N. M. Jacobs, "Gender and Layered Narrative in *Wuthering Heights* and *The Tenant of Wildfell Hall*," in *The Brontës*, ed. Patricia Ingham (Harlow: Pearson Education, 2003), 216–33; Catherine Quirk, "Consent and Enclosure in *The Tenant of Wildfell Hall*: 'You Needn't Read It All; but Take It Home with You,'" *Victorians: A Journal of Culture and Literature*, no. 138 (Winter 2020): 231–41.
29. A. Brontë, *Tenant*, 419, 14, 183, 106, 109, 401, 422.
30. A. Brontë, 23.
31. Perrault, *Contes*, 228.
32. Perrault, 219.
33. A. Brontë, *Tenant*, 136. Perrault's heroine is the daughter of a "dame de qualité" ("woman of quality"; *Contes*, 219), though subsequent versions of the story have often lowered her social standing, surely in order to better explain her decision to marry someone as suspicious as Bluebeard.
34. A. Brontë, *Tenant*, 149.
35. A. Brontë, 365.
36. Like Bluebeard's last wife, Helen escapes with the help of her brother. Frederick Lawrence functions in *Wildfell Hall* both to escalate Gilbert's desire for Helen and to rescue his sister from the monstrous husband—albeit through

less dramatic means than running him through with a sword as the fairy-tale brothers do.

37. A. Brontë, *Tenant,* 331.
38. Robin Gilmour, *The Idea of the Gentleman in the Victorian Novel* (London: Allen & Unwin, 1981).
39. A. James Hammerton, *Cruelty and Companionship: Conflict in Nineteenth-Century Married Life* (New York: Routledge, 1992); Marlene Tromp, *The Private Rod* (Charlottesville: University Press of Virginia, 2000); J. Carter Wood, *Violence and Crime in Nineteenth-Century England* (New York: Routledge, 2004); and Lisa Surridge, *Bleak Houses: Marital Violence in Victorian Fiction* (Athens: Ohio University Press, 2005).
40. A. Brontë, *Tenant,* 350.
41. See Judith E. Pike, "Breeching Boys: Milksops, Men's Clubs and the Modelling of Masculinity in Anne Brontë's *Agnes Grey* and *The Tenant of Wildfell Hall,*" *Brontë Studies* 37, no. 2 (April 2012): 112–24.
42. A. Brontë, *Tenant,* 262.
43. Sarah Stickney Ellis, *The Wives of England* (New York: J&H Langley, 1843), 14.
44. Ellis, *Wives,* 49.
45. Charlotte Brontë herself participated, comparing Rochester, Huntingdon, and Heathcliff in this 1848 letter to William Smith Williams: "The foundation of each character [Rochester and Huntingdon] is entirely different. Huntingdon is a specimen of the naturally selfish sensual, superficial man whose one merit of a joyous temperament only avails him while he is young and healthy, whose best days are his earliest, who never profits by experience, who is sure to grow worse, the older he grows. Mr Rochester has a thoughtful nature and a very feeling heart; he is neither selfish nor self-indulgent; he is ill-educated, misguided, errs, when he does err, through rashness and inexperience: he lives for a time as too many other men live—but being radically better than most men he does not like that degraded life, and is never happy in it. He is taught the severe lessons of Experience and has sense to learn wisdom from them—years improve him—the effervescence of youth foamed away, what is really good in him still remains—his nature is like wine of a good vintage, time cannot sour—but only mellows him. Such at least was the character I meant to pourtray [*sic*].

    "Heathcliffe [*sic*], again, of 'Wuthering Heights,' is quite another creation. He exemplifies the effects which a life of continued injustice and hard usage may produce on a naturally perverse, vindictive and inexorable disposition. Carefully trained and kindly treated, the black gipsey-cub [*sic*] might possibly have been reared into a human being, but tyranny and ignorance made of him a mere demon. The worst of it is, some of his spirit seems breathed through the whole narrative in which he figures: it haunts every moor and glen, and beckons in every fir-tree of the 'Heights.'" Margaret Smith, ed., *The Letters of Charlotte Brontë,* vol. 2 (Oxford: Clarendon Press, 2000), 99.
46. Parallels with *Wuthering Heights* are the most obvious: like Emily's novel, Anne's is named after one of its central locations (initials W. H.), features an

abusive central male figure, and teems with male characters whose names begin with H. Although the first two elements apply to many novels, the profusion of H-names is unlikely to be a coincidence. As for *Jane Eyre*, critics compare the checkered pasts of Huntingdon and Rochester, as well as the heroines' flights from and returns to these men.

47. Priti Joshi, "Masculinity and Gossip in Anne Brontë's *Tenant*," *SEL: Studies in English Literature* 49, vol. 4 (Autumn 2009): 907–24; Quirk, "Consent"; Claybaugh, "Everyday," 124.
48. Chitham, *Life*, 142–43.
49. Langland, *Other*, 58.
50. Janina Hornosty, "Let's Not Have Its Bowels Quite So Quickly, Then: A Response to Maggie Berg," *Brontë Studies* 39, no. 2 (April 2015): 130–40; Deborah Denenholz Morse, "'I Speak of Those I Do Know': Witnessing as Radical Gesture in *The Tenant of Wildfell Hall*," in *New Approaches to the Literary Art of Anne Brontë*, ed. Julie Nash and Barbara A. Suess (Aldershot, UK: Ashgate, 2001), 121; Grace Pregent, "Peripheral Voices in *The Tenant of Wildfell Hall*," *Victorians: A Journal of Culture and Literature*, no. 138 (Winter 2020): 224.
51. Pike, "Breeching," 119–22; Butterworth, *Trials*, 95.
52. Perrault, *Contes*, 228n1.
53. Perrault, *Contes*, 228.
54. Doreen Thierauf, "Guns and Blood: Reading *The Tenant of Wildfell Hall* in the Age of #MeToo," *Nineteenth-Century Gender Studies* 16, vol. 2 (Summer 2020): https://www.ncgsjournal.com/. See also Elizabeth King, "'Uncivil Usage': Shifting Forms of Control in *The Tenant of Wildfell Hall*," *Victorians: A Journal of Culture and Literature*, no. 138 (Winter 2020): 124–40.
55. A. Brontë, *Tenant*, 3.
56. Deborah Logan's introduction to the 2020 special bicentennial issue of *Victorians* on Anne Brontë observes, "A primary theme readers of this collection will find is the well-entrenched tradition of marginalizing Anne Brontë as the 'other' sister who (as some have claimed) would likely not be on the literary map at all, except for her kinship with Charlotte and Emily" ("Review," 1).

Chapter 8: A Personage in Disguise: Villette *and the Narrative of Enchantment*

1. Charlotte Brontë, *Villette* (New York: Penguin Classics, 2004), 341.
2. C. Brontë, 341.
3. Margaret Smith, ed., *The Letters of Charlotte Brontë*, vol. 3 (Oxford: Clarendon Press, 2004), 137.
4. C. Brontë, *Villette*, 85.
5. C. Brontë, 128.
6. On this aspect of the novel, see Talia Schaffer, *Communities of Care: The Social Ethics of Victorian Fiction* (Princeton, NJ: Princeton University Press, 2021).

7. C. Brontë, *Villette*, 130.
8. Review of *Villette* in *Spectator*, in *The Brontës: The Critical Heritage*, ed. Miriam Allott (New York: Routledge, 1974), 183.
9. Charise Gendron, "Harriet Martineau and Virginia Woolf Reading *Villette*," in *The Brontë Sisters: Critical Assessments*, ed. Eleanor McNees, vol. 3 (Bodmin, UK: Helm Information, 1996), 697.
10. Heather Glen, *Charlotte Brontë: The Imagination in History* (Oxford: Oxford University Press, 2002), 201.
11. Penny Boumelha, *Charlotte Brontë* (New York: Harvester Wheatsheaf, 1990), 100.
12. Ezra Dan Feldman, "Weird Weather: Nonhuman Narration and Unmoored Feelings in Charlotte Brontë's *Villette*," *Victorians* 130 (Fall 2016): 79.
13. Feldman, 89, 97, 93.
14. Talia Schaffer is observing the same phenomenon when she suggests that "Lucy continues to act when narrating to us." Schaffer, *Communities*, 109.
15. *Oxford English Dictionary Online*, s.v. "enchant (*v.*), Etymology," 2023, https://doi.org/10.1093/OED/4511149518.
16. I build here, too, on Heather Glen's examination of the many "images of visual bedazzlement" in *Villette*; she convincingly demonstrates that Brontë was interested in bedazzlement's "challenge to perceptual mastery, [and] its connotations both of splendour and of annihilation," as discussed in contemporary debates in the visual art world (*Imagination*, 285). Although Glen does not explore the possibility that narrator-Lucy may be attempting to "dazzle" the reader, this strikes me as a logical extension of her argument.
17. The language with which some critics have discussed *Villette* anticipates my argument about the enchanting quality of the narrative: for Gilbert and Gubar, "we submit to the spell of the novel"; for John Hughes, the novel "works on us" because we are "enthralled readers." Sandra M. Gilbert and Susan Gubar, *The Madwoman in the Attic: The Woman Writer and the Nineteenth-Century Literary Imagination*, 2nd ed. (New Haven, CT: Yale University Press, 2000), 439; John Hughes, "The Affective World of Charlotte Brontë's *Villette*," *SEL: Studies in English Literature* 40, no. 4 (Autumn 2000): 716, 715. Although such phrasing is common enough in describing anything powerful, these critics are on to something. Micael Clarke has used the language of enchantment more substantially in discussing the British Protestant conflation of Catholicism and magic in the novel: "*Villette* takes place in a world that, for Lucy Snowe, is disenchanted" because she is not Catholic, but due to the supernatural elements Brontë introduces into the novel, "the enchanted world exists side-by-side with the disenchanted world." Micael M. Clarke, "Charlotte Brontë's 'Villette,' Mid-Victorian Anti-Catholicism, and the Turn to Secularism," *ELH* 78, no. 4 (Winter 2011): 985. I concur, and I argue that narrator-Lucy deliberately introduces these elements in order to contribute to the enchantment she performs on the reader throughout the novel.
18. C. Brontë, *Villette*, 62.

19. C. Brontë, 62. This alliterative axiom is not quoted from a preexisting text but rather mimics the style of sayings children were required to write to practice their penmanship.
20. Consider, too, the example of the Romantics, whom we know Brontë read voraciously. Samuel Taylor Coleridge, in particular, tends to reveal truth through enchantment. The eponymous heroine of "Christabel" is rendered unable to speak of her thrall to the serpentine Geraldine; she magically loses control over her speech as she has genuinely lost control over her behavior and the sovereignty of her self. Christabel's vocal paralysis is matched by the mariner's compulsion to speak in "The Rime of the Ancient Mariner"; his supernaturally mandated need to tell his story over and over again literalizes the natural guilt and trauma he experiences in the wake of the event. Brontë would have encountered revelatory enchantment, then, in prestigious poetry as well as in fairy tales flagged as fantastical.
21. Abigail Heiniger, *Jane Eyre's Fairytale Legacy at Home and Abroad: Constructions and Deconstructions of National Identity* (New York: Routledge, 2016), 2.
22. C. Brontë, *Jane Eyre*, 390.
23. C. Brontë, *Villette*, 166, 124, 280.
24. C. Brontë, *Villette*, 208.
25. Katherine J. Kim, "Corpse Hoarding: Control and the Female Body in 'Bluebeard,' 'Schalken the Painter,' and *Villette*," *Studies in the Novel* 43, no. 4 (Winter 2011): 406–27.
26. C. Brontë, *Villette*, 151.
27. C. Brontë, *Villette*, 268, 270. Throughout this book, I have noted instances of male narrators and characters accusing female characters of the "caprice" associated with fairies, sprites, and similar creatures. Astonishingly, in *Villette*, Lucy deems a man a capricious sprite—and not just any man, but the man she will later desire to marry. This is nearly unprecedented in literature of its kind and speaks to Lucy's uniqueness as a narrator and as a character.
28. C. Brontë, *Villette*, 188.
29. In a nod to western fairy tales, Brontë also gives Lucy something of a fairy godmother: Graham's mother, Mrs. Bretton. The first words of the novel, in fact, are "My godmother" (7). Mrs. Bretton is a benefactor for Lucy in that she takes Lucy into her home on more than one occasion. In a specific episode, she not only arranges for Lucy to go out to a concert with her and Graham but also provides her with a dress à la Cinderella's fairy godmother in Perrault's tale (231).
30. Recall from chapter 2 that Branwell Brontë refers to the tale of the Barmecide's feast as well in "The Life of Field Marshal the Right Honourable Alexander Percy."
31. C. Brontë, *Villette*, 431.
32. Sally Shuttleworth, *Charlotte Brontë and Victorian Psychology* (Cambridge: Cambridge University Press), 1996, 226.

33. C. Brontë, *Villette*, 118.
34. Christina Crosby, "Charlotte Brontë's Haunted Text," *SEL: Studies in English Literature* 24, no. 4 (Autumn 1984): 703.
35. Gilbert and Gubar, *Madwoman*, 426.
36. Anna Neill, *Primitive Minds* (Columbus: Ohio State University Press, 2013); Emily W. Heady, "'Must I Render an Account?' Genre and Self-Narration in Charlotte Brontë's *Villette*," *Journal of Narrative Theory* 36, no. 3 (Fall 2006): 341–64; Mary Jacobus, "The Buried Letter: Feminism and Romanticism in *Villette*," in McNees, *The Brontë Sisters*, 673–88.
37. See Heady, "Must"; Robert A. Colby, "*Villette* and the Life of the Mind," in McNees, *The Brontë Sisters*, 632–49; Ruth Robbins, "How Do I Look? *Villette* and Looking Different(ly)," *Brontë Studies* 28, no. 3 (2003): 215–22; and Ruth D. Johnston, "Dis-Membrance of Things Past: Re-Vision of Wordsworthian Retrospection in *Jane Eyre* and *Villette*." *Victorian Literature and Culture* 22 (1994): 73–102.
38. Feldman, "Weird," 93.
39. Recall the example of revelatory enchantment in "Hansel and Gretel," which is useful for my purposes here because of the doubling or splitting of the female threat. Hansel and Gretel's problem is their mother or stepmother (depending on the version), who wants to lose them in the woods because she and their father can no longer afford to feed them. The children's subsequent conflict with the witch in the woods works out their problems with their (step)mother. When the children return home after killing the witch, they discover that their (step)mother has died as well: defeating the one entails defeating the other. Witches with edible houses are creatures of fiction; inadequate parents are not. Something similar is going on in *Villette*: the fairy tale's witch has a functional equivalent in the novel's mysterious nun.
40. C. Brontë, *Villette*, 273.
41. C. Brontë, 281.
42. Crosby, "Haunted," 702.
43. C. Brontë, *Villette*, 517.
44. Gilbert and Gubar, *Madwoman*, 416; Nina Auerbach, "Charlotte Brontë: The Two Countries," in McNees, *The Brontë Sisters*, 672.
45. C. Brontë, *Villette*, 51.
46. Karen Chase, *Eros and Psyche: The Representation of Personality in Charlotte Brontë, Charles Dickens, and George Eliot* (New York: Methuen, 1984), 67.
47. Rachel Ablow, *Victorian Pain* (Princeton, NJ: Princeton University Press, 2017), 72–73.
48. C. Brontë, *Villette*, 108.
49. Ablow, *Pain*, 73.
50. C. Brontë, *Villette*, 546.
51. Lucy's initial reference to the banshee involves an odd assertion: "Epidemic diseases, I believed, were often heralded by a gasping, sobbing, tormented, long-lamenting east wind. Hence, I inferred, arose the legend of the Banshee"

(43). Although negative associations with the east wind go back to Genesis and appear in other Victorian texts, including Dickens's *Bleak House*, the notion that this wind is particularly loud and perhaps engendered the legend of the banshee appears to be unique to the Brontë sisters. Instead of an informative statement, this is a flourish in Lucy's enchanted narrative.

Conclusion

1. Annie Hiebert Alton, ed., *Peter Pan*, by J. M. Barrie (Peterborough, ON: Broadview Press, 2011), 244.
2. Alton, 21.

Bibliography

Ablow, Rachel. *Victorian Pain*. Princeton, NJ: Princeton University Press, 2017.

"About the Folklore Society." *The Folklore Society*. Accessed March 26, 2021. https://folklore-society.com/about/.

Alexander, Christine, ed. *An Edition of the Early Writings of Charlotte Brontë*. Vol. 1. Oxford: Basil Blackwell, 1987.

———, ed. *An Edition of the Early Writings of Charlotte Brontë*. Vol. 2, Part 1. Oxford: Basil Blackwell, 1991.

———, ed. *An Edition of the Early Writings of Charlotte Brontë*. Vol. 2, Part 2. Oxford: Basil Blackwell, 1991.

———, ed. *Tales of Glass Town, Angria, and Gondal*. Oxford: Oxford University Press, 2010.

Alexander, Christine, and Margaret Smith. *The Oxford Companion to the Brontës*. Oxford: Oxford University Press, 2018.

Ali, Muhsin Jassim. *Scheherazade in England: A Study of Nineteenth-Century English Criticism of the Arabian Nights*. Washington, DC: Three Continents Press, 1981.

Allott, Miriam, ed. *The Brontës: The Critical Heritage*. London: Routledge & Kegan Paul, 1974.

———, ed. *The Poems of John Keats*. London: Longman, 1970.

Al-Rawi, Ahmed K. "The Arabic Ghoul and Its Western Transformation." *Folklore* 120, no. 3 (2009): 291–306.

Alton, Annie Hiebert, ed. *Peter Pan*. By J. M. Barrie. Peterborough, ON: Broadview Press, 2011.

Anderson, Amanda. "Trollope's Modernity." *ELH* 74, no. 3 (2007): 509–34.

Anderson, Victoria. "Investigating the Third Story: 'Bluebeard' and 'Cinderella' in *Jane Eyre*." In *Horrifying Sex: Essays on Sexual Difference in Gothic Literature*, edited by Ruth Bienstock Anolik, 111–21. Jefferson, NC: McFarland, 2007.

Anonymous. Review of *Wuthering Heights* in *Atlas* (1848). In *Wuthering Heights*, edited by Alexandra Lewis, 5th ed., 273–75. New York: W. W. Norton, 2019.

———. Review of *Wuthering Heights* in *Eclectic Review* (1851). In *Wuthering Heights*, edited by Alexandra Lewis, 5th ed., 346–48. New York: W. W. Norton, 2019.

Argyle, Gisela. "Gender and Generic Mixing in Charlotte Brontë's *Shirley*." *Studies in English Literature 1500–1900* 35, no. 4 (1995): 741–56.

Arms, Drew Lamonica. "Anne Brontë's Labors." *Victorians: A Journal of Culture and Literature*, no. 138 (Winter 2020): 169–80.

Armstrong, Nancy. "Emily Brontë in and out of Her Time." *Genre* 15, no. 3 (Fall 1982): 243–64.

———. *Fiction in the Age of Photography: The Legacy of British Realism*. Cambridge, MA: Harvard University Press, 1999.

———. "Imperialist Nostalgia and *Wuthering Heights*." In *Wuthering Heights: Case Studies in Contemporary Criticism*, edited by Linda H. Peterson, 428–49. Boston: Bedford / St. Martin's, 1992.

Auerbach, Nina. "Charlotte Brontë: The Two Countries." In *The Brontë Sisters: Critical Assessments*, edited by Eleanor McNees, vol. 3, 659–72. Bodmin, UK: Helm Information, 1996.

Auerbach, Nina, and U. C. Knoepflmacher, eds. *Forbidden Journeys: Fairy Tales and Fantasies by Victorian Women Writers*. Chicago: University of Chicago Press, 1992.

Azim, Firdous. *The Colonial Rise of the Novel*. New York: Routledge, 1993.

Bacchilega, Cristina. *Postmodern Fairy Tales: Gender and Narrative Strategies*. Philadelphia: University of Pennsylvania Press, 1999.

Baldridge, Cates. "*Agnes Grey*: Brontë's *Bildungsroman* That Isn't." *Journal of Narrative Technique* 23, no. 1 (Winter 1993): 31–45.

Barker, Juliet. *The Brontës: A Life in Letters*. London: Viking, 1997.

———. *The Brontës*. 2nd ed. New York: Pegasus Books, 2013.

Barzilai, Shuli. *Tales of Bluebeard and His Wives from Late Antiquity to Postmodern Times*. New York: Routledge, 2009.

Beaton, Kate. "Dude Watchin' with the Brontës." In *Hark! A Vagrant*, Comic 202. Montreal: Drawn & Quarterly, 2011.

Beaumont, Jeanne-Marie Leprince de. "La Belle et la bête." In *La Belle et la bête, suivi de l'oiseau bleu*, 9–42. Paris: Livres de Poche Jeunesse, 2014.

Benvenuto, Richard. "'The Child of Nature, the Child of Grace, and the Unresolved Conflict of *Jane Eyre*." In *The Brontë Sisters: Critical Assessments*, edited by Eleanor McNees, vol. 3, 210–25. Bodmin, UK: Helm Information, 1996.

Benwell, Gwen, and Arthur Waugh. *Sea Enchantress: The Tale of the Mermaid and Her Kin*. New York: Citadel Press, 1965.

Berg, Maggie. "'Let Me Have Its Bowels Then': Violence, Sacrificial Structure, and Anne Brontë's *The Tenant of Wildfell Hall*." *Literature Interpretation Theory* 21, no. 1 (2012): 20–40.

Berg, Temma. "Reading Amazon Fragments: Queering *Shirley*." *Brontë Studies* 41, no. 3, (September 2016): 216–28.

Berry, Elizabeth Hollis. *Anne Brontë's Radical Vision: Structures of Consciousness*. Victoria, BC: English Literary Studies, 1994.

Bersani, Leo. *A Future for Astyanax*. Boston: Little, Brown, 1969.

Bonnell Collection. Papers. Brontë Parsonage Museum, Haworth, UK.

Bottigheimer, Ruth. *Fairy Tales: A New History*. Albany: SUNY Press, 2009.

Boumelha, Penny. *Charlotte Brontë*. New York: Harvester Wheatsheaf, 1990.

Bown, Nicola. *Fairies in Nineteenth-Century Art and Literature*. Cambridge: Cambridge University Press, 2001.

Bray, Anna Eliza. *Traditions, Legends, Superstitions, and Sketches of Devonshire on the Borders of the Tamar and the Tavy, Illustrative of Its Manners, Customs, History, Antiquities, Scenery, and Natural History, in a Series of Letters to Robert Southey, Esq*. London: John Murray, 1838. GoogleBooks.

Briggs, Katharine. *An Encyclopedia of Fairies*. New York: Pantheon, 1976.
———. *The Fairies in English Tradition and Literature*. Chicago: University of Chicago Press, 1967.
"The British Settlements in Western Africa." *Blackwood's* 26 (September 1829): 341–50.
Brontë, Anne. *Agnes Grey*. New York: Modern Library Classics, 2003.
———. *The Poems of Anne Brontë*. Edited by Edward Chitham. London: Macmillan, 1979.
———. *The Tenant of Wildfell Hall*. Edited by Stevie Davies. London: Penguin Classics, 1996.
Brontë, Charlotte. *Jane Eyre*. 4th ed. Edited by Deborah Lutz. New York: W. W. Norton, 2016.
———. *The Poems of Charlotte Brontë*. Edited by Tom Winnifrith. Oxford: Shakespeare Head Press, 1984.
———. *The Professor*. Edited by Heather Glen. London: Penguin Books, 1989.
———. *Shirley*. Edited by Margaret Smith. Oxford: Oxford World's Classics, 1981.
———. *Tales of Angria*. Edited by Heather Glen. London: Penguin Classics, 2006.
———. *Tales of the Islanders*. New York: Hesperus Press, 2011.
———. *Villette*. New York: Penguin Classics, 2004.
Brontë, Emily. *The Complete Poems*. Edited by Janet Gezari. London: Penguin Books, 1992.
———. *Wuthering Heights*. Edited by David Daiches. London: Penguin Books, 1985.
Brooks, Peter. *Reading for the Plot*. New York: Alfred A. Knopf, 1984.
Butcher, Emma. *The Brontës and War: Fantasy and Conflict in Charlotte and Branwell Brontë's Youthful Writings*. Basingstoke: Palgrave Macmillan, 2019.
Butterworth, Robert. *Anne Brontë and the Trials of Life*. Oxford: Peter Lang, 2017.
Buzard, James. *Disorienting Fiction: The Autoethnographic Work of Nineteenth-Century British Novels*. Princeton, NJ: Princeton University Press, 2005.
Capuano, Peter J. "Networked Manufacture in Charlotte Brontë's *Shirley*." *Victorian Studies* 55, no. 2 (Winter 2013): 231–42.
Caracciolo, Peter. "Introduction: 'Such a store house of ingenious fiction and of splendid imagery.'" In *The Arabian Nights in English Literature: Studies in the Reception of the Thousand and One Nights into British Culture*, edited by Peter Caracciolo, 1–80. New York: St. Martin's, 1988.
Carlton-Ford, Cynthia. "Intimacy without Immolation: Fire in *Jane Eyre*." In *The Brontë Sisters: Critical Assessments*, edited by Eleanor McNees, vol. 3, 342–51. Bodmin, UK: Helm Information, 1996.
Chase, Karen. *Eros and Psyche: The Representation of Personality in Charlotte Brontë, Charles Dickens, and George Eliot*. New York: Methuen, 1984.
Chitham, Edward. "The Irish Heritage of the Brontës." In *A Companion to the Brontës*, edited by Diane Long Hoeveler and Deborah Denenholz Morse, 403–15. Chichester, UK: Wiley Blackwell, 2016.
———. *A Life of Anne Brontë*. Cambridge, MA: Blackwell, 1991.

Clarke, Micael M. "Charlotte Brontë's 'Villette,' Mid-Victorian Anti-Catholicism, and the Turn to Secularism." *ELH* 78, no. 4 (Winter 2011): 967–89.

Claybaugh, Amanda. "Everyday Life in Anne Brontë." In *Narrative Middles: Navigating the Nineteenth-Century British Novel,* edited by Mario Ortiz-Robles and Caroline Levine, 109–27. Columbus: Ohio State University Press, 2011.

———. *The Novel of Purpose: Literature and Social Reform in the Anglo-American World.* Ithaca, NY: Cornell University Press, 2007.

Clayton, Jay. *Romantic Vision and the Novel.* New York: Cambridge University Press, 1987.

Colby, Robert A. "*Villette* and the Life of the Mind." In *The Brontë Sisters: Critical Assessments,* edited by Eleanor McNees, vol. 3, 632–49. Bodmin, UK: Helm Information, 1996.

Coleridge, Samuel Taylor. *Samuel Taylor Coleridge: The Major Works.* Oxford: Oxford World's Classics. 2000.

Conover, Robin St. John. "Creating Angria: Charlotte and Branwell Brontë's Collaboration." *Brontë Society Transactions* 24, no. 3 (1999): 16–32.

Corbett, Mary Jean. *Family Likeness: Sex, Marriage, and Incest from Jane Austen to Virginia Woolf.* Ithaca, NY: Cornell University Press, 2008.

Coriale, Danielle. "Charlotte Brontë's 'Shirley' and the Consolations of Natural History." *Victorian Review* 36, no. 2 (Fall 2010): 118–32.

Cortés Vieco, Francisco José. "A Changeling Becomes Titania: The Realm of the Fairies in Charlotte Brontë's *Jane Eyre.*" *Anglia,* 138, no. 1 (2020): 20–37.

Croker, Thomas Crofton. *Fairy Legends and Traditions of the South of Ireland.* 2nd ed. Vols. 1–3. London: John Murray, 1828. HathiTrust Digital Library.

Crosby, Christina. "Charlotte Brontë's Haunted Text." *Studies in English Literature* 24, no. 4 (Autumn 1984): 701–15.

Cunningham, Allan. *Traditional Tales of the English and Scottish Peasantry.* Vol. 2. London: Taylor and Hessey, 1822. HathiTrust Digital Library.

Darton, F. J. Harvey. *Children's Books in England.* Cambridge: Cambridge University Press, 1958.

d'Aulnoy, Marie-Catherine. "La Biche au bois." In *Contes de Madame d'Aulnoy,* 48–62. Paris: Garniers Frères, 1882. Gallica.

———. "The White Cat." In *Beauties, Beasts, and Enchantment: Classic French Fairy Tales,* translated and edited by Jack Zipes, 515–44. Maidstone, UK: Crescent Moon, 2009.

David, Deirdre. *Rule Britannia: Women, Empire, and Victorian Writing.* Ithaca, NY: Cornell University Press, 1995.

Davison, Carol Margaret. "Emily Brontë's *Ars Moriendi.*" *Victorians: A Journal of Culture and Literature,* no. 134 (Winter 2018): 151–65.

DeFord, Miriam Allen. *Thomas Moore.* New York: Twayne, 1967.

Dickson, Melissa. *Cultural Encounters with the Arabian Nights in Nineteenth-Century Britain.* Edinburgh: Edinburgh University Press. 2019.

Dorson, Richard. *The British Folklorists.* Chicago: University of Chicago Press, 1968.

Duckett, Bob. "Branwell Brontë, *BST* and *Brontë Studies*: An Annotated Bibliography." *Brontë Studies* 42, no. 3 (2017): 261–72.

———. "The Library at Ponden Hall." *Brontë Studies* 40, no. 2 (2015): 104–49.

Eagleton, Terry. *Myths of Power*. London: Palgrave Macmillan, 1975.

Eliot, George. *Middlemarch*. Oxford: Oxford World's Classics, 1991.

Ellis, Sarah Stickney. *The Wives of England*. New York: J&H Langley, 1843.

Feldman, Ezra Dan. "Weird Weather: Nonhuman Narration and Unmoored Feelings in Charlotte Brontë's *Villette*." *Victorians: A Journal of Culture and Literature*, no. 130 (Fall 2016): 78–99.

Forsberg, Laura. "The Miniature World of Charlotte Brontë's Glass Town." In Pike and Morrison, *Charlotte Brontë from the Beginnings*, 44–58.

Fraser, Rebecca. *The Brontës: Charlotte Brontë and Her Family*. New York: Crown, 1988.

Frawley, Maria. "'It Seemed as If They Looked on Vacancy': Life Writing in *Agnes Grey*." *Victorians: A Journal of Culture and Literature*, no. 138 (Winter 2020): 242–52.

Gallagher, Catherine. *The Industrial Reformation of English Fiction: Social Discourse and Narrative Form, 1832–1867*. Chicago: University of Chicago Press, 1985.

Gaskell, Elizabeth. *The Life of Charlotte Brontë*. New York: Penguin Classics, 1987.

———. *Mary Barton*. Edited by Jennifer Foster. Peterborough, ON: Broadview Press, 2000.

Gendron, Charise. "Harriet Martineau and Virginia Woolf Reading *Villette*." In *The Brontë Sisters: Critical Assessments*, edited by Eleanor McNees, vol. 3, 696–703. Bodmin, UK: Helm Information, 1996.

Gérin, Winifred. *Branwell Brontë*. London: Thomas Nelson and Sons, 1961.

———. *Charlotte Brontë*. London: Oxford University Press, 1967.

Gezari, Janet. *Last Things: Emily Brontë's Poems*. Oxford: Oxford University Press, 2007.

Gilbert, Sandra M., and Susan Gubar. *The Madwoman in the Attic: The Woman Writer and the Nineteenth-Century Literary Imagination*. 2nd ed. New Haven, CT: Yale University Press, 2000.

Gilmour, Robin. *The Idea of the Gentleman in the Victorian Novel*. London: Allen & Unwin, 1981.

Glen, Heather. *Charlotte Brontë: The Imagination in History*. Oxford: Oxford University Press, 2002.

Gordon, Jan B. "Gossip, Diary, Letter, Text: Anne Brontë's Narrative Tenant and the Problematic of the Gothic Sequel." *ELH* 51, no. 4 (Winter 1984): 719–45.

Gose, Elliott B. *Imagination Indulged: The Irrational in the Nineteenth-Century Novel*. Montreal: McGill-Queen's University Press, 1972.

Grenby, M. O. *The Child Reader, 1700–1840*. Cambridge: Cambridge University Press, 2011.

Grimm, Jacob, and Wilhelm Grimm. *The Complete Grimm's Fairy Tales*. New York: Pantheon, 1972.

Grove, Robin. "'It Would Not Do': Emily Brontë as Poet." In *The Art of Emily Brontë*, edited by Anne Smith, 33–67. London: Vision Critical Studies, 1976.

Grudin, Peter D. "*Wuthering Heights:* The Question of Unquiet Slumbers." *Studies in the Novel* 6, no. 4 (Winter 1974): 389–407.

Hammerton, A. James. *Cruelty and Companionship: Conflict in Nineteenth-Century Married Life*. New York: Routledge, 1992.

Hardy, Barbara. "The Lyricism of Emily Brontë." In *The Art of Emily Brontë*, edited by Anne Smith, 94–118. London: Vision Critical Studies, 1976.

———. *Wuthering Heights*. Oxford: Basil Blackwell and Mott, 1963.

Harman, Claire. *Charlotte Brontë: A Fiery Heart*. New York: Alfred A. Knopf, 2016.

Harries, Elizabeth Wanning. *Twice Upon a Time: Women Writers and the History of the Fairy Tale*. Princeton, NJ: Princeton University Press, 2001.

Harris, Jason Marc. *Folklore and the Fantastic in Nineteenth-Century British Fiction*. New York: Routledge, 2008.

Hartland, Edwin Sidney. *The Science of Fairy Tales: An Inquiry into Fairy Mythology*. London: W. Scott, 1891. HathiTrust Digital Library.

Hatfield, C. W. *The Complete Poems of Emily Jane Brontë*. New York: Columbia University Press, 1995.

Heady, Emily W. "'Must I Render an Account?': Genre and Self-Narration in Charlotte Brontë's *Villette*." *Journal of Narrative Theory* 36, no. 3 (Fall 2006): 341–64.

Hearne, Betsy. *Beauty and the Beast: Visions and Revisions of an Old Tale*. Chicago: University of Chicago Press, 1989.

Heilman, Robert B. "Charlotte Brontë's 'New Gothic.'" In *From Jane Austen to Joseph Conrad: Essays Collected in Memory of James T. Hillhouse*, edited by Robert C. Radiburn and Martin Steinmann Jr., 118–32. Minneapolis: University of Minnesota Press, 1958.

Heiniger, Abigail. *Jane Eyre's Fairytale Legacy at Home and Abroad: Constructions and Deconstructions of National Identity*. New York: Routledge, 2016.

Helsinger, Elizabeth K. *Rural Scenes and National Representation: Britain, 1815–1850*. Princeton, NJ: Princeton University Press, 1997.

Hermansson, Casie E. *Bluebeard: A Reader's Guide to the English Tradition*. Jackson: University Press of Mississippi, 2009.

Hillard, Molly Clark. "Dangerous Exchange: Fairy Footsteps, Goblin Economies, and *The Old Curiosity Shop*." *Dickens Studies Annual* 35 (2005): 63–86.

———. *Spellbound: The Fairy Tale and the Victorians*. Columbus: Ohio State University Press, 2014.

Hoeveler, Diane Long. "Charlotte Brontë and the Anxious Imagination." In *Time, Space, and Place in Charlotte Brontë*, edited by Diane Long Hoeveler and Deborah Denenholz Morse, 85–102. New York: Routledge, 2016.

———. *Gothic Feminisms: The Professionalization of Gender from Charlotte Smith to the Brontës*. University Park: Pennsylvania State University Press, 1998.

———. "The Not-So-New Gothic: Charlotte Brontë's Juvenilia and the Gothic Tradition." In Pike and Morrison, *Charlotte Brontë from the Beginnings*, 85–98.

Hogg, James. *Anecdotes of Scott*. Edited by Jill Rubenstein. Edinburgh: Edinburgh University Press, 1999.

———."The Brownie of the Black Haggs." *Blackwood's Edinburgh Magazine* 14 (October 1828): 489–96.

———. "Fairies, Brownies, and Witches." *The Shepherd's Calendar*, Class 9, *Blackwood's Edinburgh Magazine* 23 (February 1828): 214–27.

———. "Fairies, Deils [Devils], and Witches." *The Shepherd's Calendar*, Class 9, *Blackwood's Edinburgh Magazine* 23 (April 1828): 509–19.

———. "The Magic Mirror." *Blackwood's Edinburgh Magazine* 30 (October 1831): 650–54.

———. "The Origin of the Fairies." *Blackwood's Edinburgh Magazine* 28 (August 1830): 209–17.

———. *The Queen's Wake: A Legendary Poem*. Edinburgh: George Goldie, 1813. HathiTrust Digital Library.

———."Shepherd's Calendar, April 1827." *Blackwood's Edinburgh Magazine* 21 (1827): 434–48.

Homans, Margaret. *Women Writers and Poetic Identity*. Princeton, NJ: Princeton University Press, 1980.

Hornosty, Janina. "Let's Not Have Its Bowels Quite So Quickly, Then: A Response to Maggie Berg." *Brontë Studies* 39, no. 2 (April 2015): 130–40.

Huang, Mei. *Transforming the Cinderella Dream*. New Brunswick, NJ: Rutgers University Press, 1990.

Hughes, John. "The Affective World of Charlotte Brontë's *Villette*." *SEL: Studies in English Literature* 40, no. 4 (Autumn 2000): 711–26.

Imlay, Elizabeth. *Charlotte Brontë and the Mysteries of Love*. New York: St. Martin's, 1989.

Inboden, Robin L., ed. *Agnes Grey*. By Anne Brontë. Peterborough, ON: Broadview Press, 2020.

Jackson, Mary V. *Engines of Instruction, Mischief, and Magic: Children's Literature in England from Its Beginnings to 1839*. Lincoln: University of Nebraska Press, 1989.

Jacobs, N. M. "Gender and Layered Narrative in *Wuthering Heights* and *The Tenant of Wildfell Hall*." In *The Brontës*, edited by Patricia Ingham, 216–33. Harlow, UK: Pearson Education, 2003.

Jacobus, Mary. "The Buried Letter: Feminism and Romanticism in *Villette*." In *The Brontë Sisters: Critical Assessments*, edited by Eleanor McNees, vol. 3, 673–88. Bodmin, UK: Helm Information, 1996.

Jaffe, Audrey. *The Victorian Novel Dreams of the Real*. London: Oxford University Press, 2016.

Janu, Philippa. "Plotting the Governess: The Lessons of *Agnes Grey*." *Brontë Studies* 48, no. 4 (2023): 336–46.

Johnston, Ruth D. "Dis-Membrance of Things Past: Re-Vision of Wordsworthian Retrospection in *Jane Eyre* and *Villette*." *Victorian Literature and Culture* 22 (1994): 73–102.

Joshi, Priti. "Masculinity and Gossip in Anne Brontë's *Tenant*." *SEL: Studies in English Literature* 49, no. 4 (Autumn 2009): 907–24.

Jung, Sandro. "Knowledge Economies in *Agnes Grey*." *Brontë Studies* 36, no. 3 (2011): 224–34.

Keats, John. "La Belle Dame Sans Merci." *The Longman Anthology of British Literature: The Romantics and Their Contemporaries*, edited by Susan Wolfson and Peter Manning, 3rd ed., vol. 2A, 948–49. London: Pearson Longman, 2006.

Kettle, Arnold. *An Introduction to the English Novel, Vol. 1*. New York: Harper & Row, 1951.

Kim, Katherine J. "Corpse Hoarding: Control and the Female Body in 'Bluebeard,' 'Schalken the Painter,' and *Villette*." *Studies in the Novel* 43, no. 4 (Winter 2011): 406–27.

King, Elizabeth. "'Uncivil Usage': Shifting Forms of Control in *The Tenant of Wildfell Hall*." *Victorians: A Journal of Culture and Literature*, no. 138 (Winter 2020): 124–40.

Knoepflmacher, U. C. "Introduction: Literary Fairy Tales and the Value of Impurity." *Marvels and Tales* 17, no. 1 (2003): 15–36.

Krebs, Paula M. "Folklore, Fear, and the Feminine: Ghosts and Old Wives' Tales in *Wuthering Heights*." *Victorian Literature and Culture* 26, no. 1 (1998): 41–52.

Kreilkamp, Ivan. "Petted Things: *Wuthering Heights* and the Animal." *Yale Journal of Criticism* 18, no. 1 (2005): 87–110.

Langer, Nancy Quick. "'There Is No Such Ladies Now-a-Days': Capsizing 'The Patriarch Bull' in Charlotte Brontë's 'Shirley.'" *Journal of Narrative Technique* 27, no. 3 (Fall 1997): 276–96.

Langland, Elizabeth. *Anne Brontë: The Other One*. London: Macmillan, 1989.

Leaver, Elizabeth. "The Critique of the Priest in Anne Brontë's *Agnes Grey*." *Brontë Studies* 37, no. 4 (2012): 345–51.

Leavis, Q. D. "A Fresh Approach to *Wuthering Heights*." In *Critical Essays on Emily Brontë*, edited by Thomas John Winnifrith, 205–15. New York: G. K. Hall, 1997.

———. "How We Must Read *Great Expectations*." In *Dickens the Novelist*, by F. R. Leavis and Q. D. Leavis, 277–331. London: Chatto & Windus, 1970.

———. Introduction to 1966 Penguin Classics edition of *Jane Eyre*. In *The Brontë Sisters: Critical Assessments*, edited by Eleanor McNees, vol. 3, 131–49. Bodmin, UK: Helm Information, 1996.

Levine, George. *The Realistic Imagination: English Fiction from Frankenstein to Lady Chatterley*. Chicago: University of Chicago Press, 1981.

Lewes, George Henry. "Currer Bell's *Shirley*," *Edinburgh Review* (1850). In *The Brontë Sisters: Critical Assessments*, edited by Eleanor McNees, vol. 3, 462–74. Bodmin, UK: Helm Information, 1996.

———. "Recent Novels: French and English." *Fraser's Magazine for Town and Country* 36 (December 1847): 686–95.

Llewellyn, Tanya. "'The Fiery Imagination': Charlotte Brontë, the *Arabian Nights* and Byron's Turkish Tales." *Brontë Studies* 37, no. 3 (2012): 216–26.

Lodge, David. *The Modes of Modern Writing: Metaphor, Metonymy, and the Typology of Modern Literature.* Ithaca, NY: Cornell University Press, 1977.

Lofthouse, Jessica. *North-Country Folklore in Lancashire, Cumbria and the Pennine Dales.* London: Robert Hale, 1976.

Logan, Deborah A. "Review Essay: New Work on Anne Brontë." *Victorians: A Journal of Culture and Literature,* no. 138 (Winter 2020): 316–20.

Mack, Robert L., ed. *Arabian Nights' Entertainments.* Oxford: Oxford University Press, 2009.

Macpherson, James. *The Poems of Ossian.* London: J. Walker and Other Proprietors, 1819.

Marcus, Sharon, ed. Introduction to *Jane Eyre.* By Charlotte Brontë. New York: Norton Library, 2022. E-book.

Marsden, Simon. *Emily Brontë and the Religious Imagination.* London: Bloomsbury, 2014.

———. "Ghost Writing: Emily Brontë and Spectrality." *Brontë Studies* 45, no. 2 (April 2020): 144–55.

Martin, Robert K. "*Jane Eyre* and the World of Faery." *Mosaic* 10, no. 4 (1977): 85–95.

Maynard, John. *Charlotte Brontë and Sexuality.* New York: Cambridge University Press, 1994.

McKee, Patricia. "Racial Strategies in Jane Eyre." *Victorian Literature and Culture* 37, no. 1 (2009): 67–83.

Meyer, Susan. *Imperialism at Home: Race and Victorian Women's Fiction.* Ithaca, NY: Cornell University Press, 1996.

Miele, Gina M. "Intertextuality." In *Marvelous Transformations: An Anthology of Fairy Tales and Contemporary Critical Perspectives,* edited by Christine A. Jones and Jennifer Schacker, 499–502. Peterborough, ON: Broadview Press, 2013.

Mikolajcik, Deirdre. "Mooring Points: Manly Leaders, Trade, and Charlotte Brontë's *Shirley.*" *Victorians: A Journal of Culture and Literature,* no. 131 (Summer 2017): 57–67.

Miles, Rosalind. "A Baby God: The Creative Dynamism of Emily Brontë's Poetry." In *The Art of Emily Brontë,* edited by Anne Smith, 68–93. London: Vision Critical Studies, 1976.

Miller, J. Hillis. *Fiction and Repetition: Seven English Novels.* Cambridge, MA: Harvard University Press, 1982.

Miller, Lucasta. "The Brontës and the Periodicals of the 1820s and 1830s." In *A Companion to the Brontës,* edited by Diane Long Hoeveler and Deborah Denenholz Morse, 285–301. Chichester, UK: Wiley Blackwell, 2016.

Moglen, Helen. *Charlotte Brontë: The Self Conceived.* Madison: University of Wisconsin Press, 1984.

Moore, Tara. "Women and Myth Narratives in Charlotte Brontë's *Shirley.*" *Women's Writing* 11, no. 3 (2004): 477–92.

Moretti, Franco. *The Way of the World: The* Bildungsroman *in European Culture.* London: Verso, 1987.

Morse, Deborah Denenholz. "'The Mark of the Beast': Animals as Sites of Imperial Encounter from Wuthering Heights to Green Mansions." In *Victorian Animal Dreams*, edited by Deborah Denenholz Morse and Martin A. Danahay, 181–200. London: Routledge, 2017.

———. "'I Speak of Those I Do Know': Witnessing as Radical Gesture in *The Tenant of Wildfell Hall*." In *New Approaches to the Literary Art of Anne Brontë*, edited by Julie Nash and Barbara A. Suess, 103–26. Aldershot, UK: Ashgate, 2001.

Moynahan, Julian. "The Hero's Guilt: The Case of *Great Expectations*." In *Victorian Literature: Selected Essays*, edited by Robert O. Preyer, 126–45. New York: Harper & Row, 1966.

Neill, Anna. *Primitive Minds*. Columbus: Ohio State University Press, 2013.

Neufeldt, Victor, ed. *The Works of Patrick Branwell Brontë*. Vol. 1. New York: Garland, 1997.

———, ed. *The Works of Patrick Branwell Brontë*. Vol. 2. New York: Garland, 1999.

———, ed. *The Works of Patrick Branwell Brontë*. Vol. 3. New York: Garland, 1999.

"Noctes Ambrosianae." *Blackwood's Edinburgh Magazine* 17 (January 1825): 123–30.

North, Christopher. "Hints for the Holidays, No. III." *Blackwood's Edinburgh Magazine* (September 1826): 397–426. HathiTrust Digital Library.

O'Brien, Lee. "Letty Garth's Little Red Book: 'Rumpelstiltskin,' Realism, and *Middlemarch*." *Victorian Literature and Culture* 45 (2017): 549–68.

Oxford English Dictionary Online, s.v. "enchant (*v.*), Etymology," 2023, https://doi.org/10.1093/OED/4511149518.

Oxford English Dictionary Online, s.v. "fantastic (*adj., n.*)," 2023, https://www.oed.com/dictionary/fantastic_adj?tab=meaning_and_use#4752657.

Oxford English Dictionary Online, s.v. "thing (*n.1*)," 2023, https://www.oed.com/dictionary/thing_n1?tab=meaning_and_use#18542603.

Padilla, Yolanda. "Dreaming of Eve, Prometheus, and the Titans: The Romantic Vision of Shirley Keeldar." *Brontë Society Transactions* 21, no. 1/2 (1993): 9–14.

Perera, Suvendrini. *Reaches of Empire: The English Novel from Edgeworth to Dickens*. New York: Columbia University Press, 1991.

Perrault, Charles. *Contes*. Edited by Catherine Magnien. Paris: Librairie Générale Française, Livre de Poche Classiques, 2006.

Piciucco, Pier Paolo. "*Wuthering Heights* as a Childlike Fairy Tale." *Brontë Studies* 31, no. 3 (November 2006): 220–29.

Pike, Judith E. "Breeching Boys: Milksops, Men's Clubs and the Modelling of Masculinity in Anne Brontë's *Agnes Grey* and *The Tenant of Wildfell Hall*." *Brontë Studies* 37, no. 2 (April 2012): 112–24.

———. "Disability in Charlotte Brontë's Early Novellas, *Jane Eyre* and *Villette*: The Legacy of Finic's Disabled and Racialized Body." *Brontë Studies* 43, no. 2 (2018): 114–24.

———. "Redefining the Brontë Canon: A Tribute to Christine Alexander." In Pike and Morrison, *Charlotte Brontë from the Beginnings*, 14–29.

———. "Rochester's Bronze Scrag and Pearl Necklace: Bronzed Masculinity in *Jane Eyre, Shirley,* and Charlotte Brontë's Juvenilia." *Victorian Literature and Culture* 41, no. 2 (2013): 261–81.

Pike, Judith E., and Lucy Morrison, eds. *Charlotte Brontë from the Beginnings: New Essays from the Juvenilia to the Major Works.* New York: Routledge, 2017.

Pionke, Albert D. "Reframing the Luddites: Materialist and Idealist Models of Self in Charlotte Brontë's *Shirley.*" *Victorian Review* 30, no. 2 (2004): 81–102.

Plasa, Carl. *Charlotte Brontë.* London: Palgrave Macmillan, 2004.

Pollock, Lori. "(An)Other Politics of Reading *Jane Eyre.*" *Journal of Narrative Technique* 26, no. 3 (Fall 1996): 249–73.

Pregent, Grace. "Peripheral Voices in *The Tenant of Wildfell Hall.*" *Victorians: A Journal of Culture and Literature,* no. 138 (Winter 2020): 212–30.

Propp, Vladimir. *Morphology of the Folktale.* Translated by Laurence. Revised and edited by Louis A. Wagner. Austin: University of Texas Press, 1968.

Pykett, Lyn. *Emily Brontë.* Basingstoke, UK: Macmillan, 1989.

Pyrhönen, Heta. *Bluebeard Gothic: "Jane Eyre" and Its Progeny.* Toronto: University of Toronto Press, 2010.

Quirk, Catherine. "Consent and Enclosure in *The Tenant of Wildfell Hall:* 'You Needn't Read It All; but Take It Home with You.'" *Victorians: A Journal of Culture and Literature,* no. 138 (Winter 2020): 231–41.

Ralph, Phyllis. "'Beauty and the Beast': Growing Up with Jane Eyre." In *Approaches to Teaching Brontë's "Jane Eyre,"* edited by Diane Long Hoeveler and Beth Lau, 56–61. New York: MLA, 1993.

Ratchford, Fannie E. *Gondal's Queen: A Novel in Verse.* Austin: University of Texas Press, 1955.

"Review of *Shirley.*" *Atlas,* November 3, 1849. Reprinted in *The Brontës: The Critical Heritage,* edited by Miriam Allott, 119–21. London: Routledge & Kegan Paul, 1974.

"Review of *Shirley.*" *Westminster Review* 52 (January 1850). Reprinted in *The Brontë Sisters: Critical Assessments,* edited by Eleanor McNees, vol. 3, 475–76. Bodmin, UK: Helm Information, 1996.

Review of *Villette* in *Spectator.* In *The Brontës: The Critical Heritage,* edited by Miriam Allott, 181–84. New York: Routledge, 1974.

Rich, Adrienne. "Jane Eyre: The Temptations of a Motherless Woman." In *The Brontë Sisters: Critical Assessments,* edited by Eleanor McNees, vol. 3, 226–39. Bodmin, UK: Helm Information, 1996.

Ritson, Joseph. *Fairy Tales.* London: Thomas Davison, 1831. HathiTrust Digital Library.

Robbins, Ruth. "How Do I Look? *Villette* and Looking Different(ly)." *Brontë Studies* 28, no. 3 (2003): 215–22.

Rogers, Philip. "'My Word Is Error': 'Jane Eyre' and Colonial Exculpation." *Dickens Studies Annual* 34 (2004): 329–50.

Rosengarten, Herbert. "Charlotte Brontë's *Shirley.*" In *A Companion to the Brontës,* edited by Diane Long Hoeveler and Deborah Denenholz Morse, 167–82. Chichester, UK: Wiley Blackwell, 2016.

Ross, Shawna. *Charlotte Brontë at the Anthropocene.* Albany: SUNY Press, 2020.

Rowe, Karen E. "'Fairy-Born and Human-Bred': Jane Eyre's Education in Romance." In *The Voyage In: Fictions of Female Development,* edited by Marianne Hirsch and Elizabeth Langland, 69–89. Hanover: University Press of New England, 1983.

Said, Edward. *Orientalism.* New York: Vintage Books, 1979.

Schacker, Jennifer. *National Dreams: The Remaking of Fairy Tales in Nineteenth-Century England.* Philadelphia: University of Pennsylvania Press, 2003.

———. *Staging Fairyland: Folklore, Children's Entertainment, and Nineteenth-Century Pantomime.* Detroit: Wayne State University Press, 2018.

Schaffer, Talia. *Communities of Care: The Social Ethics of Victorian Fiction.* Princeton, NJ: Princeton University Press, 2021.

Scott, Sir Walter. *The Lady of the Lake.* Edited by William J. Rolfe, 1883. Project Gutenberg.

———. *The Lay of the Last Minstrel.* London: Longman, 1806. HathiTrust Digital Library.

———. *A Legend of Montrose; The Black Dwarf.* Classic Reprint Series. London: Forgotten Books, 2012.

———. *Letters on Demonology and Witchcraft.* London: John Murray, 1830. HathiTrust Digital Library.

———. *Marmion.* London: Cassell & Company, 1888. Project Gutenberg.

———. *Minstrelsy of the Scottish Border.* Kelso, UK: Ballantyne, 1802. HathiTrust Digital Library.

———. *The Monastery.* Edinburgh: Longman, [1820] 1910. HathiTrust Digital Library.

———. *The Pirate.* Bibliophile Edition, The Waverley Novels, edited by Andrew Lang. Boston: Estes & Lauriat, 1893.

———. *The Vision of Don Roderick.* Edinburgh: Ballantyne, 1811. HathiTrust Digital Library.

Seelye, John. Jane Eyre's *American Daughters.* Newark: University of Delaware Press, 2005.

Shakespeare, William. *A Midsummer Night's Dream.* Edited by Russ McDonald. The Pelican Shakespeare. New York: Penguin Books, 2000.

Sharpe, Jenny. *Allegories of Empire: The Figure of Woman in the Colonial Text.* Minneapolis: University of Minnesota Press, 1993.

Shuttleworth, Sally. *Charlotte Brontë and Victorian Psychology.* Cambridge: Cambridge University Press, 1996.

Silver, Anna Krugovoy. *Victorian Literature and the Anorexic Body.* Cambridge: Cambridge University Press, 2002.

Silver, Carole. "'East of the Sun and West of the Moon': Victorians and Fairy Brides." *Tulsa Studies in Women's Literature* 6, no. 2 (Autumn 1987): 283–98.

———. *Strange and Secret Peoples: Fairies and Victorian Consciousness.* Oxford: Oxford University Press, 1999.

Simpson, Jacqueline, and Stephen Roud, eds. *A Dictionary of English Folklore.* Oxford: Oxford University Press, 2000.

Sitter, Zak. "On Early Style: The Emergence of Realism in Charlotte Brontë's Juvenilia." In Pike and Morrison, *Charlotte Brontë from the Beginnings*, 30–43.

Smith, Margaret, ed. *The Letters of Charlotte Brontë*. Vol. 2. Oxford: Clarendon Press, 2000. EBSCOhost.

———, ed. *The Letters of Charlotte Brontë*. Vol. 3. Oxford: Clarendon Press, 2004.

Smith, Sheila. "'At Once Strong and Eerie': The Supernatural in Wuthering Heights and Its Debt to the Traditional Ballad." *Review of English Studies*, n.s., 43, no. 172 (November 1992): 498–517.

Spark, Muriel, and Derek Stanford. *Emily Brontë: Her Life and Work*. London: Peter Owen, 1960.

Spivak, Gayatri Chakravorty. "Three Women's Texts and a Critique of Imperialism." *Critical Inquiry* 12, no. 1 (Autumn 1985): 243–61.

Staten, Henry. *Spirit Becomes Matter: The Brontës, George Eliot, Nietzsche*. Edinburgh: Edinburgh University Press, 2014.

Stedman, Jane W. "The Genesis of the Genii." *Brontë Society Transactions* 14, no. 5 (1965): 16–20.

Stewart, Susan. "The Ballad in *Wuthering Heights*." *Representations* 86 (Spring 2004): 175–97.

Stolpa, Jennifer M. "Preaching to the Clergy: Anne Brontë's *Agnes Grey* as a Treatise on Sermon Style and Delivery." *Victorian Literature and Culture* 31, no. 1 (2003): 225–40.

Stone, Harry. *Dickens and the Invisible World: Fairy Tales, Fantasy, and Novel-Making*. Bloomington: Indiana University Press, 1979.

Stoneman, Patsy. "A Peculiar Illusion: Narrative Technique and the Lovers in *Wuthering Heights*." *Brontë Studies* 45, no. 2 (2020): 196–208.

———. "*Shirley* as Elegy." *Brontë Studies* 40, no. 1 (January 2015): 22–33.

Sullivan, Paula. "Fairy Tale Elements in *Jane Eyre*." *Journal of Popular Culture* 12, no. 1 (Summer 1978): 61–74.

Summers, Mary. "Fact to Fiction: Anne Brontë Replicates La Trobe's Biblically Inspired Advice in Scenes from *Agnes Grey*." *Brontë Studies* 37, no. 4 (2012): 352–58.

Sunderland, Jane. "Canine Agency and Its Mitigation in the Characterization of Dogs in the Novels by Charlotte, Emily and Anne Brontë." *Brontë Studies* 48, no. 3 (2023): 189–206.

Surridge, Lisa. *Bleak Houses: Marital Violence in Victorian Fiction*. Athens: Ohio University Press, 2005.

Talairach-Vielmas, Laurence. *Fairy Tales, Natural History and Victorian Culture*. New York: Palgrave Macmillan, 2014.

Tatar, Maria. *The Hard Facts of the Grimms' Fairy Tales*. Expanded 2nd ed. Princeton, NJ: Princeton University Press, 2003.

———. *Secrets beyond the Door: The Story of Bluebeard and His Wives*. Princeton, NJ: Princeton University Press, 2004.

Thierauf, Doreen. "Guns and Blood: Reading *The Tenant of Wildfell Hall* in the Age of #MeToo." *Nineteenth-Century Gender Studies* 16, no. 2 (Summer 2020). https://www.ncgsjournal.com/.

Thomas, Sue. *Imperialism, Reform, and the Making of Englishness in "Jane Eyre."* London: Palgrave Macmillan, 2008.

Thomson, David. *The People of the Sea*. London: Canongate Books, 2017.

Thormählen, Marianne. *The Brontës and Religion*. Cambridge: Cambridge University Press, 1999.

"Tieck's Bluebeard. A Dramatic Tale, in Five Acts." *Blackwood's Edinburgh Magazine* 33 (February 1833): 206–23.

Tillotson, Kathleen. *Novels of the Eighteen-Forties*. Oxford: Clarendon Press, 1954.

Trollope, Anthony. *The Eustace Diamonds*. Oxford: Oxford World's Classics, 1983.

Tromp, Marlene. *The Private Rod*. Charlottesville: University Press of Virginia, 2000.

Uther, Hans-Jörg. *The Types of International Folktales, Part I: Animal Tales, Tales of Magic, Religious Tales, and Realistic Tales, with an Introduction*. Helsinki: Folklore Fellows Communications, 2011.

van Ghent, Dorothy. *The English Novel: Form and Function*. New York: Rinehart, 1953.

Wagner, Tamara Silvia. "Charlotte Brontë's *Ashworth*: From Adapted Angrian Villains to Recurring Sibling Pairs." In Pike and Morrison, *Charlotte Brontë from the Beginnings*, 126–40.

Whipple, E. P. "Novels of the Season" (1848). In *Wuthering Heights*, edited by Alexandra Lewis, 5th ed., 289–92. New York: W. W. Norton, 2019.

Whone, Clifford. "Where the Brontës Borrowed Books." *Brontë Society Transactions* 11, no. 60 (1950): 344–58.

Wilcockson, Colin. "'Fair(y) Annie's Wedding': A Note on Wuthering Heights." *Essays in Criticism* 33, no. 3 (July 1983): 259–61.

Wilson, Kristian Nicole. "Reading Charlotte and Branwell Brontë's Early Writings as Colonialist Fantasy." Master's thesis, Clemson University, 2019.

Wood, J. Carter. *Violence and Crime in Nineteenth-Century England*. New York: Routledge, 2004.

"Works of Hans Christian Andersen." *Blackwood's Edinburgh Magazine* 63 (October 1847): 387–407.

Yeazell, Ruth Bernard. "More True Than Real: Jane Eyre's 'Mysterious Summons.'" In *The Brontë Sisters: Critical Assessments*, edited by Eleanor McNees, vol. 3, 240–53. Bodmin, UK: Helm Information, 1996.

Zipes, Jack. *The Irresistible Fairy Tale: The Cultural and Social History of a Genre*. Princeton, NJ: Princeton University Press, 2012.

Zlotnick, Susan. "Luddism, Medievalism and Women's History in *Shirley*: Charlotte Brontë's Revisionist Tactics." *Novel* 24, no. 3 (Spring 1991): 282–95.

Zonana, Joyce. "The Sultan and the Slave: Feminist Orientalism and the Structure of 'Jane Eyre.'" *Signs* 18, no. 3 (Spring 1993): 592–617.

Index

Index